41 G's righteousness + law

67 election + assurance!

3ff the church

74 Jacob's grabbing Esau's ankle

16 Isaac's constancy

81ff Isaac's love for Esau
(assurance)

100 Jacob + the birthright

106 " 's fast

122 our f. tested (121ff)

124 common analysis

126 will Dei is clear

131 The Lord's way w/us

133 ff Paul's interp of Abr + Isaac

136 G's swearing - accomm. ✓

145 Isaac's mistrust

168 OT rehearsed to us to teach us G's care

174 providence

192 Happiness in G (192 - 198ff)

193ff the need for visions | 194 accomm ✓

195 "Fear not"

199 ff our father Abraham

203ff overcoming weak faith

214 observ. on Isaac's situation

233 church is small

237,8 multiple wives - no ment. of accomm.

239 Isaac's love for Esau

244,5 - G's use of means!

247ish - 49 the faults of Isaac + Rebecca

250 - 52 ff - faith mixed w/flaws

253 contra implicit faith

4 f. def + discussed | weakness

257 on certainty of faith

266 (and 65) - Jesus foretold in blessing of Jacob by Isaac.

125 + 268 - Deut 8:3 food strengthens us by G's work!

268 - 70 ff Isaac like a preacher of the gospel!

274ff - OT/NT

288ff - on G's choice of Jacob
Isaac's wonder!

293,4 f. almost quenched

301,2 nec. of repentance

Jon Balserak

(0131) 556 - 5751

Given to me upon
my departure to New
College, Fall '97

upon completion of
M.Th.) summer '96

¶*Thirteene*
SERMONS OF
Maister Iohn Caluine,

Entreating of the Free Election
of God in *Iacob*, and of
Reprobation in Esau.

A treatise wherein euery Christian
may see the excellent benefites of God to-
wardes his children, and his maruelous
iudgements towards the reprobate
firste published in the French toung, &
now Translated into Englishe by
Iohn Fielde, *For the*
comfort of all
Christians

ROM. 11.33
O the deepenes of the riches, both of the vvisdome and
knovvledge of God! Hovve vnsearcheable are his
iudgements, and his vvayes past finding out.

SERMONS ON
ELECTION & REPROBATION
by
JOHN CALVIN

Foreword by:

The Rev. David C. Engelsma,
Professor of Dogmatics and Old Testament Studies
Theological School of the Protestant Reformed Churches

Old Paths
Publications

Old Paths Publications
223 PRINCETON RD.
AUDUBON, NEW JERSEY 08106 USA
...ask for the old paths... Jer. 6:16

Original English Edition 1579
This Old Paths Edition 1996

ISBN 0-9632557-9-7

Foreword

Table of Contents

Publisher's Note

The time for Calvin's *Sermons Entreating of the Free Election of God in Jacob and of Reprobation in Esau* has come, in fact, has been too long in coming. This awe-inspiring English edition, done by John Field in the year 1579, has apparently been overlooked for over 400 years, yet belongs to the same family of Calvin's sermons on various books and Scripture sections of the Bible which have been reprinted in this century. The collection of sermons on the subject of election and reprobation is one of a series of reprints of Calvin's sermons recently undertaken by Old Paths Publications, and makes a fine compliment to his *Sermons on Galatians*, and *Sermons on Psalm 119*. An explanation is no doubt in order as to the particulars of the present volume, editorial decisions, and the publisher's decision to present this work in a form not characteristic of either a simple photolithographed facsimile or a new translation from the original French.

Firstly, a word about translations. We decided to forego the task of a new translation for two primary reasons. The first is that there existed a translation which was

I

believed to be adequate and reasonable. The second is that there is more to translation than simply translating. What we mean by this is that in our age anything with the name "new" is assumed to have some special and improved significance. As in the case of modern translations of the Bible, the onslaught of new versions or new translations has done anything but justice to the original language or to the older translations. As for the spiritual writings of men, criticism may arise regarding the faithfulness of a translation made 400 years ago, and the capabilities of the translator himself. The translation was performed by one, namely John Field, who was responsible for the Christian productions of other learned men of his day, which includes translations of many of Calvin's Sermons, such as *Foure Sermons, with a Briefe Exposition of the lxxxvii Psalme - 1579*. Additionally, this translation was undertaken within a generation of the original sermons, and published in English only fifteen years after Calvin's death.

The qualifications of Field, who was familiar with the times in which these sermons of Calvin were written and the religious circumstances to which they applied, are strengthened for such an undertaking. Field was a contemporary of Calvin, having lived during the author's own lifetime (being approximately nineteen in the year of Calvin's death). He also performed this task of translation with access to the collection of sources, at his command, by the author. Furthermore, there is something to be said for the fact that Field was knowledgeable of the vulgar language of that day, both in English for his translation and the original French. This further supports his credentials. The approach to translation employed by Field no doubt had characteristics like that which is taken by many who are acquainted with an author's writings, theology, and circumstances. Further, Field was a Puritan. Hence, his theological leanings were complementary, if not indebted to Calvinism. According to an article in *The Oxford Dictionary of the Christian Church*, it is said of Field that he was "the organizing genius of extreme Elizabethan Puritanism." Benjamin Brook's, biographical work entitled, *The Lives of Puritans*, introduces Field saying "[t]his excellent divine was a great sufferer in the cause of nonconformity."

Secondly, a word about facsimile reprints. If one could obtain a mint copy of an original antiquarian book, that is to say, one without any stains, tears, creases, worming, or markings of any sort, then he has an ideal copy from which to produce his reprinted volumes. Obtaining such a pristine copy is difficult, particularly if the book is rare, expensive, printed or bound in a less than adequate fashion, of poor quality paper, exposed to elements of inclement weather, war, or frequent use by its owners, etc. These are far more easily overcome than the obstacle of the hesitant, disinclined and reluctant reader who chooses not to endure the product of the ancient printing press. As the saying goes, "you can lead a horse to water, but you cannot make him drink." We decided that it is a larger disservice to placate the modern reader with a watered down edition suitable for milky appetites than to challenge him with the meat necessary to develop beyond the limited literacy characteristic of the present day. Moreover, our age is one which is not only largely responsible for the wholesale destruction of the remembered past, but is guilty of rewriting and altering the meaning of Christian history as well.

In light of this, a publisher is faced with the dilemma of how to best accomplish the goal of getting sound Christian writings into the hands of God's people, providing the stimulus to actually read the writings, and to having the Christian qualitatively yet comprehensively benefit from the writings. Therefore we attempted to bring the ancient forward and carry the modern backward. That is to say, the work itself has been left complete and unabridged, except that the text of the sermons has been newly typeset and edited to reflect contemporary spelling, and bracketed words *in italics* inserted following some antiquated terms or phrases, The task of modernizing spelling required identifying old texts that used (y for i), (u for v), (v for u), (vv for w), (I for J), and characters with loops on the top such as (ꝛ ſh ſl ſt and ſt). Also you will see something that looks like the letter "f" when in fact it is a letter "s" (note the difference): "f" and "ſ". Examples of spelling changes are *"sonne"* to *"son"*, *"deere"* would be *"dear"*, *"Iesus"* would appear as *"Jesus"*, and *"Paule"* should be *"Paul"*. However, exceptions to this were made for other names such as Esay, Moyses, Malachie, Isaack, Ismael, etc., which have been left intact. Other exceptions are for the use of *"eth"* at the end of a word, such as *"behooveth"*, or *"blesseth"*. All of these remain unchanged. In the original the Apostle Paul is referred to as "S. Paule", "Sainte Paul" and "Sainꝍ Paule". In this reprint, "Saint Paul" is used throughout. Additionally, capitalization and punctuation techniques that were the current practices of that era and the printing industry were left intact. For example, there are inconsistencies (or rather nuances, if you will) such as *"GOD"* or *"God"* or *"god"*, and *"Gospel"* and *"gospel"*. Capitalization differences are most likely attributable to the availability of letters for layout on the movable type printing press. In the example just mentioned, the letter "G" frequently would be used in the manuscript and so in some cases would be replaced by a "g". There are instances, however, where it is reasonable to assume that the translator or even Calvin himself employed capitalization to emphasize a particular point, or simply to refer to more than one characteristic or attribute of God (not unlike the varying occurrences of capitalization used by the translators of the Authorized Version). Scripture references quoted by Calvin and found in the side margins of the original edition have been checked and in some cases corrected. They appear at the bottom of each page as daggered footnotes to the sermons.

As was customary with older writings, a section would be placed at the beginning of the work entitled "Erata" or in the present work "Faultes escaped". This section would identify any printing errors later identified after printing, but before the final binding of the book. Rather than reprinting the work, this section would serve as an aid to the reader, and would provide instruction such as "Fol. 33. b, line 16. *for euill diſpoſed, reade better diſpoſed.*" In this reprinting the corrections have all been made thereby eliminating the use of the "Faultes escaped" section.

Another area of decision pertains to the brief Scripture sections of Genesis chapters 25-27 preceding each sermon. These verses have been stylishly typeset to approximate their original appearance. This was done for two primary reasons. Firstly, to maintain an accurate reproduction of Field's English text of these verses in Genesis translated from Calvin's French version which Calvin translated himself from the original languages. Secondly, to offer the reader a taste of antiquity by viewing the rich and full majesty that so beautifully flows from translations of the Reformation era.

The production of this work was through the joint efforts of many, most of whom probably would rather remain anonymous; however, we feel it is only appropriate to identify the instruments that accomplished the finished work. We are grateful first of all for the generous assistance of Thomas Rockhill, and David Clum, who largely financed this work. There was also the typing by Sheryl Hand who slaved over photocopies of a 416 year-old book with all its antiquity. The painstaking task of proof-reading was undertaken by Willard Neel, Randy Olson, and Mark Trigsted. We also are thankful for the quality artwork and design of the dust-jacket by Peter Nicolas. The publisher also wishes to thank his wife April and children for the time so generously sacrificed while husband and father was buried for countless hours in the production of this work.

Ernie Springer
Old Paths Publications

Foreword

by

The Rev. David J. Engelsma
Professor of Dogmatics and Old Testament Studies
Theological School of the Protestant Reformed Churches

The thirteen sermons of John Calvin on God's election of Jacob and reprobation of Esau were originally part of Calvin's series of sermons on Genesis. Calvin began preaching through Genesis in September, 1559. These sermons, therefore, give us the fully developed biblical insight and doctrinal thought of Calvin at the end of his ministry.

The sermons on Genesis were taken down as Calvin preached them and then transcribed by the famed scribe, Denis Raguenier.

At once the thirteen sermons on election and

reprobation were lifted from the series on Genesis and published as a separate volume. They were published in French in 1562. In 1579, they were published in English by a London publisher. The translator was John Field. This was the only English publication of the sermons until now. It is this translation in modernized form that Old Paths Publications now makes available after more than 400 years (see T. H. L. Parker, *Calvin's Preaching*, Westminster/John Knox Press, 1992 and W. de Greef, *The Writings of John Calvin: An Introductory Guide*, Baker Books, 1993).

For all practical purposes, Calvin's sermons on Genesis 25:12-27:38 are now available in English for the first time. It is important to remember that Calvin's sermons on Genesis are different from his (earlier) commentary on the book of Genesis.

Calvin's Preaching Style

There is a great deal more in this valuable work than only instruction concerning divine predestination. For one thing, we learn something of the nature and style of Calvin's preaching. Working his way through an entire book passage by passage, Calvin carefully explained Scripture.

The exposition was applicatory. Calvin's preaching was intensely practical. From the very outset of a sermon, Calvin was applying the teaching of the passage to the experience and life of the congregation. The tenth sermon, on Isaac's peaceful reception of Abimelech as found in Genesis 26, begins with the observation that most of the evils men endure in this world "proceed from themselves, everyone of them being as a wolf to his companion."

Throughout the sermon, Calvin warns against the "desire of revenge" and exhorts his audience "to appease all strifes and quarrels."

In keeping with his conviction that the Word forms the lives of the people of God, Calvin's style was vivid, forceful, and, thus, popular. Old Isaac "loved (Esau) . . . for his tooth's sake." When men disobey God, they "spit in God's face." God's prohibition against mixed marriages is due to His determination that the house of the believer not be "mingled and mashed" with the ungodly. In his marriages with two heathens, Esau "wallowed . . . a swine upon a dung-hill." In his grief over the loss of the blessing, "Esau cried out, yea, by yelling and roaring, and . . . howled as it were a wild beast." This makes for interested listening to the sermon.

Doctrinal Preaching

Practical as Calvin was in preaching the Old Testament, he did not view Old Testament history as a mere collection of illustrations for a godly life. For Calvin, Old Testament history has a covenantal center and is, therefore, prophetic of Jesus Christ. Commenting on Rebekah's attempt to gain the blessing for Jacob by "craft and lying," Calvin said, "The matter was here of the salvation of the world, the question was of having Jesus Christ whom God should send for a Redeemer" (sermon eleven).

The sermons, therefore, are doctrinal. Nor is predestination the only doctrine taught. Indeed, the title of the set of sermons can be misleading. Sermons six through nine contain little or nothing that explicitly concerns predestination, treating as they do of the trial of Isaac in Gerar. Only at the very end of sermon ten, where he explains Esau's marriages to two heathens as a manifestation of his reprobation, does Calvin return to the subject of predestination.

Even the sermons that proclaim predestination give instruction also in other, important doctrines. In the sixth sermon, Calvin goes on at some length contending that God's covenant with Abraham does not depend upon Abraham's obedience but upon God's free grace. In sermon eleven, Calvin defines faith ("an understanding which we have of the goodness and favor of God, after that He has illuminated us by His Holy Spirit") and explains that faith is the instrument, not the ground, of salvation. Sermon thirteen defends the truth of the perseverance of saints.

Here and there, Calvin drops intriguing observations about the good, material gifts that God bestows on the ungodly. In sermon seven, he speaks of "God's favor, which is common to all" in the sunshine and fruits of the earth. In sermon eight, Calvin notes that God's blessing of His people with physical prosperity is enjoyed by their wicked neighbors, so that it is foolish for the wicked to drive the people of God away, as Abimelech did to Isaac. At the same time, in sermon nine, Calvin asserts that to have "all the blessings" without the assurance of the favor of God is to have "nothing." "If God do not testify unto us the love that He bears us, though we should be in an earthly paradise, we should be in a hell."

Running through the entire exposition, as through all of Calvin's theology, is the theme that binds all together:

the sovereignty of the God and Father of Jesus Christ. This sovereignty is divine purpose and power governing all that takes place, the disobedience of the reprobate as well as the obedience of the elect, for the sake of God's glory in the salvation of the church of Jesus Christ.

> And so we see that God waiteth not upon men, neither dependeth upon them, when the matter standeth for the performance of His counsel. It is very true, that He will use them to serve His turn; but He sheweth notwithstanding that He worketh all alone and of Himself. And when His creatures serve Him as instruments, it is no farther than it pleaseth Him, and not as though He were bound by any necessity. Yea, and albeit that things in respect of men go quite backward as it seemeth, yet this sheweth that His power is sufficient, so that it needeth no help from others (sermon twelve).

Sovereign Predestination

This sovereignty, which was as real, constant, and urgent to the mind of Calvin as was God Himself, is manifested and magnified above all in predestination. Following the apostle in Romans 9, John Calvin saw in the inspired history of Jacob and Esau the revelation of God's eternal predestination of some particular individuals unto salvation and of other particular individuals unto damnation.

This divine discrimination from eternity between person and person—brother and brother! *twin* brother and *twin* brother!—applies to the history of the covenant, that is, to the physical children of believers. Calvin's opening words in this section of the series on Genesis were, "We have here to consider the difference that Moses puts betwixt *the children of Abraham*" (my emphasis—DJE). The instruction of the history of Rebekah's twins is that "they, who for a time have place in the church and bear the title of the faithful and of the children of God, may well be so accounted before men, but they are not written in the book of life: God knoweth them not, nor avoucheth them for His" (sermon two).

There is, for Calvin, close relationship between election and covenant. Membership in the covenant is determined by election.

> And, moreover, we are taught a far greater thing, and that is in the first place that albeit God had established His covenant with Abraham, yet notwithstanding He would declare that this was not all, to have made offer of His grace, but that it behooved that He choose according to His liberty such as He thought good, and that the rest should remain in their cursed state (sermon two).

Calvin found the nature of predestination to be clearly revealed in the history of God's dealings with Jacob and Esau. Predestination is a decree in eternity: God loved Jacob and hated Esau "before He created the world and before the fall of Adam" (sermon two). That the decree is unconditional is evident from the fact that God loved the one and hated the other while they were yet in their mother's womb, before they were born or had done good or evil. The decree appoints to everlasting bliss and everlasting woe. It is personal, referring to individuals—the person, Jacob, and the person, Esau.

Calvin repudiated the notions that God's predestination is conditioned by humans' worth; that it concerns mere "earthly or transitory inheritance"; that it refers to "peoples," or nations, rather than individuals; and that it depends upon foreknowledge in the sense of God's knowledge beforehand as to who would believe. Concerning this last error, Calvin proved from several passages of Scripture that faith is due to election. Those who oppose predestination by appeal to foreknowledge as though God's election depends upon foreseen faith, said Calvin, "have no drop of the fear of God" (sermon two).

In Defense of the Faith

As this quotation indicates, the sermons are vigorously polemical. Calvin was no smiling, positive preacher. He defended the truth of God—predestination—against God's enemies. In sermon two, he notes that there are two main kinds of enemies, dogs and hogs. The dogs are the theological opponents of predestination. These are the preachers and professors who by their teaching try to "make this doctrine odious." They bark against election and reprobation.

The hogs are those who, while professing election-- and themselves elect!—"overthrow this doctrine of election by their loose and lewd life." Nominal members of a Reformed church, they are profane persons, as Esau, given to the same earthlimindedness and adultery.

In addition to the defense of predestination that is found throughout the sermons themselves, there is the fascinating "Answer to Certain Slanders and Blasphemies" that is appended to the thirteen sermons. The complete heading is, "An Answer to certain slanders and blasphemies, wherewith certain evil disposed persons have gone about to bring the doctrine of God's everlasting Predestination into hatred." This is a little-known but significant defense of predestination by Calvin against an attack on the doctrine in an anonymous writing that was "scattered about, to abolish this article of our faith." Calvin supposed that the author of the offending piece was Sebastian Castellio.

Whether Castellio or "some such like," this enemy of predestination maintained that God "created all the world to be saved" and "labors to draw unto Him all that went astray." Calvin agreed that God "propounds" the doctrine of faith and repentance "to all in general." However, God has two purposes with this general "propounding": "to draw His elect unto Him, or to make other inexcusable."

The enemy appealed to Ezekiel 33:11 ("I have no pleasure in the death of the wicked; but that the wicked turn from his way and live"), in every age the "buckler," as Calvin put it, of the foes of predestination. Calvin denied that this text stands against predestination. Rather, it

> very well confirmeth my saying for . . . (it)
> signifieth that God biddeth and exhorteth all
> which are gone astray to return to the right way.
> But not that in deed He leadeth them all to

Himself by the power of His Spirit. The which
He promiseth not but to a certain number, which
appeareth as well in the 31st chapter of Jeremiah,
as in the 37th of Ezekiel, and in the 11th, and
throughout the whole Scripture.

To the argument that all men have the ability to
believe inasmuch as all naturally retain the image of God,
thus denying that faith and salvation rest squarely upon
sovereign, particular election, Calvin replied by affirming
the complete loss of the image by fallen humanity.

Albeit there remain yet some trace of the image
of God in us, yet . . . the whole is disfigured, so as
reason is blind and the heart perverse.
Wherefore by nature we are wholly accursed.

This implies, thought Calvin, a logical theologian,
that faith is a gift that God gives only to some according to
His election.

A weighty objection grounded rejection of
reprobation in the call of the gospel to all: "God hath not ...
predestinated any man not to believe, seeing He calleth
everyone." Calvin refuted this objection by distinguishing
between "the outward preaching" and "the secret calling of
God whereby He touches the hearts within." The external
call does not indicate or express a will of God to save all to
whom it comes. And this distinction, remarked Calvin,
belongs to "the A B C of Christians."

It is interesting that the enemy of predestination
whose slanders Calvin answered evidently appealed to
Philip Melanchthon in support of his rejection of

predestination. It is equally interesting, and of some historical and theological value, that Calvin referred the "simple and weak" souls who were troubled by the slanderous writing to "a little book that our brother, master Beza, hath made" for a full and satisfactory defense of predestination.

The Preaching of Predestination

What Reformed and Presbyterian preachers should learn from these sermons is that predestination can and must be preached to the congregation. It may not be shut up in the confines of mind, study, and seminary. The reason, in addition to the inclusion of the doctrine in Holy Scripture, is the importance of this fundamental truth. Election is "the root and beginning of the church" (sermon two). Predestination is the ultimate explanation of the different effects of the preaching of the gospel:

> Concerning those to whom the gospel is preached, the one receive it with obedience, and they are touched therewith to the quick and persevere in it to the end; and the other remain blockish, or rather will be full of outrage, to strive against God, or else will be fickle and give themselves over to all iniquity, throwing off the yoke, when they shall be brought into the good way. And from whence cometh this diversity? We must come to this fountain that the Holy Scripture sheweth us, that is, that the like grace hath not been shewed to all (sermon three).

Election is the source of faith, holiness, and every Christian virtue. Upon election must the assurance of salvation be founded:

> It behooveth us (I say) to have our foundation upon the election of God, that we may be so settled thereon that we know that our Lord, being our Father, will not suffer that we perish, seeing we are His children (sermon three).

"The principal thing which we have to observe is this, that God will have the whole praise of our salvation to be attributed to Him" (sermon two).

Shall predestination not then be preached?

Calvin's *Sermons on Election & Reprobation* is an eminently worthy companion-volume to Old Paths Publications' recent edition of Calvin's *Sermons on Galatians*.

To the right Honorable

and my very good Lord, the Earl of Bedford,
one of her Majesty's most honorable privy Counsel,
and to the Honorable, godly, and virtuous Lady,
the Countess his wife: John Field *wisheth*
encrease of godliness and constancy
by Jesus Christ forever.
AMEN.

 *Ecause I cannot (my very good* Lord and Lady, whom the Lord I say by the profession of this glorious Gospel hath made right Honorable) by any other means testify the duty that I owe you, but in such poor sort as this is, I most humbly beseech you to accept of it. Look not upon it as it is in itself: but value it according to the hearty affection of the giver, who with all duty protesteth his humble service towards your Honor, to the uttermost that he shall be able for the advancement of your knowledge, increase of godliness and spiritual gain, in the true practice of God's blessed and holy truth the greatest benefit that ever God in mercy could have bestowed upon you. I am sorry that my skill is no better, to help you forward in that so excellent a work: but forasmuch as God accepteth us according to that measure we have received, I hope you of your Honorable courtesy, will

likewise take it well, that I show this remembrance of you in presenting such a present as he hath bestowed upon me. And this I will say: though in respect of my labor it be homely, yet in respect of the matter it is most excellent: a work of one of the rarest instruments whom god hath raised up, in these last times to give light amidst our great ignorance, and to draw many to that blessed knowledge, which I beseech God we may both thankfully accept of: and also diligently conform ourselves with all obedience, to live according to it: that the Lord do not either take this blessing from us, or else bring upon us severe judgments, for abusing so excellent a treasure. I know some unthankful wretches, puffed up with pride and a vain opinion of themselves, will hardly endure that I should speak thus either of the work, or of this singular instrument of God. For the nature of men's corruption is such, and specially of such as seek to be magnified one of another, that they tread under their feet God's glory: and being behind others in gifts, they pout and swell against them whose shoe latchets they are not worthy to loose: Besides that they are so corrupt, either being open Papists, counterfeit professors or manifest heretics, that they can abide no sincerity. Of the first sort I will not say much, because now I mind not at large to dispute with them, as being the open and hopeless enemies of God (I mean the obstinate ones) who set themselves not only against his servants, but against his holy word. For what should a man say to such, whom nothing can please, but that they have received either from their own brains, or else from their sottish [*stupid, foolish*] doctors, who are destitute of all truth and godliness? what they tell them, be it never so silly, nay so false, they will receive with all greediness: No

Legend so lying, no opinion so gross, no motive so light, no life so villainous, as they will not accept of, maintain and defend, both with tooth and nail, if it come from themselves and from their own polshorne [*shaven, tonsured*] generation. But alack it should be otherwise, if they would be content to have all things tried by that undeceivable touchstone that god hath appointed: If the everlasting word of god which of right (proceeding from god) ought to have his preeminence of perfection to judge all did beat the bell, as also god hath appointed it should do, this matter would be soon at an end. For whatsoever building should be found, either in the one or the other, that had not his foundation therein, it should quickly vanish, and every man's work should appear. But if men will come with prejudicate minds, to be admirers of men's Persons, and will only look to a personal and local succession and be carried away with the empty and bare titles of their names and professions, without examination of that they bring, men shall easily offend both in the one and in the other. Let all men therefore be examined, let the word of God discuss according to his[†] prerogative: when God speaketh let all men hold their peace, and if he teach, let all flesh be confounded. In matters of faith and religion, let that word only be heard which is the true instructor, having been set down by men as writers, yet by the holy ghost the true inditer, who came not to suggest a peace, and so to leave an imperfect work, but to lead us into all truth, and to teach us whatsoever was necessary for our salvation: not leaving things doubtfully to be received from hand to

---

† "her" in the original English edition—Ed.

hand by way of tradition, but plainly written to remain to all the sons of God as god's sufficient and perpetual Testament. Fy [*def., exclamation expressing disgust*] upon these blasphemous mouths that will accuse God of infidelity, of cruelty of lack of care to his Church in providing for his: that like high traitors dare clip and adulterate his coin, wringing the scepter of his kingdom out of his hand, and bounding his government to some one people, city and country, as did the *Donatists*: challenging to themselves with the old *Chatarists*, and new *Anabaptists* and such as are of the *Family of love*, that they cannot err, when the most of their Popes (and specially such as followed him that proudly to show himself Antichrist, challenged the name of universal Bishop) were Sorcerers, Conjurers, Whoremongers and incestuous liars, Heretics, Murderers, Sodomiters, covetous Harlots, and cruel blasphemers in all their doings. I stand not to cite the places out of their own stories, they are manifest, and all the world may know them. And as for their Counsels they were nothing but wranglings and repeals one of another's Laws and Canons: their customs drawn from men's errors, and therefore (as *Cyprian* saith) being without truth, though they were never so old, are but old errors. And yet we leave the fountain, and go to the stinking puddles that they have digged unto themselves: we must leave the light of God, and go to the darkness of men: the instruction of the holy Ghost, and rest upon these Dunces, that know not what they say, nor whereof they affirm. The word of God must be drawn in and out by them as they think good, and therefore they speak most despitefully of it. They call it a dead letter, a nose of Wax, a Shipman's hose, a School mistress of error, dark, hard, insufficient of itself, and I cannot tell what. And yet as I said, if anything come from their Dunces, they receive it and never distrust it. The name of a Catholic is enough to authorize unto them anything be it never so false, absurd, peevish and contrary to the known and express truth of God. They cry the Church, the Church, no otherwise than crafty strumpets that will most scold for their honesty, when they never came where it grew. And then they brabble [*dispute obstinately*] with us about the translation, O, it is corrupted, it is not according to the Hebrew text, and to discredit that which maketh most against them: besides that, they forbid the people the reading of it, they bear the world in hand, that they have observed so many and so many faults, when all men of learning and judgment know that the time wherein their errors were most palpable and rife, all kind of good learning was worn out, the knowledge of tongues decreased, they whom they most spitied were the lighters of their Candles before all the world. For to themselves Hebrew letters though (as they say) they were as big as Oaks, yet they were Pitchforks and staples: and as for Greek, they were so far from understanding of it, that not one amongst a thousand could read it. I speak not of the latter times, for now good learning being brought to light, with the knowledge of the Gospel many of them have tinded [*kindled, lighted*] their Candles at our lights, and many (thanks be to God) are converted, and more should be, had not God in his justice for their wicked Rebellion made the means fruitless, reserving them to a farther judgment.

But let us see, where they ever amended anything they blamed. Their common translation hath been amended by us, to which yet so obstinate they are, that all upon pain of the black curse in their conspiracy of *Trent*, must be bound only to hold themselves: when as in many places for their lives, they are not able to make any construction or sense of it. But the obscurer it was, the better liked of them, and the more to their profit: and therefore they kept it under and forbad the reading of it, lest the light thereof should discover their faults and filthy corruptions. And this is the principal cause that *Calvin* and such notable men are so ill liked, and with such violence condemned amongst them. But what should good men look for other of these blind *Balamites*, but such condemnation? The other sort are those, that having once tasted of the sweet doctrine of the Gospel, are yet through an indisciplinate kind of life, be also devoid of true humility, carried away from the sincerity of the truth, some slugging still in dark ignorance, and sodding themselves in their own persuasions, believing nothing but that which they can compass and receiving nothing but that which standeth to the liking of their humors and graveled consciences, following like Swine their own beastly and carnal appetites. These men would be awakened. And when the Lord shall open their eyes, they shall see that the profession of the gospel of God, consisteth not in a bare confession, they shall find that the counsel of God in part revealeth itself, by our vocation: which also is from him, and then they shall know themselves to be effectually called, when they find sanctification as a continual companion in them: which is approved and known by mortifying the old Adam in us, and by quickening the inward man, in that daily reparation that maketh us as dear Children to resemble our heavenly father. Indeed we shall come short in the perfection thereof, but he that is perfect shall supply our wants [*lack*], both strengthening us to will and perform whatsoever is good, and also perfecting in himself that which is imperfect in us. These men would be warned not to abuse the Gospel of grace, and the glad tidings of their everlasting salvation to their own perdition: who whilst they speak of Christ should endeavor to know him as he is: that his bare name deceive them not, to lull them asleep in sin, and whilst they seek to comfort the oppressed, should likewise take heed that they strengthen not the wicked, to continue in their cursed security and fleshly liberty. It is very true that in Christ we have all things, but Christ with all his riches only belongs to his children, and to them he is applied with all his benefits, through a true and lively faith: and he hath sundry offices, to which, his must submit themselves. They must acknowledge his kingdom to be ruled by his word, and they must be subject to his law, who hath thoroughly and continually provided for their government. They must rest in that which he teacheth, because he is their only Prophet, their only Priest, in whose only sacrifice the father is pacified and well pleased. And Christ is the mark to whom the law leadeth, the end and perfection thereof, that they in him should walk in obedience. The last sort which are as ill as the worst, I mean either open or else close and crafty Heretics, they can as ill brook the sincere word of God as any of the others, bleating also against his government and discipline, because it restraineth, correcteth and bridleth their heretical opinions and manners. They allege overmuch surety, continually abusing his mercy, and like fanatical wretches, because they would be left to themselves to spew out their heresies, they continually bark against this wholesome correction and holy obedience. These fellows pick many quarrels, making it subject to the inconstant wiles of Popes and ignorant Princes, as though it were a Shipman's hose, to be altered and changed at their pleasure. But alack they do but catch the wind in a net: For it must needs be that Christ's scepter bruise them, and it prevail. And specially they cannot abide such men as this good *Calvin* was, because he rubbed them on the gawle [*subdued or broke their spirit*], and brake even the skull (as I may say) of their heretical corruptions. For some of them are *Arians*, other some *Anabaptists*, and *Servetians, Davidians* and *Sylvanists, Pelagians,* and *Freewill men, Libertines* and of the *Family of Love*, joining with them infinite heresies, and secretly in this security of the Church, disperse their poison, which I fear me, will one day so break forth when we least think of it, to the trouble of the whole Church of God, that it will be a long time or ever it be purged and appeased. I would to God there were none in England, I would to God they had fewer favorers, and we more judgment and zeal to defend the sincere truth of our God, then should they not give such evident tokens of the venom that is within them, in defending *Servetus* that Dog that hath renewed all the old heresies of the *Arians*, that so much troubled the Church in time past: neither would they themselves in their own fantasies with such impudence condemn the dear servants of God, for procuring and calling upon the magistrate for his lawful execution against Heretics and empoisoners of the Church. They would not make a mash and hotchpotch [*hodgepodge*] of the civil and ecclesiastical state, and so jumble them together. They would not deny the power of the magistrate's sword, committed to his ministers not in vain, but to be used in cutting off the rotten members thereof, for the preservation of the whole body. They would not bark so like Dogs against the everlasting predestination and election of God, the most comfortable doctrine that can be, being the foundation of all the rest, where it is wisely taught according to the word, and learned within that sober compass that it is prescribed: joining and jumping so near with *Anabaptists*, the spiritual illuminate, *Pelagians*, and other merit mongers, who howsoever they differ in some particular marks, yet are birds of one and the same feather. This shall always be found true that they follow the corruptest men of our age in all these matters. But whatsoever they say, God's truth is of sufficient power to overcome all their heretical blasphemies. *Moyses* rod shall devour their Sorcerers serpents. *Dagon* shall break his neck where his truth is received. And this sun arising shall scatter all their darkness. These excellent instruments shall live when they shall be forgotten, unless it be in immortal shame and opprobry [*reproach, disgrace*]. Let us not therefore be discouraged but hold fast the truth of our good God, and with fear and reverence, let us seek after those things he hath revealed unto us. There can be no danger if we keep ourselves within the compass of the holy Scriptures. For this doctrine of God's eternal election and Predestination is most comfortable. O, but say they with the old Heretics, if I be elected and predestinated, what need I to avoid evil works, they shall neither further nor hinder me: God is sure and what need I torment and vex myself to do well and to lead a straight and godly life, we like not these peppered consciences! Such Heretics there were long ago that so wrote and taught that occasioned Saint *Augustine* to write that excellent work of the Predestination of God's Saints, confuting such caitiffs [*despicable wretches, villains*] as these. Saint *Augustine* therefore answereth them, that this doctrine is a most comfortable doctrine, necessary to be known, to be published and preached to the people in his due time and place. For it is that same everlasting and unchangeable decree of GOD, whereby he hath undoubtedly determined in the time that he himself best knoweth, to call his elect to the knowledge of his truth, that his mercy and glory might be declared in them. And this hath the Scripture confirmed *Rom.8,verse 30!* Whom he hath predestinated those he hath called, and whom he hath called those he hath justified. And again in the first Chapter to the *Ephesians*, we are elected before the foundations of the world, and in the ninth to the *Romans* speaking of *Esau* and *Jacob* (of whom these Sermons especially entreat) he saith that one was elected and the other rejected before they had done either good or evil. The foundation hereof, is only the purpose of his will: not foreseeing (as the Papists say) any worthiness or unworthiness of man; but for just causes known to himself, and in himself not in us, in which without further inquiry we ought to rest, acknowledging him to be only good, wise and most righteous, who is and shall be blessed and justified forever. Now for them that are either rejected or elected, we wade no farther to judge of them than may appear by the effects, neither do we judge absolutely of them, but with condition unless upon those peculiar lost ones of whom God himself in his word hath pronounced. Read *Ephe. 1* and *1.Pet. 1.* Now if any Potsherd [*pottery fragment*] will reason with the potter, which not resting in his will, would wade further to know the secret causes of this, we say unto him with the Apostle: O wretched man who art thou that disputest with God. Shall the thing formed say to him that formed it, why hast thou made me thus? For further satisfaction in this question, I refer all Christians to the Books that are written hereof, and namely to these excellent Sermons: M. *Knox* hath learnedly answered the objections of the adversaries in a Book printed at *Geneva*. We have also home writers, that have dealt fully and plainly therein, as *Veron* of Predestination, and M. *Crowly* in his book against *Cerberus*, rightly so called for his barking blasphemies, against this most comfortable and excellent doctrine: others that are learned may further satisfy themselves, with those learned answers of M. *Beza* against that impure Apostata *Castalio*.

And now to return to your Honours, I most humbly beseech you to accept my poor labors, which I offer under your Honours names to the whole Church of God. And I beseech your honours, as God hath called you to the knowledge of his glorious Gospel, which is a token of your election, so go forward more and more in the growth thereof: that the Gospel being truly rooted in your hearts, it may bring forth sanctification, the true seal of your adoption, that you may feel his goodness in the assurance of that everlasting and blessed inheritance. God hath called you to high honor, not so much by your places and calling amongst men (which yet is somewhat, because it is a great benefit of God) but in that he hath made you his adopted children, it is that you should show obedience, in that he hath made you heirs with his son, and Citizens with his Saints, it is that you should look up to Heaven and have your joy there despising this world, and living to righteousness and true holiness. And this will the Lord in mercy bestow upon you, thereby sealing your election, if you separate yourselves from the corruption of the world: I say not that you should go out of the world, but that you should depart from evil, and be followers of God as dear children, walking in love, even as he hath loved you. Beware of these two Cankers that corrupt the whole world, and is most likely to assail Nobility, I mean Pride and Covetousness, Let them not once be named amongst you as becometh Saints. A day will come, when the Lord will fulfill your hope in better things than all this world can give you. Stand fast in his truth in these slippery days, and above all things let his glory, and the advancement of his word, be dear and precious unto you. In God's matters, let his will be the rule thereof, and not your own wisdom and affections. Examine yourselves often by it, and neglect not holy exercises. Let other Gallants of this world, follow their foolish and fading pleasures, delight you in his law, and be good examples to others. Care not for the contempt of the world, but hold fast a good conscience that you may be approved before GOD. The Lord Jesus bless you both, that as he hath knit you together, so you may draw on forwards in one yoke towards his kingdom, that that may be your aim and mark in all your deeds, words, and thoughts. Amen. October 25, 1579

Your Honours most humble and
faithful ever to command in Christ,
John Field

❧The first Sermon of
M. John Calvin
concerning Jacob and Esau

Genesis Chap. 25. verse 12

Now these are the generations of Ismael Abrahams sonne, whome Hagar, the Egyptian Sarahs handmaide bare vnto Abraham, &c. To the end of the 22. verse.

E HAVE HERE TO CONSIDER the difference that Moyses putteth betwixt the Children of Abraham. We have seen already that the whole stock which he had by Keturah, dwelled in a country far off. Concerning Ismael he is separated far enough from the land of Canaan: notwithstanding he be yet as one rejected. For it was necessary that the inheritance which was ordained to Isaack, should remain to him. Now in the first place it is said, that Ismael had twelve sons, the which in such sort multiplied, that of them came twelve Peoples. In this we see that God not without cause said to his servant Abraham[†], that for his sake Ismael also should have a certain blessing: but that it should be transitory and fleeting, and the principal should remain to Isaack. But

---

† *Genesis 17:20-22*

I

whatsoever it be: yet so it is, that God did show himself faithful and true in his promise, the which belongeth to this temporal life. If God would that his truth and constancy should be known in these things of the world, which slip away, and have nothing else but a figure which vanisheth, as Saint Paul saith: what shall it be, when the promises are of far greater importance, as when he calleth us to the inheritance of the kingdom of heaven? Think we then that we can be frustrate of that, staying ourselves upon him? See then how we must make our profit of this place. If God will be known firm and faithful in his word towards those which are as strangers, and which he hath shut out and rejected from his church: what will he then do towards us which are his children, whom he hath adopted, and to whom it hath pleased him to show himself nigh? For if God in small things, as in the stock, and in all other things of like sort, will have his truth known? what shall it be, when in the person of our Lord Jesus Christ, he setteth out unto us the inheritance of heaven, and declareth unto us that he will be merciful unto us, and that he will pardon our faults, that we may be reconciled to him, and that by this means we may be the brethren and companions of Angels, under one head, to wit, our Lord Jesus Christ? Can God there fail in his promises? Shall they be void and without effect and execution? It is impossible. This then is that we have to hold in this first place. And further we have next to note, that God will manifest himself not only to us in these his benefits, which are most great and excellent, but also those that concern this life: and that there is nothing so small, in which he will not have some marks of his fatherly goodness imprinted. And forasmuch as he hath said that he will have care to feed us, let us wait upon him, for all that which belongeth to the maintenance of this life, and let us not think that it derogateth any whit from his majesty, in that he will have us to call upon him for drink and for food to feed upon. For he will that in all and through all we should have our recourse to him: let us not then doubt but that God (albeit our bodies be earth and ashes, rottenness and worms meat, and as the common speech is, but carrions [*dead and putrefying flesh*], which are nothing worth) will yet notwithstanding provide for all our corporal necessities. This is that we have to add as the second point. But now we must here see the comparison, which Moyses maketh betwixt Ismael and Isaack. Behold Ismael which is cut off, and is no more reputed among the children of God, and yet notwithstanding we see that he prospereth, and that he hath a great train. For of twelve sons which he hath begotten, behold twelve peoples that came from them. And with all of Isaack, what? Isaack married at forty years old: and after that his wife was barren, and that not for one year, nor for two, but even for twenty years space, he had no children. God had said unto him: *I will multiply thy seed, as the stars of heaven, and as the sand of the sea.* This was pronounced to his father Abraham: but this was of special favor toward him. But he might have been before this time increased, as he hoped, notwithstanding he saw that his wife was barren, and it seemed as though god minded to mock him, and declare unto him that the thing which he hoped for, was nothing worth. When therefore he saw that his brother Ismael, who had no root in the church, who was a stranger from all hope of salvation: when he saw him (I say) to flourish in his seed, and it seemed that God had poured forth all his graces upon him: and in the meantime, that he was left in his own house all alone, and had none to succeed him: it is certain that he might be in great perplexity, as if it had been much better for him to have been like his brother Ismael.

This was to make him give over all, and after to be without hope, and to have contemned God: he had falne [*fallen*] even to the uttermost extremity, if he had not been holden in by a singular patience. Now then, we have here to behold as in a glass, the condition of God's Church, how it beginneth, and how God upholdeth it, and multiplieth it, that is to say, after so strange a fashion, that it seemeth at all assays, that that same appearance which God shall have given us, is nothing (as a man would say) but to deceive us. For (instead that the children of this world have a goodly show, and a man shall find them to encrease to the eye) the church shall be hidden under the Earth: a man shall see the earth full replenished by unbelievers, of contemners of God and profane people: and where shall a man find the faithful? They shall be very thin sown and a man shall not be able to perceive them, they shall be despised, men shall tread them almost under their feet, and men shall think that God hath no care of his Church, and that further he taketh pleasure that the wicked should make their triumphs, and should have their brave and pompous shows.

Now then this is showed unto us in the persons of Isaack and of Ismael, to the end that the strangeness of it troubles us not beyond measure, and that we should fight constantly against all doubtings which might arise in our imagination, as often as we do see a small number of people which worship God, and that we see almost an infinite number of those which stubbornly set themselves against him, and which know not what it meaneth to bear his yoke. Now this doctrine is very necessary for us at this day. For how doth God work in our time? For when he meant to rear up against his Gospel, at what end began he? What people called he? And yet now, if we cast our eye upon the whole world, we shall find in the first place, that in Asia (which is the greatest part thereof) all is disordered and confused, and that there, there is nothing but superstitions on the one side, and so unruly barbarousness on the other, as pity it is to behold. Mark also the other part of the world, to wit, Africa, which is in the same order. And as concerning Europe (which men call Christendom) let a man behold that which is in Italy, in France, and other places, and a man shall find that the Devil beareth there the sway, and that the upholders of Antichrist, who are deadly enemies of the Church, what profession soever they make, a man shall see them to be as the Stars of Heaven, and as the sand of the sea: so as a man might say that there is nothing but for their use. And indeed they are very skillful to make their vaunt thereof: for they make a buckler of this to contemn God, and also to harden themselves in their rebellion. They mock and deride us for this, that we are so few people, and that notwithstanding we will be holden for the Church. But for our part we are despised and rejected: and moreover, we are far off from approaching to this great people, which advance themselves against us: To be short, a man would say, that we are as three grains of Corn under a great heap of Chaff. And yet for all this it is so, that we have this testimony of God, that he keepeth us and avoweth us to be his household servants. For it is no Church, unless it be joined to our Lord Jesus Christ, who is the head thereof. When this faileth, all the rest goeth to wrack and to ruin, as Saint Paul saith: *Now we are united to the son of God, through the faith of his Gospel*, which is the certain and undeceiveable bond. And how shall we judge that we are the Church, seeing that we are nothing in comparison of the unfaithful, who are puffed up by reason of their greatness, and of all their other qualities, which they know well enough how to set out with full mouth? But let not us be astonished for all this, seeing that God hath given us an allowance in the person of our father Isaack, that the Church was as a forsaken house, and that he had no stock and that he had not a great number of people, and yet for all that he ceased not to hold it as an hidden treasure: let us content ourselves herewith. And now for that which followeth, the person of Ismael ought also to be well marked: for he came out from the house of Abraham, which at that time was the only Church in the whole world: he bare also circumcision, as if he had been an inheritor of the kingdom of God: yea he was the firstborn, and had the swinge [*sway, influence, authority*] in the house, yea, insomuch that he mocked his brother, as we have seen already. Now it is even so likewise at this day concerning the Papists: for they are not strangers from the church, but they are as bastard children. They will say also that they have antiquity on their side, and they went before us: and we see how they trust in their succession which they have from the Apostles (as they say:) that at all times there have been Bishops and prelates in their church, and that hereupon a man might certainly conclude, that the title of the church belongeth to them. And yet for all this they are but bastards as Ismael was, forasmuch as they were not begotten by the gospel as we have heard, which is the seed of freedom: but have corrupted themselves. Behold, how we may account them for Ismaelites. For albeit they be great peoples, and that we in the meantime remain as poor untimely fruits, yet let us know that our Lord Jesus Christ hath given us such an example thereof, that at this day we might not be ashamed. This then to be short, is that we have here to remember. And hereunto we ought also to apply that which we read in the prophets. For it is not for once that this happened, that the Church hath been brought to a small number, yea and that it had nothing but horrible desolation in it: as in the time of the captivity of Babylon, what was it? For thereupon it is said: by Esay[†], *Rejoice O barren that didst not bear: break forth into joy and rejoice, thou that didst not travail with Child: For the desolate hath more Children than all the married wives: Albeit thou hast been as a widow, God shall multiply thee, and thou shalt be a people, as it were by miracle, and above the judgment and opinion of men, and when thou shalt have stretched out thy Pavilions here and there, all shall be filled and replenished.*

    When therefore we hear that this is spoken to the Church, let us know that if God at this day to humble us or to punish our offences, do diminish the number of them that call upon him: we must not therefore quail, but rather follow always our vocation without any astonishment at all. And further let us note that we see (specially in the state of the church) that which is spoken of in the hundred and

---

† *Isaiah 54:1*

thirteenth Psalm[†]: That God filleth the houses of those that were barren before, with goodly children and a great offspring. Let us wait then till our Lord doth his work, and then we shall have occasion to glorify him, knowing that it is not in vain that he hath said: that Abraham's seed shall be multiplied: but that this must come after such a sort as is incomprehensible unto us, and that the beginnings are small, and as it were nothing. When then we shall have this patience, it is certain that God will work in such sort, as we shall have always whereby to be confirmed in his promises, seeing that the effect shall show itself, yea and more than we could have thought or wished for. Furthermore this we have to mark here in this place. But there is another difficulty: to wit, that although Ismael be so advanced, that he seeth so many successors as is wonderful, (for he lived an hundred, thirty and seven years, and had twelve sons) and might see a people already descended of his stock. Although for a time he were so lifted up, yet within a while after he was as one taken away: For Moyses indeed rehearseth those children he had, but when he speaketh thereof in the holy history, they are rejected and have no fellowship with that true stock of Abraham which was blessed: even so let us note that it is nothing to have like authority, and to have a great show, and goodly hue among men, and to be in reputation, namely so as men wonder at us, yet all this is worth nothing in comparison of the durable state of the Church.

God setteth up his house in such force, that it

---

† *Psalm 113:9*

seemeth as a play of little Children: notwithstanding the foundations are perpetual. And further he continueth his grace, in such sort, that a man may very well see, that it is he which is the founder of his Church, which buildeth, finisheth, and upholdeth it. This plainly appeareth: yet the unbelievers have their discourses and determinations: in such sort, that they are as the grass which groweth upon the house tops, like as it is said in the hundred and twenty-ninth Psalm[†]: The corn shall be trodden under feet, and men cast it into the earth, and it remaineth there in a low place, and in the meanwhile, behold the grass which shall grow very high upon the house tops: but inasmuch as it is nearer to the Sun it taketh no root: so that it must needs wither, in such sort that there cometh no fruit of it, as the Prophet there showeth. Even so then, when we see that the Lord keepeth us in this poor and low condition, and that not only we are despised, but as it were utterly rejected of all: let us know, that it ought to suffice us, that we have a root in our God, to live by his grace forever: that we are maintained by him; and that we are as a tree planted by the river's side, which always shall be moistened with water to draw out nourishment therefrom. Let us content ourselves herewith. And so this comparison is not made without cause, when Moyses expressly saith that Ismael begat twelve sons, which were gathered into twelve peoples, and after that, he stays there, and so leaves them. Further he saith: *Behold the generations of Isaack.*

And why? it is for that his wife was barren, until that

---

† *Psalm 129:6*

he was come to the age of sixty years. Behold a wonderful thing, yea but we shall find, that after God had ratified his promise, to wit, that he should be multiplied in such sort, as he had showed unto him, that he had not spoken in vain. For what was it to see such a multitude of people in Egypt, as if grass had grown in the midst of an hot burning Oven? For this was as a furnace, (as the scripture speaketh) which was the tyranny and bondage of Egypt. Behold the people as chaff, and see the fire which is kindled in every place all about, and yet for all this the people is not consumed, like as is showed in the figure of the Bush, which was as it were burning on a light fire, and yet the bush remained whole and was not consumed†. We see likewise how the people multiplied, being under such oppression and anguish, that then was not only question of an hundred thousand, or of three or four hundred thousand, but behold six hundred thousand issuing out under such a captivity. And how was this possible? Behold a miracle to ravish us in astonishment. Now then let us know, that as God after this manner tried the faith and patience of Isaack, so in the end he found a means to accomplish his promise, yea beyond the reach of man. For this came to pass after a strange fashion, and which a man would not have thought. Let us also at this day apply this to ourselves, and let us practice that which is spoken in the thirty-seventh Psalm††. If we see the wicked and the contemners of God to be advanced as the Cedars of Lebanon, let us wait: for there needs no more,

---

† *Exodus 3:2-4 & Acts 7:30*

†† *Psalm 37:10*

but even to turn our eyes, and lo, they are razed [*erased*] and cut off, and one shall not see so much as the place where they were. And why so? Because they were not planted in God. We hear that which our Lord Jesus Christ saith, Matt. 15[†]. *Every plant which my heavenly father hath not planted shall be rooted up.*

So let us not envy the Children of this world, when we shall see them in high estate, when we shall see them advance to nobility and to dignity, and in all other things: let us wait patiently and bear our condition peaceably: and if the world do mock us, make no account of us, and disdain us, let it suffice us notwithstanding to be esteemed before God and his Angels. And in the meantime let us wait, till God accomplish that he hath spoken in another place, *The righteous shall flourish like a Palm tree, and shall grow like a Cedar in Lebanon*[††]: yea, after another fashion: for he saith, he shall be multiplied in the courts of the house of the Lord. When it is said, that they shall be planted in the house of God, that is to say, they shall be blessed of him: For, behold also wherein our continual felicity consisteth, so as from age to age, we may always stand fast, as it is said in the hundred and twelfth Psalm[†††]. That inasmuch as God abideth forever one, and changeth not as doth the world which waxeth old and groweth in corruption: but that God is always like himself: The Prophet thereupon concludeth, that the

---

[†] *Matthew 15:13*

[††] *Psalm 92:12,13*

[†††] *Psalm 112*

faithful shall have their abiding: and that albeit at the first blush a man see not that the grace of God is showed upon them, yet in the end, it shall be known.

This therefore hitherto is that we have to learn of this place, and of this difference which Moyses putteth here between the stock of Ismael, and that of Isaack. Behold these beginnings of the church which are as a thing of nothing, but the finishing thereof is wonderful. Now the beginnings of the children of this world are mighty and noble, and such as astonish all men: but all comes to nothing. And why so? Because they have no continuing in the promise of God. This is the fountain of life: and behold how we may continue to the end: this also is the means to make us to be advanced above the world. For when the question is, of our rejoicing in God, and of contenting ourselves with his fatherly goodness, that he hath showed unto us, Let us not be as fools to busy ourselves about that which we now see with the eye: For these present things of the world pass away and vanish: but let us behold that which is invisible, as the true nature of Faith is, as the Apostle saith. Now Moyses addeth,

> That Ismael dwelt over against his brethren, or in
> their presence.

It is true that one hath translated this *to dwell*, and the word importeth *to fall*: but it signifieth to rest, to dwell, and to have a house. This then is the true and natural meaning, that Ismael was not far off (as already we have seen) from the children of Keturah, but that he remained a near neighbor of the land of Canaan, which was promised to Isaack: notwithstanding this is true also, that he possessed not that land there, for it was meet that he should be barred from thence. And who is it that had driven him thence? For after the death of Abraham, it is certain, that he might have tarried there if he would. Isaack had nothing but the Sepulcher which is father had gotten: he was not lead thence to have any great and large possessions: he had nothing, unless it were altogether borrowed and by the leave of the inhabitants.

Ismael therefore might well have made his abode and nested there, if he had listed [*desired*]. But he went from thence: was this to obey GOD? No, For he was full of pride and rebellion. So he would rather have blasphemed God, when he had thought I am here put apart, as though I were not of my father's house. Therefore I must stay myself in the country where I was born. But God doth lead him thither without his knowledge, wherefore he goeth thither, yea by a secret inspiration. See how God worketh towards the unbelievers: he turneth them, he windeth them from one side to another.

We do not see apparently that it is so: but we must by faith consider therein a providence of GOD, and if we were very attentive therein, it is certain that we should have proof of that which is here written and that daily. For how is it that we are not destroyed of these mad beasts, which compass us on every side? We see what their cruelty is, and how insatiable they are in their covetousness: Whereupon then stayeth it, that we are not all swallowed up: but that God turneth away their fury, and that he knoweth how to direct them as seemeth good unto him? he will make them sometimes to push one another: further he keepeth them there as Lions that are enchained and holden within Iron bars.   See then how God also at this day driveth and chaseth the unbelievers, where he will without violence at least, so as they perceive it not, even as he did that at time with Ismael. For we have already declared, that he desired nothing more then to overthrow and abolish the promise of God, which was made unto Isaack, and yet for all that he goeth not about it.   And why so?   Because it was not permitted unto him from above, and because God doth place him there in a dwelling out of the way, saying, *Thou shalt dwell near thy brethren*: but howsoever it be, thou shalt not hinder, but that they shall enjoy the region which I have assigned unto them for an inheritance.   But he speaketh specially of Brethren, and yet for all that he had none but Isaack: this is to show that God had no regard to one or to two, when he so shut up Ismael: but as if the people had already inhabited the land of Canaan: the people I say, which was not yet born, yea, which was not born a long time after.

This is the sum of that we have further to note here. Now hereupon we may be confirmed and strengthened, as often as we see the wicked and condemners of God (who are so deadly enemies to us) to cast out their froth, in that we know that our Lord can stay and hold them in well enough, and that he will turn them some other way, and when it shall seem that they are to cast and banish us out of the world that our Lord will hold them as Captives, albeit they know not how.   To be short, this that is here set out of Ismael, we shall have trial of, so that we be patient, and call upon God, and nothing doubt, but that he hath means of his own in himself to save us, the which we at the first perceive not. But now let us come to that which Moyses reciteth concerning Isaack. It is true that thereof he had already spoken something, but it is requisite that it be deducted more at large. He hath said, *That Isaack was forty years old, when he took Rebecca to wife*, and further that she was barren. Now it is like that Ismael was married sooner. For we have already seen that Hagar his mother had given him wife, without mention of his age, and a man may well gather that he was then very young. Isaack cometh to the age of forty years and might already be enfeebled before he entered into marriage. See then how he was kept back. Now let us note that all this while passed not, but he often entered into reckoning, to inquire of this promise, which was made unto him, that his seed should be multiplied as the stars of Heaven and the sand of the sea, and all this while he found no wife, for he durst not take one in the country. And it is like that God showed him that he would keep her barren even till the end. But yet when he was married, it seemeth that then at the least God would bless him, and increase and augment him in his stock. But his wife is barren, yea by the space of twenty years. If any such temptation should come unto any of us, it is certain that the best of us should hardly resist it one day: we lightly pass over that which is here recited by Moyses. And why so? It is because we be not exercised with many conflicts, yea and because we shun them, and also God spareth us by reason of infirmity and rudeness. Nevertheless we ought to make our profit of such examples, when we come to any entry or trial of our faith, we are altogether undone. And why? Because in time and place we are not so fenced as were necessary. Now it is said here, that for the space of twenty years it seemed that Isaack was accursed of God, and that he was in a manner a dead stock, and that he had no hope of having any children during the space of twenty years. For here is not question of having children only. As when men and women do marry, they will be glad to have children: And this is also a token of God's favor, but here was a special reason in Isaack. For he waited not only for the people that should descend of him, but he waited for the salvation of the world. See then Jesus Christ, which is after a sort in his reins, as the Apostle saith: for he useth the same manner of speech there. Isaack saw that he was barren, and yet he had no other hope to be saved, he is as it were a cursed creature, and as it were at the pits brink, except he have issue, and all this while, that God which had made promise thereof in the person of his father, seemeth to mock him and leaveth him there, where he must needs languish: and that as often as he beheld his wife he might thus think with himself, Lo, a glass, wherein I see that God hath rejected us, and that he maketh no account of us, and that he hath turned his back towards us, that his promise is frustrate, that it hath no force or efficacy towards us.

See (I say) how Isaack had daily to bear with such assaults: and we ought well to weigh all these things (as I have already said:) but forasmuch as we do not regard to what end the holy Ghost speaketh unto us of Isaack, and because we know not how to apply that to our instruction which is here spoken of him: see why it ought to make us lose no courage at all: but when there is but one Blast of wind, by and by we are beaten down. And why so? for we ought to have thought thus on this sort. Go to, how is it that Isaack hath so firm constancy, and that for the space of twenty years? he quailed not, albeit, it seemed to him that GOD had mocked him: this was because that he was patient, and because he knew, it behooved him not to set God the time wherein he had to perform his promise: but that he must submit himself to him and do him this honor to know that his works are incomprehensible, and that he knoweth the fit times and seasons, to perform that he hath pronounced: to be short, that it is not our part to set him a law: but that it is meet that we keep silence, and that we murmur not, if things fall not out according to our appetite and desire: but that we must wait till he accomplish his own works, yea, although we see all things contrary: Nevertheless, it behooveth that our faith prevail against all the world, even as Saint John saith in his Canonical Epistle. Now inasmuch as all this is nothing, and it vanisheth from before our eyes: and when we read this history, it is so coldly done, that we receive no fruit by it. See, also why GOD punisheth us for our ingratitude: because we are so delicate, that as soon as there cometh, not a storm or some great Whirlwind, but a little puff, behold we are forthwith shaken, and in the end do fall away.

So much the rather then it behooveth that we mark well that which is here spoken: to wit, that Isaack continued to trust in GOD, although that by the space of twenty years, it seemed that he could have no issue. Now that he persevered, it appeareth by that which Moyses saith.

For Isaack prayed unto the Lord for his wife, and was heard, so as his wife conceived.

When it is said, that he prayed to the Lord, we must

not think that he only waited till that time was accomplished: but seeing that his wife was barren, he had his recourse to GOD, which was the only remedy. What? seemeth it then that he lost his time, and that he cast his Prayers in the Air, and that they never came to God's ears? For a man would say so. For if he had been heard, would not God then have declared by experience, that which he had promised him? But he saw nothing of all that. Then when Isaack had prayed one year, and twain: it is all one, as if he had spoken to a Rock or to a wall: God making wise as though he were deaf: that is to say, he showed not himself in any sort to have a favorable care to receive Isaack's requests: and this continued. But when this cometh unto the end of ten or twelve years, what would a man say, but that it were better to give over? For this is a marvelous hard and great temptation, that God should do nothing of that that he had promised at the end of fifteen years. But although he had put off to do it even to the twentieth year, yet nevertheless Isaack ceased not to pray, but always continued, and his prayer was a sure seal of his Faith. For he prayed not after the manner of the unbelievers, which ever wait to rage against God: but he followed the rule that is given us by Saint Paul (although it was not yet written). And that was to join thanksgiving with our prayers, referring ourselves wholly unto God, and quietly waiting for such an issue from him as could not yet be seen. Like as then when Isaack continued still to cast all his heaviness into the bosom of God, and all the care that oppressed him, and all the sorrows, griefs and anguishes, wherein he was enclosed: when he reposed all this in the bosom of God, this was a sure trial of his faith.

This then is that we have to learn by his example: to
wit, that we think not that God hath bound himself unto us
to do all that he hath spoken at the first dash: but after that
he hath once spoken, he will not give any sign to
accomplish his work and we will think that all that he had
promised was nothing else (as men say,) but words and
wind. It behooveth then that we be holden in, with such
patience: (as also the Apostle exhorteth us hereto, in the
tenth Chapter to the Hebrews[†]) that from day to day, from
year to year, and all our life long, and as if nothing were,
that we hold ourselves there in quiet and hold our peace
before God, to the end we skirmish not, nor make any broil,
nor plead against him, nor summon him, according as our
fickle appetites would move us. And hereupon we have to
put that in practice which the Apostle allegeth out of the
Prophet Habacuc[††]: That if he forslow his promise, we
should wait, and it shall not linger. He there setteth down
two things: he saith in deed that the promise of God shall
not be foreslowed: that is to say, that it shall have a certain
and undoubted execution, and in it, season: But concerning
us and our sense or feeling, he saith, it shall linger: so that
we have need patiently to wait. Behold then how our faith
must be tried. For if we hope that God will show himself
faithful towards us, and that we remain firm and constant,
it behooved that we be often again and again exercised in
prayers and supplications: for faith must not be idle, to be
short, if we have to live here beneath, as poor miserable

[†] *Hebrews 10:37*

[††] *Habakkuk 2:3*

wretches, and that some must be afflicted with diseases, and others with poverty, that everyone hath to endure many afflictions and miseries: that nevertheless we go forward, and that we know, when God promiseth us to be our father, it is not that he meaneth to show it always apparently to the eye. He will give us indeed some taste of his goodness, as much as shall be necessary, yea we shall have therein to satisfy ourselves, so that our faith be always joined thereunto: in such sort that we shall feel, that that which he hath pronounced is not to deceive us. Open thy mouth and I will fill it[†]. But howsoever it be, it behooveth that we wait always by faith, for that which yet appeareth not, and which is as it were far from us, and seemeth to be impossible. Again, when we shall be thus grounded and stayed upon the truth of God, and that we shall suffer ourselves to be afflicted by many miseries, that yet, we have that care and zeal to pray and call upon God both morning and evening, and have our recourse unto him: for this is our only comfort. This therefore is not a thing lightly to be passed over, when Moyses rehearseth, that Isaack prayed unto god for the bareness of his wife, and that God heard him. For on the one side we see the perseverance which Isaack had in staying himself upon God, and making request unto him: on the other side we see that God was not deaf to his requests: but this was not, for that he showed himself at the first dash. For a man would have said, that Isaack was abused to run so unto God morning and evening, and that it had been better that he had given over all: but at the end of twenty

---

† *Psalm 81:10*

years, God came suddenly, to the end he might show that men are too hasty and headlong in their desires: and here see, what is the cause that often times his name is blasphemed, and men will accuse him for that he worketh not according to our fantasy: this (say I) proceedeth of impatience. Now we have also to note, that Isaack knew that it was a great benefit of God, to give his issue. For when God had pronounced, *Encrease and multiply*†, according as we have seen, it is to show that neither men nor beasts could bring forth and increase, but by his power, that we should not think that it came by adventure. If therefore Bulls, horses, and Asses cannot engender [*beget, procreate*] unless God shed out his blessing and secret power, what shall be of men? For we are far more noble creatures, inasmuch as god hath formed us according to his own image. So that when we see that both men and beasts are increased by generation, we must thereby call to memory that this is from the word of God, which hath issued out of his mouth, *Encrease and multiply*, which yet even at this day showeth itself, but we must go farther: to wit, that God keepeth this blessing and liberality to himself, to the end to distribute it as he seeth good. For we see that all engender [*beget, procreate*] not alike: Some have no children, others one or two, and others again have them by dozens. So then when see such an inequality, it behooveth is too acknowledge that it is a special benefit of God to have children: as also it is expressly said in the Psalm††, that the

---

† *Genesis 1:28*

†† *Psalm 127:3*

fruit of the womb (for so the Scripture speaketh) is a reward
of God. And so we must in this behalf, have recourse unto
him. And therefore those that desire so greatly to have
children, they must follow always the example of Isaack.
For they will say indeed, O I would have Children: but of
thinking upon God, there is neither mention, nor news.
And forasmuch as God is defrauded of his honor, lo, why he
withdraweth his hand: or rather if he give an offspring,
forasmuch as they are a profane people, he will give them
children which shall scratch out their eyes. For their
children are as young serpents, or thorns, for to prick and
pierce them even to the heart. Behold therefore what is the
cause that many have no offspring to succeed them: or if
they have, it is for their farther evil: forasmuch as they have
not addressed themselves to God, to obtain all of his
blessing. Let us therefore mark well, that that which is here
showed as concerning our father Isaack, is that he seeing his
wife barren, prepared himself to God knowing very well,
that it was of him that he ought to demand issue. And
indeed, what will men allege here against this blessing? If
we mark that which is written in Job[†], that when a child
cometh into the world, it is a lively image of the
incomprehensible power of God, which cannot be
sufficiently esteemed. For whereof is it that an infant is
engendered [*begat, procreated*], and after it is conceived, how
liveth it in the womb of the mother? And further, how is it,
that he cometh forth? If a man mark all these things, who
will be so brutish, to say that men engender [*beget, procreate*]

---

† *Job 14*

them by their own strength and industry? Let us then hold fast this lesson: which is that they that are married and desire offspring, that they ask it of God: and that for two reasons. The first, because God has reserved this in his own hand, as we have even now alleged out of the Psalm. The second is that it is not enough that their houses be full of children, unless that God always govern them. For it were much better that they had no offspring at all, than to have a perverse seed, accursed and full of mischief. So then let fathers learn (in this behalf) to follow the example of Isaack. But let us also diligently note, that Isaack prayed not for an offspring, only after the natural appetite of men: But he looked up higher: that is to say, because that it behooved that of him should proceed the salvation of the world in the person of our Lord Jesus Christ, the which shall be deducted more at large hereafter.

But now let us fall down before the holy majesty of our good God, in acknowledging our faults, and praying him that he will make us to feel them more and more, and that it may be to humble us, and to bring us to true repentance: and that we may be in such sort touched with fear, that we may desire nothing but to be stripped of all our earthly affections and lusts to the end we may be clothed with his righteousness, until that he shall have drawn us to a full and perfect perfection. And that he will not only do this good unto us, etc.

❧The second Sermon

Genesis 25. Chapter.

So that Rebecca his wife conceaued.

21. *And when the Children ſtroue within her, ſhee ſayde, If it be ſo, to what end is it? & ſhe went to aſke counſell of the Lord.*

22. *To whome the Lord ſaid: There are two peoples in thy wombe, and two nations brought foorth out of thy wombe ſhalbe deuided, of whome one ſhall be mightier than the other, and the elder ſhall ſerue the younger.*

E SAW YESTERDAY HOW GOD proved the faith of Isaack, before he gave him any offspring, to wit, for the space of twenty years. Now to the end we should know that he prayed not to God in vain, seeing that God heard his request, the which tended to this, that God might send the savior of the world by means of the seed that he had promised him. Now lo, wherein it was that Isaack might rejoice, and not after the common manner. For his wife had been barren a long time, and he saw that she had conceived, and that God had declared that he had not forgotten his promise, and after he knew that this was granted him, forasmuch as he had his recourse to God. But see a new temptation, and which is more hard and more grievous to be borne, than if his wife had remained barren. For she conceived two children, the which struggled and strove together in her belly. Now this was very hideous thing, and as it were against nature. And see wherefore also she said, that it had been better that she had been dead, and this was not of any impatience that she spake thus, as if she had felt horrible torments and sorrows that had constrained her unto it: but she looked up higher. For she bare in her womb all the hope that might be had of the salvation of the world. Now in the meantime she seeth such a combat, that it seemeth that GOD overthroweth all, and that he would show therein a sign of his wrath. To be short, the thing is detestable of itself, that there should be such a strife and battle in the womb of a woman: and this came not naturally, but God would now do (as we have seen) to Isaack and to her, that all they that should come of their seed after the flesh, should not therefore be reputed of the number of the faithful: but rather that there should be mortal war amongst them. Now therefore when she saw (instead of having the salvation of the world in her womb) such a sign of God his wrath, and as it were a devilish fight of deadly enemies of the Church, she could not know the whole: but she perceived, that if she had conceived to have such a combat, that this was, as if GOD had been against her, and come with a main army, to say: Thou art unto me as a detestable creature, and I have cast thee off and refused thee. In what case then is she, when she imagineth all these things? And so we ought not to think it strange, if in such anguish, she would rather have chosen to die, than to see so monstrous a thing, which was altogether contrary to the order of nature. Notwithstanding it is said, that in this so great heaviness, she left not off, to have recourse unto God.

And in very deed she obtained an answer to comfort her: not but that there was also some grief mingled therewith, but yet God did moderate this passion, that was so grievous unto her, and said, that she had two peoples in her womb: as if he should have said, that his was not only for the two children's sakes, which she bare, but that this had a farther respect: that is to say, that they should be divided the one from the other.   And howsoever both two were the sons of Abraham, and that it had been said unto Abraham, that in his seed all the nations of the earth should be blessed, yet it must needs be that from Isaack such must descend, as God should cut off from his Church, who should be rejected, and so consequently should be the enemies of the Church of God.   Now it is very true that this might have wounded both Isaack and Rebecca with a deadly sorrow: but yet in the meantime they see that the goodness of God was no whit quenched and that God showed himself faithful in that he had once pronounced.   For he had said.

The elder shall serve the younger.

Wherein Rebecca knew, that of her, howsoever it should be, should come that blessed seed, which had been promised. See in brief the whole that is here rehearsed. But all would be dark, if it were not declared particularly. Let us note here then, that they that are called into the Church, does not always remain there, as we have seen a notable example in Ismael: who was the eldest son of Abraham, notwithstanding he was banished from the family, and it was said, that he should not be here. And this was not of the riches of the world, nor of those possessions, which

Abraham had. For he was rich in cattle, in gold and silver: but he had not one foot of land. This heritage therefore, to what had it respect? Even to the spiritual promise: that is to say, that God had chosen the seed of Abraham, which was as much to say, as this shall be a people that shall be dedicated to my service: and those that shall come of them, will I receive and accept for my children, to the end I may gather them into everlasting life. Mark then how Ismael with his birthright is cast from the hope of life: and it remaineth only to Isaack. And even so is it herein, concerning Esau and Jacob: For both these were descended of Abraham, yea they were twins, their mother bare them in one belly: yet that one is received, and the other rejected: one is chosen, and the other refused.

So then we see that they, who for a time have place in the church, and bear the title of the faithful and of the children of God, may well be so accounted before men, but they are not written in the book of life: God knoweth them not, nor avoucheth them for his. Hereby we are admonished, not proudly to vaunt ourselves, nor to be drunken with sottish [*stupid, foolish*] presumption, when God shall show us this favor, to bring us into his church: but let us walk in purity, and labor to make sure our election, and to have the testimony thereof in our hearts, by the holy Ghost, and not to trust only to the outward title and appearance, which we may pretend before the world: see what we have here to mark. And moreover we are taught a far greater thing: and that is in the first place: that albeit God had established his covenant with Abraham, yet notwithstanding he would declare that this was not all, to have made offer of his grace: but that it behooved that he chose according to his liberty, such as he thought good, and that the rest should remain in their cursed state. And therefore Saint Paul allegeth this place to apply it to the secret election of God, through which before the foundation of the world, he chose those as seemed good unto him. Now this is a very high and profound matter, but when it shall be farther declared, everyone may make his profit of it, so that we be attentive unto it. And for the remnant, let us receive that, which the holy scripture showeth unto us, with sobriety, and let us not desire to be wiser, than is lawful for us: but let us rest in that which God shall speak unto us, and moreover let us be humble, not to reply against him, nor to bring forth our fantasies before him, as though we would plead against God: but acknowledging that his judgments are bottomless: let us not search farther therein, than is permitted unto us. Now it behooveth that we handle these things in such sort, that that which at the first show seemeth to be dark, be made more easy to us. We have already seen that God hath chosen Abraham's seed. Now if a man would ask, why or by whom he was brought so to do: he shall not find that Abraham was any worthier than others: as we have already largely enough handled this matter. Lo then a privilege which was given to a certain family, not flowing from any merit, neither for that God found anything in their persons, wherefore they ought to be preferred: for they were no better nor more excellent than others, but it pleased him so. Now, it is very true the this will be hard for us to digest, if we bring in our own judgment as there are a great sort of fanatical heads which cannot abide this doctrine: For it seemeth good to them to reply against God: But what profit they thereby in the end?

We have alleged that herein we must bring with us an humility, for to reverence that which is hidden from us. And indeed Saint Paul hath well showed us this by his example. For instead of disputing the matter he crieth out. O how wonderful are the judgments of God: Behold Saint Paul who was altogether amazed, he found himself astonished, he that had been rapt [*lifted, carried*] up above the heavens, he that had seen the secrets of God which was not lawful for man to utter. Saint Paul then, who was (as a man would say) a companion of Angels, was found in this case to marvel, and to be altogether confounded: and what shall become of these Scullions, who have scarcely licked with the tip of their tongue one word of the law and Gospel, and yet nevertheless would go beyond Saint Paul? And yet men shall find this pride in very many. But for our part let us return to that which is here showed us. *O man who art thou.* When therefore we will make comparison betwixt God and us: who is God? within what compass shall we enclose him? Shall it be within the compass of our brain? And we have scarcely half an ounce of wit, and in mean season God, who closeth his fist, to hold the whole world as a grain of dust (as Esay the prophet saith†) and is not comprehended neither in heaven nor in earth, who hath an infinite power, and infinite justice and wisdom, and hath incomprehensible counsels: and yet for all that we must come to make him subject to our foolish fantasy. And whereto will this grow? Moreover who are we? Men, (saith Saint Paul) By which word he meaneth, that we are nothing

---

† *Isaiah 45*

at all: as if he should say, must it be that thou presume so much, as to dare to inquire of the bottomless secrets of God, seeing thou art nothing but clay and dung? And again, what is thy understanding? Thou art full of sin and iniquity, thou art a poor blind one: and yet thou wilt that God shall make an account to thee: and wilt thou conclude, that if thou find not that which he doeth good and reasonable, that thou mayest accuse him, and must he needs hold up his hand at thy bar? Now let us mark this admonition in the first place, and let us know that our Lord Jesus Christ teacheth us, that we cannot do amiss to harken and open our ears, to inquire and search after that, that it hath pleased him we should know: but let us take heed that we go not beyond it: For there is no rage so great and outrageous, as when we will know more than God doth show us. And moreover we shall have spun a fair thread if we apply all our senses and all our studies thereto: whether is it that we shall come. This shall be always to enwrap us so much the more in a Labyrinth, and maze unless, we have the direction of God to show us the way.

Let us therefore keep this mean: that is to say, to hearken to that which God doth propound unto us: and as soon as he shall once shut his mouth, let us have all our understandings locked up and captive, and let us not enterprise to know more, than that he shall have pronounced unto us. Now therefore see how the stock of Abraham was chosen before all the rest of the world, forasmuch as God so would: but this was not yet enough: For it behooveth that his free election be yet better confirmed unto us. And this is it that is here showed unto us, in the person of two brethren. For behold Rebecca which bare Jacob and Esau: was the one better than the other? Saint Paul expounding this place saith[†]: *And they were not yet born.* How then could they have obtained favor and grace before God for their merits? For Jacob had done neither good nor evil no more than Esau. Why then doth God make him the greater? It behooveth not that we enter into any deeper disputation of this matter, unless it be to adore with astonishment the secret counsel of God, through which, those which seemed good to him are elected, and the other rejected. See then how God would yet give greater glory and beauty to his mercy, when he had chosen Jacob before Esau. For indeed he might have well placed Jacob the foremost when the Infants should come forth from their mother's womb. Men may well understand, that this was not by any adventure: as it is said in the Psalm[††]: *Thou hast drawn me out from my mother's womb:* And God manifesteth a singular power, when children come into the world. And why then did not he permit and ordain that Jacob should have the privilege of birthright? For this was meet since he meant to banish Esau out of the church, and would have Jacob to remain there, and to succeed in the place of his father Isaack and Abraham. And why doth God then pull him back, and make him inferior to his brother, as touching the law of nature, and afterwards setteth him above him? In this we see that God would shut out all glory of man, that he would that all height should be thrown down, and that men should bring nothing of their own: to the end to

---

† *Romans 9:11*

†† *Psalm 22:9*

say: I have attained such or such a good thing. I have gotten it by mine own industry. We see then that which I have already touched: that is to say, that we have here a glass, wherein we may behold, that all they that are of the church, are not advanced thereto by their own virtue, and that they have not obtained this favor by their merits: but that God hath chosen them before they were born: See then briefly what we have to hold out of this place. But now a man might here move some doubt: For Moyses saith expressly that this was extended to two peoples, and that it was not only in respect of Jacob and Esau, that this struggling combat was moved, as touching their persons: but that it was in respect of their successors, and each others posterity. Now it is so, that many which descended of Jacob were nevertheless rejected. For he stayeth upon that that is spoken here: to wit, that the stock and offspring of Jacob was chosen and that of Esau rejected: and yet notwithstanding a man may see, that the most part of those that descended of Jacob, were disallowed of god, and that he pronounceth them bastard children, the children of an harlot, and such as were sprung of fornication, and that they belonged nothing at all unto him, and that it was a vain thing for them, to glory or boast of his name. Now how can these agree together? Let us mark that god setteth such a spectacle before the eyes of Jacob and Rebecca, to show them what the condition and state of the church should be: For God in few words testifieth unto them, that his church should come of Jacob and not that all they which he should beget concerning the flesh must be of the church: but it was enough that he remained there, and that God kept him: and that Esau was driven out in time, as afterwards we shall see. This shall be better understood by that exposition which Saint Paul giveth[†]: he taketh this sentence thus: *All they which are of Jacob after the flesh, are not for all that, true Israelites*: that is to say, they are not of the people of God. For he had two names, as we shall see hereafter, to wit, Jacob and Israel. And that it is so, before the children were born, lo God, which severeth the one from the other, and showeth that this is not one body, and that they were not united together: but that one was reserved, and the other rejected. Saint Paul therefore well understood, that they which should be born of Jacob, were not all elected of God: for he sendeth us to the beginning, and saith that the one was separated from the other by the secret counsel of God, and that we cannot comprehend and set forth the reason thereof: forasmuch (as I have already said) that he keepeth his liberty, in such sort that it well sufficeth that the Church be engendered [*begat, procreated*] of his stock, albeit that all do not appertain unto it. We have before declared that there was a double grace or favor in this stock of Abraham: one was, that God had in general declared, that he would be their father. Circumcision also was common to them all. Now circumcision was not in vain: but it bare witness of the remission of sins and of the righteousness that all the faithful must obtain through our Lord Jesus Christ. Lo then Ismael who was circumcised: as much as was on god's behalf, he received the sacrament that might assure him that God accounted him of the number of his children, that he was a member of Jesus Christ, that the

---

† *Romans 9:6*

curse which he had drawn from Adam, was abolished: yea
but this stood him in no steed at all. As much may be said
of Esau, and of all their like: but howsoever it was, we must
not despite the benefit that he showed towards all the stock
of Abraham.   As at this day when we speak of the
inestimable blessing that God hath bestowed upon us, when
his Gospel was preached: this same shall be spoken unto all
indifferently.   Men will say that God hath used a very
singular mercy towards us, inasmuch as he hath lightened
us by his word, that we should know the way of salvation.
In the meantime, we see others that wander in darkness and
confusion, as if God had forgotten and altogether cast them
off.   Behold the Papists, albeit they be full of pride and
rebellion, yet they are tossed to and fro of Satan: so as they
know neither way nor path: and in meantime god calleth us
to him daily, and there is mention of his covenant, to the
end that we should know that he is always merciful unto us,
and that we may call upon him in a true certainty, not
doubting, but that he will be our father. Behold then a
benefit, which we ought not the esteem lightly of: and yet
there are great many, to whom this serveth not, but to
condemnation: For   there   is   so   much   the   more
unthankfulness, if they be rebels against God, and disdain
to accept the fatherly favor that he offered unto them. So
then, behold such a favor already bestowed upon us, as that
was upon the stock of Abraham: but yet there was also a
second grace, the which must be restrained to these bounds:
to wit, that God hath chosen of this stock, those that hath
seemed good unto him, as he received Isaack to himself, and
Ismael had no place in his house: he might well be
accounted for a time a member of his house: but in the end

he was cut off. As much may be said of the children of
Keturah: and behold although Esau were the firstborn, yet
God shut him out. See therefore a second favor which was
in Abraham's family: that is, that God held to himself, those
that he thought good. For Jacob was as the root of this
stock which sprung afterwards. And farther mark for what
cause all the elect were figured in his person, and that God
setteth forth unto us, that they have not that of themselves,
which he through his only goodness giveth unto them, and
that they cannot brag, that this was of their own moving,
that they attained to salvation: but that they were drawn to
it, yea inasmuch as they were chosen before the creation of
the world and consequently before their birth. Behold,
wherefore Saint Paul, in this place that we have alleged, for
the more full declaration adjoineth the testimony of
Moyses[†]: I will have mercy on him on whom I will have
mercy: and I will have compassion on him, on whom I will
have compassion. It should seem that this is a broken
speech and from the purpose: but it is of great importance:
For it is as much as if GOD had said, I know whom I will
refuse, and there is no need that any come in this case to
plead with me: For this consisteth in my liberty. When we
shall mark our common speech, this shall not be dark at all.
For if a man say, I will do that, I will do: that is to say, I will
do that which I think good to do, by this he showeth, that
he will not submit himself to any person: he showeth that
he is neither tied nor bound to open his counsel and
purpose, in that he hath to do. So God saith, *I wilt show*

---

† *Exodus 33:19*

mercy to him, that I will show mercy: as if he should say: My
mercy dependeth neither upon this or that, neither must the
cause be sought in any other, nor I bound to any law: For I
know what I ought to do: and in the meantime my mercy
shall have place, and I will show mercy to whom I will show
mercy. That is to say: I mark not who is worthy of it. For
there is not one: But yet I will not cease to show mercy to
some, to wit, to such as I shall have chosen. Mark then how
precisely God speaketh: and this is to beat down whatsoever
men can allege to shut the door against all curiosity, and set
a bar against all presumption: and that we do simply
reverence him, leaving that to him which he hath reserved
to himself: that is to say, when he saveth, it is of his free
goodness: and when he condemneth, that we should not
enterprise to bark against God, but that we shut up our
mouth: unless it be to glorify him. Now let us mark that
this was spoken by Moyses when the people already
multiplied, and after that God had brought them out of
Egypt. Behold a Church descended from the race of Jacob:
For from this same barren house, and which was as it were
desolate, GOD had drawn so great a multitude therefrom,
that this seemed rather to be a notorious miracle, and that
this promise was verified: that *Abraham's seed should be as the
stars of Heaven.* Was not this in a goodly show in respect of
men? God saith of this multitude here, I will retain as
many as I shall think good: I will show mercy to whom I
will show mercy, and let no man ask the reason thereof. It
is true indeed that God hath reason, but it followeth not
therefore that we can comprehend it, or that we must break
out beyond our bounds into his secrets. We must therefore
know that in respect of us, there is no reason: but the

counsel of God ought to be unto us in all respects the rule of righteousness, wisdom and equity. Mark therefore how the exposition of Saint Paul agreeth very well to that which is here pronounced: that is to wit, that there were two peoples in the belly of Rebecca, and that from her bowels two nations should be divided: and this was as much as if God had testified, that there should be such a divorce, that yet the stock of Jacob should remain blessed: Not altogether without exception, but those whom it should please GOD to keep to himself, as he had chosen them before the creation of the world. See then the sum of that which is contained here. But before we go any farther, let us well note that which hath been said: that is to say, that the principal thing which we have to observe, is this, that God will have the whole praise of our salvation to be attributed to him. For what is the root and beginning of the church? It is his election. See whereto Moyses calleth us, yea according to the interpretation of Saint Paul: and the text also herein is most plain. For here (as I have said) there is not any question of any earthly or transitory inheritance: it is of everlasting life that Abraham had hoped for according to that he had received through the promise. Now see Jacob an heir: and why so? was it because he put himself in the favor of God, or for that he had purchased favor for anything he brought? It was not so. See then Moyses's text without any gloss, which showeth sufficiently, that the Church springeth from the pure grace of God: and so that all the praise of our salvation, must wholly be reserved to himself. Now, for all this, they that would overthrow and darken this doctrine say, although that God knew no merit in Jacob: yet he foresaw well enough that he should be such a one. Behold for what cause they say he was chosen, and Esau rejected. To be short, inasmuch as a great sort of those Dogs dare not openly and flatly deny the election of God, they would that there should be a superior cause, to wit, his foreknowledge. And what is that foreknowledge? It is that God foreseeth what manner of one everyone must be: and he choseth (say they) those whom he hath foreseen to be of a good nature and affection: and it is no marvel if he accept them before others: For he knoweth the good which appeareth not yet, but is to come. But such kind of men have no drop of the fear of God. For they manifestly blaspheme against the holy ghost, who hath spoken by the mouth of Saint Paul, and these mock at that which Saint Paul hath spoken as if it were a fable. For if a man accept their solution, then hath Saint Paul spoken as an ignorant and unadvised man: For he taketh this reason, he found neither good nor evil, neither in Isaack nor in Esau, nor in Jacob. Notwithstanding God chose the one and rejected the other. But the reply shall be easy, in the opinion of these fanatical persons. And how? It is true that there was neither good nor evil: but there must be either good or evil, and God did so foresee it. But Saint Paul presupposeth that this be true, to wit, that we are all damned, and that until that God had chosen us, it must needs be that we should remain as Serpents full of venom, and that there was nothing in us but matter of wrath and of the vengeance of God, and that we are altogether confounded, and full of poison and iniquity.

Lo Jacob's case as well as Esau's. For what shall we find in the race of Adam, but all corruption? We are therefore infected before God: and inasmuch as the root is

accursed and vicious and altogether rotten, it must needs be
that the fruits be of the same sort. So then when God shall
leave us such as we are, it must needs be that we all perish,
and that there remain not one, but that we be all lost and
consumed.

To be short, this doctrine is common enough in the
holy Scripture, that we are all the children of wrath. It
followeth then that there was no diversity in Esau and
Jacob, and that God had not distinguished the one from the
other, for that he found or foresaw any good either in the
one or other. For what could he foresee, but this corrupted
mass of Adam, that brings forth no other fruit but
malediction? See therefore what he foresaw as well in the
one as in the other indifferently. It followeth then, that he
had put in Jacob that which is found in him, and that he
left Esau such a one as his birth brought him forth. See also
why it is said in another place†, *That God hath chosen us, to
the end that we should be holy and unblamable before him.* He
saith not, because God foresaw that we should be holy, he
hath chosen us: but contrariwise he deriveth all our holiness
and righteousness, and all the good which shall be found in
us, he deriveth it from this root: to wit, from the election of
God, to the end we should walk in his fear, that we should
have some integrity in us, that we should have some zeal
and affection to do well. If this be so, it followeth then that
God hath foreseen nothing in us. For let us take away
election, and what shall there remain? As we have declared,
we remain altogether lost and accursed. And not without

---

† *Ephesians 1:4*

cause: For God saw nothing in us but corruption: and it must needs be that he must disallow us, and renounce us, as it is said, that he repented that he had made man. Behold then what we may allege on our part. So then, this is too trifling a folly to say, that God hath chosen his, according as he foresaw they should become afterwards: for it must needs be, that he put in them that which is good, and place it there, because he hath chosen them. Mark therefore the first step whereby we must begin: that is to say, that we nothing differ one from another, unless in this, that God hath discerned us. Mark also for what cause Saint Paul disannuleth all the glory the which men may usurp: Who is it (saith he) that doth discern thee? he hath nothing but this word there to beat down and disannul all pride. And why so? For hast thou anything (saith he) which is thine own? Hereby he showeth that men cannot choose their own place, to say, I will dispose myself to do good, and God shall have pity upon me, and I will come unto his grace, I will have a good motion, I will have this preparation. Now Saint Paul excludeth all this, in saying that we are all lost, that one with another, we must be all thrown down, and enter into the gulf of hell, except it please God to discern us. Lo from whence all our dignity and excellence cometh: that is, for that it pleaseth God to lend us his hand. Again let us hold fast this principle, and apply all this doctrine which we have rehearsed to this purpose, how God hath set forth unto us, in Jacob and Esau, a glass to look into. Likewise let us content ourselves, that these two persons may be unto us, as two lively images, to show us that the world in itself, is of like condition: but that one sort is called and not the other, because it hath so pleased God. And specially (as I have noted) Jacob was the younger, and it seemed rather that he should be subject to his brother, according to the order of nature: notwithstanding mark that he was placed in the degree of the firstborn: and Esau not only was put under him, but he was utterly rejected: For in the end he had no part nor portion in the church. This thing showeth very well unto us, that God would hold us always convicted, that there is no question of bringing anything before God on our part, to thrust in ourselves there, as if we had any value and worthiness in us: For God is not contrary to himself: nevertheless he would show here a certain kind of repugnancy and contrariety. It is he which ordained that the firstborn of the house, should be the head. Now he set down this law: and yet in the meantime he overthroweth it: but (as I have said) all this agreeth very well: For God is above his ordinary law, and yet he would change that which was accustomed by a common rule: and he doeth it to the end that we should know that it is (as Saint Paul also hath said[†]) neither of the willer, nor of the runner: but only of him which showeth mercy. Now when Saint Paul saith, that it is neither of him that willeth, nor of him that runneth: he meaneth not that we may have some good will of our ourselves: as he hath declared in another place[††]: For *it is God which giveth it*: and also he meaneth not that we can enforce ourselves: but he showeth that men have nothing, and therefore they can bring nothing to God.

There is nothing then but his mercy alone. For if

---

† *Romans 9:16*

†† *Philippians 2:13*

men had anything to set against it, there must be a parting of stakes, and that must be known which is from God, and that which is from men. And then it might be said, that we have not all from the only mercy of God: but that therein there is our good will, our good running and our good zeal. Men might so speak: But Saint Paul would here make frustrate, whatsoever men might bring of themselves, and show that nothing hath dominion herein, but the only mercy of GOD. It is very true that many people will enforce themselves, yea and they allege the example of the Jews, who were swollen as Toads with a devilish kind of pride, thinking that God was bound as it were to them, and who would be accounted righteous according to their works: but herein they deceive themselves, and shall do nothing but go back instead of going forward. When men presume so of themselves, it is certain that they rob God of his honor. See then these sacrilegious persons and worse than these, and moreover until God shall have renewed us, whatsoever goodly show we have, it is certain, that there is nothing in us but stench, and we shall be as vile vermin before GOD.

So then let us not pretend that we can either will or run: but it behooveth that God find us as lost, and that he recover us from that bottomless pit, and that he separate us from them with whom we were lost, and to whom we were alike. For (as I have said) the condition of mankind is all one. It is true, that the one sort, are the Children of wrath, and the other God blesseth. But from whence cometh this separation, and this divorce? From mercy. And we must not go to inquire any farther, but we must content ourselves with this word alone, instead of all reason.

Mark then for what cause, namely the firstborn was cast out from his place: and in the mean season Jacob who was the inferior, was set in his place, yea, to remain the only heir. When Malachi the Prophet[†] speaketh of this he reproacheth unto the Jews their ingratitude. It is true that this was for an outward sign, that GOD had chosen Jacob rather than Esau, forasmuch as he had given the land of Canaan to be his inheritance, and that Esau was sent far off amidst the Mountains: but this is not the sentence whereupon the Prophet resteth: he looketh unto a thing much higher.

Saint Paul also when he useth this testimony of his, seeing that GOD had taken unto himself the stock of Jacob, he attributeth all this to his mere mercy: But the Prophet saith. And Esau, was he not the brother of Jacob? As if he should say. You are full of pride and obstinacy, yea, you burst yourselves therein, and it costs you nothing to say, O we are of the holy and sacred stock of Abraham: we are the Church, we are the people whom God hath blessed and sanctified: yea, and from whence have you this (saith he?) For was not Esau, Jacob's brother? You see the Idumeans your brethren: and are they the people of God? You say that they are strangers from the Church: and although they have circumcision, yet notwithstanding God hath cut them off. And when cometh this (saith he?) Who is it that hath so separated them? If you will go from age to age: very well, you shall find how you are the Children of Jacob. And Esau, whose child was he I pray you? Did not he descend

----

† *Malachi 1:2*

from Abraham and Isaack as well as you? But here he speaketh not only of the land of Canaan: but he goeth farther, and saith *That he loved Jacob, and hated Esau.* And this love which he bare unto Jacob, from whence proceeded it? It is certain that Jacob could not be accepted of him (as we have said) being considered in himself. For behold him the child of wrath, and bringing nothing from the womb of his mother, but this horrible curse, which was cast upon all mankind: notwithstanding God did love him. Now God loveth not iniquity, he hateth sin as we know. How then loved he Jacob? This was for that he drew him from that perdition, wherein he was. And why did he hate Esau? Now it is very true that there is just cause why God should hate all mankind: For as we have said, there is nothing in us but vice and iniquity: but yet when we will go farther, and that we will demand, why God before he created the world, and before the fall of Adam, why this should be, that he would hate or love? here we must hold ourselves mute and still: Here we must not lift up our horns. For what shall we gain, when we will enter into debate and question with God? It is certain that we shall cast stones upon our own heads, and they will fall neither here nor there, they cannot reach unto the majesty of God: but they shall return upon our own pates, and it must be that we be crushed and bruised therewith.

Behold then what we shall gain when we open our throat, to cast forth blasphemies against God: For we shall but cast out our darts and stones into the air: but they shall not reach unto him, it shall be rather that we be pierced and wounded by them, and that we remain confounded in that our rashness and overweening [*high opinion*]. Thus, let us content ourselves with that which God hath pronounced, that is to say: that he hath hated Esau and loved Jacob. Now by this the Children of Jacob were as well convinced, that they had nothing whereof they might glory in themselves, and that there rested nothing, but that they made an acknowledgment unto God of such a liberal and bountiful goodness which he had used towards them, and whereof none could find any reason, unless in this that it so pleased him. But notwithstanding they were full of impiety against God, and would hold this privilege: but God showeth them, that it doth not belong unto them, and that if they accounted him for their father, they must be his children. But hereby we are admonished, that although our salvation proceed from the only grace of God, and that therein in consisteth to the end: Notwithstanding it followeth not, that under the shadow hereof, we can let loose ourselves to evil, and give over ourselves thereto. But there are villains and dogs that bark against God, and there are also Hogs, which overthrow this doctrine of election, by their loose and lewd life. For there are two sorts of people, that are enemies to this doctrine. The one are as dogs, and the other as Hogs. The one, which are they? they which will bark and come to show their teeth, and who despite God by their wicked questions: as we see at this day in those villains who make no scruple, to rend in pieces all the holy Scripture to corrupt, pervert, falsify and adulterate all, so that they may darken the election of God, to wit, to make nothing of all. And mark whereunto this tendeth, to make this doctrine odious. For they will say, that they that thus speak, they put no more any difference betwixt good and evil, and that God by this means should become unrighteous, if he should put any difference between one and another, and that there should be acceptance of persons in him. Behold then the dogs that bark and whet their teeth against this doctrine. Now there are also Hogs which will not despise in such sort against it, but will say, very well. If I be elected I may do as much evil as I will: For God knows well how to keep me, and I can never perish: and contrariwise if I be reprobate, why should I torment myself so much to do well, seeing that I can never be saved. These then (as I have already said) come not to spew up their contradictions, to overthrow the truth of God: but they wallow there, and remain in their sins as brute beasts. But we must take heed both of the one and the other. And for this cause (as I have said) the Prophet Malachi showing to the people, that all that he had done unto them, came of the mere and free bounty of God, exhorteth them to holiness of life. And therefore as it is said unto us, that God is the author of our salvation, and that we can bring nothing to serve in that matter, and that yet we must always be kept under his guard, and that he must perfect and accomplish that which he hath begun, let not this be to the end, to let loose the bridle to our vices: but rather to keep us in his fear.

And in very deed when Saint Paul saith, that these are the hidden letters, and that it is an incomprehensible secret, to know who be the children of God, he addeth[†]: *Whosoever calleth upon the name of God, let him depart from all iniquity.* Let us mark then, that GOD would give us no

---

† *2 Timothy 2:19*

occasion to do evil, when he chose us without any regard to
our merits, and that he also maintaineth us by his mere
goodness: but this is to the end that we should honor him,
and we should walk in so much the greater carefulness. And
therefore let us return to that we have touched: to wit, that
he hath chosen us, to the end that we should be holy and
without blame before his face. It is true that he hath not
chosen us, for that he found us such: but when he chose us,
it was to the end we should be such. It behooveth therefore
that we march thither, and that this be the Mark that we
aim at all the days of our life.

But now let us fall down before the majesty of our
good GOD, in acknowledging of our faults, praying him
that he will in such sort make us to feel them, that it may
be to humble us, and to draw us to true repentance, to the
end, we may renounce all our fleshly lusts and affections:
and that being so cast down in ourselves, we may be
enlightened by the power of his holy spirit, to the end to
serve and honor him all the time of our life: and that by this
means we may so much the more be stirred up to give
ourselves wholly to him, knowing that we hold all of his
mere goodness: and that this may be to glorify his holy
name, not only in mouth but in our whole life. That not
only, etc.

❧The third Sermon of Jacob

and Esau, Genesis 25.

21. *Now when Rebecca had conceaued. The Children ſtroue within her belly. And ſhe ſaid, If it be ſo, to what end is it, or why doe I liue? and ſhe went to aſke councell of the Lord.*

22. *And the Lord ſayde vnto her, there are two peoples in thy wombe, and two nations brought forth out of thy wombe ſhalbe deuided, of whom one ſhalbe mightier then the other, and the elder ſhall ſerue the younger.*

T IS A THING that much troubleth men's spirits, when they see the estate of the world so confused, that the most part do manifestly despite God, and it seemeth that they have conspired with the devil, to the end to give over themselves to all mischief. For this is thought a thing greatly against reason, that GOD should create men to destroy them. Wherefore then is it, that he suffereth the greatest number so to fall? If it be said that this ought to be imputed not to God, but to those that of their own accord throw themselves so to perdition, yet this maketh no whit to the appeasing of those troubles, that we may conceive: For could not God remedy it? Why is it then that he doeth it not? They that allege a simple permission, that God layeth the bridle upon every man's neck, and that everyone guideth himself according to his own free will: yet they cannot well undo this knot: to wit, why God hath not created men of another sort: and wherefore he hath suffered that they should be so weak, yea and inclined to evil and corruption: and seeing that he knew their infirmity, wherefore is it, that he doth not help them and provide them some remedy? This therefore is to entangle ourselves in great torments and troubles. But it behooveth that we go yet farther: For it is certain (as the Scripture declareth) that there is nothing which doth not perish, saving that which God preserveth through his mere goodness and free bounty. But now, how cometh it to pass, that God chooseth only the tenth or the hundredth part of men, and leaveth all the rest, knowing well that they are swallowed up in hell and lost? Wherefore doth he not reach out his hand to help them, yea why hath he ordained them to destruction, as the Scripture speaketh? For mark the very words of Solomon: Behold a sentence, which driveth us from such hard questions: and many are therein entangled, as it were among thorns: And further they thrust in themselves so far, that they are altogether confounded. But yet there is a tentation [*temptation*] far greater. For besides that generality of the world, the like is seen also in the Church: that is, that when the Gospel hath been preached to a whole people, there are then many Hypocrites, the others are rebels, others become wholly brutish, in such sort that they profit but very little in this school, although God note all without exception to whom he speaketh. And beyond all these, a man shall find many, who through contempt and ingratitude will shut against themselves the gate of salvation, and will reject all the graces of God: and not only this: but men shall find deadly

enemies of the doctrine, although they be of the household,
And in very deed the prophet Esay having said, that god
would gather his church out of the world, and that he would
have so great a people as should be wonderful, instead of
rejoicing, he afterwards addeth: Alas my bowels. Now by
this he showeth, that when it shall seem that all must
flourish and prosper, and that God must be glorified both
of great and small, and that his banner must be displayed,
to gather together the whole world, to the end that with one
accord all may serve God: then he discovereth a secret
mischief. For the Prophet crieth not only alas the hands,
alas the legs: but he crieth out, alas my bowels, as though he
would say, this mischief is so rooted in the church, that it
must be as it were mingled of so sundry sorts of men, that
she must nourish in her own belly her own enemies, as we
have seen by the figure in Rebecca. Now what is to be done
therein? Everyone seeth that if we enter into such fantasies,
we cannot have any resolution, and the devil will thrust in
himself amongst, to the end to make us blaspheme against
God, or else to put such a bitterness into our heart, that we
shall seem rather to be blocks of wood, than reasonable
creatures formed according to God's image: as we do see the
experience thereof in many people, who do become as it
were mad and raging against god, because they cannot rid
themselves from difficulties and doubts. It is necessary
therefore to search out a remedy. Now it is true that we
cannot exempt fully ourselves from all passions, that at the
first blush and as it were with some puff we be not moved
and troubled, and that our thoughts do not wander, that we
do not conceive many things at random, and that we have
not many disputes, both on the one side and on the other:

to be short, that we be not tossed, as if there were some kind of tempest and whirlwind, which carried us about. We cannot have our spirits altogether quiet, nor so well guided, that they shall have no troubles. And this is declared unto us in Rebecca, when she saith.

If it be so, to what end I? or why do I live?

She desireth death, and yet she is the mother of the faithful? She representeth the Church. Now if this were in her, that bare in her belly the hope of the salvation of the world: what shall be in us? So considering that we have our minds so ready to conceive follies and vanities, and moreover so ready also to cast us off the hinges, and in the end so subject to make us storm against God, so much the rather it standeth us in hand to search out the remedy. Now that is here given us in Rebecca: For she fodes [*beguiles*] not herself in her sadness, she biteth not upon the bridle, as many do who stick there, which seek to have no means wherein to content themselves, nor to make them quiet and settled: but they wander this way and that way, and always add fantasies to fantasies, and plunge themselves so deep in their imaginations, that the Devil afterwards possesseth them, and driveth them by all violence and fury against God. Rebecca doth not so: But when she felt that this was an intolerable grief unto her, she withdraweth herself unto God, she enquireth of him, and answer was given unto her by and by. She had therefore whereupon to rest herself, when she knew that so was the good pleasure of GOD: and when she saw what he demandeth: and that one of her own children should be cut off from the Church, and the other

reserved, she knowing this, it behooveth that she rest there
and submit herself thereunto: the which thing she doth. For
she striveth not against God. Likewise we read not that at
anytime after she murmured: but we see that she hearkened
unto God: and brought forth children afterwards, and
always she rested herself in that which had been said unto
her, and set her mind and affection upon Jacob. And why
so? Because she knew that he was ordained of God to be
the blessed seed, which she had hoped for: so as she
behaved herself more manfully in this respect, than Isaack
her husband. Now this is to show us, that when we are in
any trouble, we must straightway have our recourse to God.
For our spirits are not able enough, to know these hidden
things: yea we see that in the most easiest things in the
world (as seemeth unto us) we shall be many times ravished
and astonished. And what shall it be then, when the
question shall be of the judgments of God, which are
incomprehensible, and which are of so high and profound
matter, that the holy Ghost teacheth us, instead of curious
searching after them, that we must adore them? shall men
presume of their reason, and of that they shall build upon
their good liking, and shall they examine all after their own
fantasy and opinion? It is certain that such presumption
shall not remain unpunished: and it is seen also. For
wherefore is it, that so many dogs at this day spew out their
blasphemies against this doctrine of predestination? It is
because they vouchsafe [*allow*] not to enquire at the mouth
of God, but they will give sentence as their brain will bear,
forsooth [*in truth*] as though we were fit and sufficient. So
then let us follow the example of Rebecca: that is to say,
when all these questions shall come before our eyes, and

that we shall be tormented on every side, in thinking: And how is it possible that the most part of the world shall perish, and the rest be saved? How cometh it to pass, that one is elected and another rejected? How is it that the greatest number go to destruction, and that there is but an handful of people which God reserveth to himself?

When we shall be thus tormented, let us have recourse unto God: that is to say, let us hearken to that which is showed us in the holy Scripture, let us pray God that he will open our ears and our eyes, to the end we may understand his will. And farther have we this? It behooveth us altogether to rest therein, and to be quiet. For there is no cause of disputing any farther, when God hath once pronounced his sentence. To be short, this is daily to show us, that we cannot ever dispose ourselves, to receive the instruction of the holy Scripture, and to seek all our wisdom there, unless we have this modesty and humility in us, not to desire to understand or know anything, but that which is contained therein. We need not any revelation from heaven at this day, as Rebecca had. It is very true that some conjectured that she went unto some Prophet: but they were thin sown in the world then. For a man may easily perceive that Melchizedek was dead: and that there was not anymore than Abraham and Isaack.

This then is a Dream, to think that she went to the schools of the Prophets: but she had a revelation, as our text here showeth. And our condition at this day is not altogether like, and neither have we also such need thereof. For then there was neither the Law nor the Gospel. At this day we have all perfection of doctrine: For *God in old time hath spoken unto our Fathers, and not in secret, nor in obscurity* (as saith Esay[†] the Prophet.)

And this was not in vain that he said, that men should seek him: as Moyses protesteth: *Behold the way, walk in the same: I have set before you this day, the way of salvation, and Heaven and Earth are witness unto me, that I have declared unto you what you must do, to come unto everlasting life.* And afterwards although God have his secrets (saith he in another place) yet notwithstanding this, that is to say the sum of the law, is for you and for your children: to the end that you should be taught in the way of salvation. But besides this we have yet the Gospel, wherein our Lord Jesus Christ hath shined unto us in all fullness: For he is that son of righteousness. Seeing therefore we have so sufficient testimonies, shall we demand that Angels come down from Heaven, and that God will yet open unto us that is hidden from us? But let us (as I have already said) content ourselves with the holy Scripture. And when there is any cause of inquiring after God, if we will have him for our master, let us come to the holy Scripture: and let us remember that which Moyses saith: *Thou shalt not say, Who is he that shall ascend above the Clouds? Who is he that shall descend into the depth? Who is he that shall go over the sea? The word of the Lord is in thy heart, and in thy mouth, saith he.* And seeing it is so that Moyses hath protested this in his time: at this day we have less occasion to wander here and there, and to run at all adventure to inquire after the will of God. For (as I have already said) the Gospel containeth all perfection of doctrine: and also behold the only mean,

---

whereby we may be thoroughly satisfied, and have our
minds settled and stayed: that is to say, that we hearken to
God speaking, and show ourselves teachable, to receive that
which he shall say. For it is certain, that as he hath
answered to our mother Rebecca, that which he knew to be
expedient: So the Scripture likewise will not deceive us in
this point: for it pronounceth clearly and manifestly, that
God hath chosen us in Jesus Christ before the creation of
the world, according to his good pleasure, the which he hath
purposed in himself. There needs no gloss: behold God
speaketh after this sort, that the most rude and ignorant
may know, what there is contained therein. God then hath
chosen us (saith Saint Paul) and hereby he showeth that he
hath discerned us from those which perish. And mark how
his mercy towards us hath the greater glory. For what letted
[*prevented*] that we should not remain in the same perdition
that others did, but that God was merciful unto us, without
any desert of ours?

But the better to express all, Saint Paul saith, that he
did choose us in Jesus Christ: it followeth then that this is
out of our persons. If we had been chosen in ourselves, God
should have found some matter in us to have been induced
to love us, and to have been inclined to have called us to
salvation. But what? We are chosen without ourselves:
that is to say: God had no regard to that we were or might
be, but our election is founded in Jesus Christ. And
moreover, he yet giveth a more ample declaration: that is,
according to his good purpose, which he had determined in
himself: it is certain that all that is according to the purpose
of man, is manifestly excluded: and again when he saith in
himself: this is to admonish us, that if we would know the

cause why: it is as if we would make an Anatomy of God, and go even into his heart and sound all his secrets. And can we do this? What overweening [*high opinion*] is this? So then, when we shall suffer ourselves to be taught of God, it is certain, that he will answer us, in such sort, as shall be necessary for us, concerning that which belongeth to our salvation: and namely we shall know that which surmounteth all man's understanding, how the one sort are elected, and the other rejected, and why the one have no doctrine, as the Papists and other infidels, whom God leaveth as poor blind ones, and why the other are enlightened through the Gospel. And farther, concerning those to whom the Gospel is preached, the one receive it with obedience, and they are touched therewith to the quick, and persevere in it to the end: and the other remain blockish, or rather will be full of outrage, to strive against God: or else will be fickle and give themselves over to all iniquity, throwing off the yoke, when they shall be brought into the good way. And from whence cometh this diversity? We must come to this fountain that the holy Scripture showeth us: that is, that the like grace hath not been showed to all. So then, behold our true wisdom that is, that we be God's good scholars: and we shall then be his scholars, when we seek to know nothing, but that he knoweth to be good and expedient for our salvation: and when we shall rest there, and learn to bring into captivity all our senses, and to keep an hard hand upon them. Then (say I) if we shall speak of the secret election of God, how he hath predestinated those whom he would to salvation, and how he hath cast off others: we shall never be troubled. And why so? because we having inquired of God's will, we will conclude, that we must keep ourselves to that which he showeth us, and to that which the scripture importeth, where he hath given us sufficient testimony of that which he knoweth to be good for us. Finally, there are so many testimonies of Scripture, to certify us of this doctrine that it must needs be, that all they that cannot rest there, must be as it were impoisoned [*poisoned*] of satan, and that they have conceived the spirit of venom, of pride and rebellion, to the end not to be ordered under the will of god: and that, to be short, they would despite all doctrine and instruction, and close up their eyes against the full light, and have their ears stopped, albeit God hath spoken loud and clearly, and that they have occasion to content themselves so much the more. To heap up all the testimonies, is not needful: but this is sufficient that we have had a sum, yea most evident as I have already briefly showed.

Again we have also, whereof to bless God and to comfort ourselves in him, when we know rightly to apply this doctrine as it behooveth. For instead that these fanatical and light brains, who would seem to be so subtle and sharp in fighting against god, and against his truth, instead that they search how they may gainsay him, we must mark how God doth satisfy us, and to what end he directeth this doctrine and to what purpose he would have it serve us, that is: to know that we are elected, and not all. For in the first place, when we see, that we cannot receive the Gospel, unless it be by the special gift of God, this serveth to make us so much the more to magnify his goodness towards us, and to see his just judgment against the reprobate, when he depriveth them of this doctrine: as we see in the Papacy, that men are as brute beasts, who err and wander through deserts, without keeping way or path. Now concerning us, we have sure testimony, which ought so much the more to stir us up to esteem this singular grace towards us. And also when we see some that have deaf ears, although it be daily declared unto them familiarly, and that which is requisite for their salvation be (as I may say) chawed unto them, they continue always in their estate: or rather they are not a whit touched, and they pass not to give over themselves to all licentiousness of life, as it were in despite of God: When we see this, it is certain, that our Lord hath so much the more bound us unto him, for that it hath pleased him to make us feel his goodness, and that we have taken such a taste of the hope of salvation which he hath propounded unto us: that we have renounced the world and whatsoever weakness there be in us, howsoever we are full of vices and corruption, nevertheless we hate the evil that is in us, and we delight in that which is good. When then we have this: it is certain, that if we be not harder than iron and steel, we ought to have all rebellion shivered and broken: and that we be inflamed with the love of God, and have our mouth open to bless and praise that so excellent and magnificent grace, which he hath showed towards us. See then the mark that the scripture setteth before us. Now in the meantime, these varlets [*persons of low and mean disposition*] will not stick to say. O shall God be an accepter of persons? Forsooth [*in truth*] as if God regarded in his election rich or poor, as if he regarded a noble man, more than a poor man, or a wise man more than an Idiot. For mark what it is to accept persons. This word *Person* in the holy scripture importeth *Look* or *countenance*, as also the Scripture useth it. But God chooseth us not for our fair eyes. Who is it that discern thee? We alleged yesterday that of Saint Paul: When God therefore chooseth these whom it pleased him, it is in his everlasting counsel, and in himself: that is to say, he hath his secrets which we ought to reverence, without farther inquiry why. Seeing this is so, it is certain that we cannot say, that he accepteth persons. And they which so speak are dolts, besides the malice that is in them. Now then they will say, And how is it that the one shall be saved by faith and not the other, if all depend upon the election of God? But yet herein they show to gross beastliness: For from whence proceedeth faith itself, but from the election of God? They say, O the promises of God are general, and God calleth all the world to salvation: It followeth therefore that all the world shall be saved. Yea he would that all the world should be saved: but this is to make the reprobate inexcusable. For the promises of God do undoubtedly contain our salvation: and we shall not be deceived leaning upon them. But what? We must know from whence the faith is which we have. For when the gospel is preached, why is it, that one sort profit therein, and receive it with due reverence, and humility of heart, and the other do not, but rather become worse by it? This is, forasmuch as they which were ordained to salvation (saith Saint Luke[†] speaking of the preaching of Saint Paul) they (saith he) did believe. Mark Saint Paul who preached: it is certain that if ever there were dexterity in a faithful teacher, it was Saint Paul that had it: and yet, all were not good scholars: there was but one part that received his

---

† *Acts 13:48*

doctrine. Whence came this? was it of their industry? was it because they were better disposed? It is very true that God disposeth: But that this cometh not from them, Saint Luke showeth and preventeth [*anticipates*] here all men's dotages, and saith that they which were ordained to salvation believed. And mark also wherefore our Lord Jesus Christ saith[†]: *That those that his heavenly father had given him, should not perish, but that he would keep them to the end.*

Now when he saith, they which are given me of my father: he calleth us to that eternal election. He saith also in another place[††]: *Thine they were, and thou gavest them unto me.* And wherefore is it that the one belong unto God and not the other? This is not in respect that they are mortal men: For our nature is alike: we are all created by one father: but the one belongeth unto God, and the other are cast off from him, because it so pleased him. He acknowledgeth and accepteth the one for his own: and the other although they he his creatures, nevertheless they have no acquaintance with him: he accepteth them not of his household, inasmuch as he hath shut them out from his election. We see then here, how faith is a special gift of God, which proceedeth not from our free will, not that we can of ourselves go forward, and that some are more able to comprehend than others: but for that it hath pleased God to reveal his secrets to those whom he hath elected. And

---

† *John 6:40*

†† *John 17:6*

therefore see also why it is said in Esay[†]: *Who is he that will believe our hearing?* For Esay had preached of the death a resurrection of our Lord Jesus Christ: as if he had displayed the banner, to declare that everyone should come to be reconciled to God, and that poor sinners should be received to mercy, that their satisfaction and righteousness is altogether ready, and that God desireth nothing but to be merciful to those that seek him: hath Esay preached so: but he crieth out forthwith *Who will believe our hearing?* And why so? For he saw in spirit the presumption and rebellion of unbelievers, because they cannot yield themselves to be ordered by God: but are wild and have always their mouth open to reply against God: and forthwith they have a wandering fantasy they may not obey. He showeth that his doctrine shall not be received of the greatest number: and addeth the reason: that the arm of god, that is to say, his strength and power is not revealed to all: he showeth there that it is not in ourselves that we have either moving or entrance, or preparation or anything whatsoever it be: but that it must be God that must work therein. Now if it be so in general: it must follow then that faith cometh from this root of the election of God. Now touching the rest when we shall have known this, there is no question, that we should bury all that instruction which our Lord hath given us in the holy Scripture. For after that he hath declared to us his will, he exhorteth us, he reproveth us, he threateneth us. If we were as these renegade spirits, which say: To what purpose do you preach so much unto us: If God have

---

[†] *Isaiah 53:1*

elected and chosen us unto himself, we cannot perish: and if we be reprobate, what shall all the doctrine, that shall ever be heard avail us? yea, but all agreeth very well, when we exceed not our bounds. We have already said, that faith cometh from election. Then like as God hath chosen us, so also he calleth us in time, as afterwards shall be handled more at large. For the place will serve there more fitly. But howsoever it be, God is not contrary to himself: and like as he testifieth unto us, that it is by his free mercy, that he enlighteneth us by the faith of his Gospel, and in the knowledge of our Lord Jesus Christ: so will he that we walk in fear and carefulness, that we be touched with his threatenings, that we be gathered unto him: all this he willeth. And indeed, mark these two sentences, that men with their impudence and rashness would ween [*think*] to be contrary: and nevertheless they agree very well one with the other. Jesus Christ saith[†]: *Come unto me all you that labor and are heavy loaden, and I will refresh you, and you shall find rest to your souls.* See how we are all bidden by the son of God, and not only two or three, but all in general: For he saith: *Come all you that are heavy loaden,* and yet in another place he saith[††]: *No man can come unto me, except it be given him of my father.* None therefore can come unto Jesus Christ, unless he be drawn by the heavenly father. It seemeth that this is contrary, yea he that would judge thereof according to man's reason: to say, that Jesus Christ inviteth us all unto him: and further addeth, that none can come unto him,

---

† *Matthew 11:28*

†† *John 6:44*

unless the father draw him. Very well: but (as I have already said) when God generally setteth salvation before us in Jesus Christ his only son, it is to make the reprobate so much the more inexcusable for their unthankfulness, inasmuch as they have despised so great a benefit: in the mean season the elect are touched, and God doth not only speak outwardly to them, but also inwardly. And see why in another place our Lord Jesus Christ saith[†]: *Whosoever hath been taught of God my father, the same shall come unto me.* But, as I have said, when the Gospel is preached in the name of God, this is as much as if he himself did speak in his own person: and yet all come not to Jesus Christ. There are a great many that go back the more when they have heard the Gospel: for then the devil kindleth them in such a rage, that they are more outrageous than ever before, and this cometh to pass, because there is a twofold hearing: the one is preaching: For the voice of a man will not enter into hearts of his hearers. I speak, but it behooveth that I hear myself being taught by the spirit of God: For otherwise the word which proceedeth from my mouth, should profit me no more than it doth all others, except it be given me from above, and not out of mine own head. Therefore the voice of man is nothing but a sound that vanisheth in the air, and notwithstanding it is the power of God to salvation to all believers (saith Saint Paul). When then God speaketh unto us, by the mouth of men, then he adjoineth the inward grace of his holy spirit, to the end, that the doctrine be not unprofitable, but that it may bring forth fruit. See then

---

† *John 6:44*

how we hear the heavenly father: that is to say: when he speaketh secretly unto us by his holy spirit: and then we come unto our Lord Jesus Christ. Mark then, the sum of that we have to learn: that is, when God declareth unto us his eternal election, and that he hath given us such a testimony, that we cannot doubt thereof: when he hath showed us that this is our benefit and salvation: and so that we take not too much liberty, to wrangle against him, and to enter in crooked and overthwart disputations, that then the whole shall profit us. For it is certain, that this is the true rejoicing of the faithful, to be instructed concerning this election of God. Moreover: when we see the wicked to cast forth their cavils against God, and their slanders to pervert all, and to bring this doctrine into hatred, let us not think it strange: for it must needs be that they declare themselves to reprobates. I have said, that we must rest ourselves in the everlasting counsel of God, whereby he hath chosen some, and cast off others. If now the reprobate come to fight against the truth of God, it is no new thing: For they are appointed to this, and it must needs be that they declare themselves to be such as they are: and we must call to mind that sentence of Ose[†] the which is put in the end of this Book: *The ways of the Lord are good and right:* also *The righteous will walk in them, but the wicked shall fall therein.* Now he addeth also: *Who is wise that will understand this? And who is a prudent man that will understand these things?* The Prophet showeth that when we speak of the judgments of God, it behooveth that we have a special wisdom to receive

---

† *Hosea 14:9*

them: and shall this wisdom be found in all our brains? that is far off. So then it behooveth that we have a wisdom given us by the mere mercy of God.

Now that which followeth is to show us, that this is a rare a most excellent thing, when men shall be apt to be taught and modest, and that they shall yield to be lead by God, and shall suffer themselves to be governed by his word, when they shall receive full instruction, which shall be unto them a good food for their souls: When this shall come to pass, it must be acknowledged to be a rare and singular benefit of God, and must assure us that he hath blessed us. And therefore it behooveth that we be armed and prepared against all offences, If we see that the wicked shall come to push with their Horns against GOD, and to bark and show their teeth as Mastiffs [*large powerful dogs*], when they cannot bite, then let us practice this doctrine of the Prophet, when he saith that the ways of God are righteous, and good, yea and the righteous shall walk in them. We shall always find this, so that we have not a malicious and froward spirit, that may turn us from God: but let us be quiet, and let us ask nothing, but that our Lord show us the path that we ought to follow: when we shall be such, it is certain that we shall always find even ground, and there shall be no question, that we should walk and take our pleasure. Behold, I say, the joy we shall have, when we shall walk in the Lords ways: but contrariwise it is said, that the wicked shall fall. And where? shall it be in hell? Shall it be in the Devils way? It is said that it shall be in the very ways of God, that all that shall be set forth unto them of the judgments of God, of his eternal counsel, of this providence, and of his fatherly love, he beareth to his children: in all these (saith he) the wicked

shall fall. So let us be in suchwise established, that all the
ruins and falls which we shall see before our eyes, hinder us
not from marching always forwards in that good way which
our Lord doth set before us. But it behooveth us oftentimes
to remember that which is here handled by Moyses? And
that is, he saith expressly,

> *that the one shall be stronger than the other, and
> the elder shall serve the younger.*

In speaking of the stronger, it is to show us, that
when God's election is steadfast and undoubted, and that
we are upholden by his holy spirit, we must no longer fear:
and this is a very profitable point, yea necessary. For what
is our condition? There needs not but one puff of wind to
beat us down, and there needs but a fly to dazzle our eyes:
and yet we are here laid open to so many combats, as
nothing more. Behold our enemies which are in number
infinite: and I speak not of those which we see with the eye,
but of spiritual enemies: For the air is full of devils, which
lie in wait for us, yea which are as roaring Lions, besides
their flights. Alas what shall we be able to do? It must
needs be that we be in distress and vexation continually and
without end, and that we be as poor people stricken
thorough, if we knew not that our Lord hath our salvation
in his own hand, and that he will keep it. Saint Peter saith
that it is well kept in hope, and that faith is as it were a
capecase [*traveling bag, wallet*]: but he sendeth us to God:
and our Lord Jesus Christ hath yet declared this more plain
unto us, when he saith, that all that was given unto him of
his father, shall not perish. And why so? The father who

hath given you (saith he) unto me, is stronger than all. So
then, he saith that we may rejoice in this, that God will
have pity upon us until the end, and that he will keep us:
and although he suffer us to stumble, yea so as we fall, yet
we shall be recovered and upholden by his hand. And how
is it that we can trust in this? Without election it is
impossible: but when we know that the father hath
committed us into the keeping of his son, we are certain,
that we shall be maintained by him unto the end: For we
have his promise whereby he hath bound himself unto us,
to preserve us: and farther he maketh it until the last day,
until the resurrection. And forasmuch as the beginning and
end of our salvation is in him, see in whom we may rejoice
ourselves: That is, that in acknowledging our weaknesses
and brickleness [*fragility, brittleness*], and that we are
nothing, and that we want [*lack*] all things: yet we may say:
the Lord which hath called me unto himself, will finish his
own work: as is said in the hundred and thirty-eighth
Psalm[†]: *Lord thou wilt not leave the work of thine own hands in
the midst.* So then we must hold fast this doctrine, that the
one shall be more strong: For our faith shall remain
victorious over all the world. And how? It behooveth us (I
say) to have our foundation upon the election of God: that
we may be so settled thereon, that we know that our Lord
being our Father, will not suffer that we perish, seeing we
are his children. Now Moyses addeth by and by that the
elder shall serve the younger. In this we have yet a more
ample confirmation of that which I touched even now, that

---

† *Psalm 138:7*

is, that we must be so assured of our salvation, that we doubt not thereof although that we be weak, and that the world despise us, and we have no greater show of strength. And why so? God would that we should for a time be the lesser: that is to say, that we should be little and despised to the end, that his glory might be the more known and esteemed. For if we had greatness and glory in ourselves, and dignity, it is certain that these should be as veils, to shadow the mere and free bounty of God: but when we are weak in ourselves, see wherein it is known, that it is he which doeth all: and it must needs be that his hand be in such sort advanced, that we come not to mingle ourselves therein, and that we throw not forth our clouds to hinder that the praise of our salvation be wholly attributed to him. Mark then that we have here to learn, that is on the one side, although that we be weak, that we cease not to go freely forward, knowing that our strength consisteth in God: and when he doth not fully show it, it is to the end that our weakness should be an occasion to humble us. See this for one principal point. And in very deed we should be cold, yea and quite negligent in calling upon him, if we knew not our necessity: but when we see that we can do nothing, then we must have our refuge to him, who can supply all our wants [*lack*]: and then we shall render unto him the sacrifice of praise which is due unto him, after that we have been heard of him. In the meantime also we have to note that God doth not at the first dash, show to the view of the eye our salvation: but it must be hid in appearance, and that for a time we be as castaways, and that the wicked tread us under their feet, and that they be in degree without comparison, more high than we: Notwithstanding let it suffice us, that we are as a precious treasure before God. Behold also why our Lord Jesus Christ saith: *Fear not my little flock, but rejoice, and be not as a scattered and discomforted flock.* And why so? Because the father delighteth in thee.

Mark then from whence we must have all our rejoicing: mark of whom we must be armed, to have victory, and to triumph against all temptation. When we see in these days the enemies of the Gospel, and the Devils supporters, to make their brags, and make no account of others in comparison of themselves, and when in the meantime they despise us: and not only that, but farther account us as most desperate creatures, as though we were unworthy (as men say) to be eaten of Dogs. When therefore we shall see this at this day, yea, that the greatest number shall be as poor starvelings, and that they shall have no bread to eat, that they shall not have their ease nor their commodity: Let us remember that, that is here spoken, that the greater shall serve the lesser. Now this service came not to pass at the first dash. For we shall see afterwards that Jacob came to crouch before his brother, and called him his Lord: he trembled as a poor Lamb before him, and then gave him all his goods as a prey. And where was this subjection of Esau? where was the superiority of Jacob, when he submitted himself in such sort? It seemeth that he gives up all: but he knoweth that God would not accomplish this at the first day. Mark then why he did bear his poverty so patiently: because God would (as if a man might say) that he should creep upon the earth, and yet this shall not hinder, but that he should always attain to that salvation, whereunto he was called. And why so? For God dependeth not upon all these earthly things. And which is more (as I

have already said) he will that we begin here, to humble
ourselves before him: following that which I alleged ere
while from the mouth of our Lord Jesus Christ, that so we
know that our Heavenly father be well pleased with us, we
pass not for the rest, or rather that we be not so shaken that
this do deprave us and bring us out of taste, and so hinder
us from doing good: but that we doubt not that amidst all
the troubles and griefs that may happen unto us, we have
always wherein to rejoice. For who shall separate us from
the love that God hath borne us in Christ our Lord? seeing
that God hath chosen us in our Lord Jesus Christ, and that
he hath called us to the faith of his Gospel, and hath
imprinted in our hearts the testimony of his fatherly love,
we will always defy our enemies, although we be poor and
feeble, yea though we be nothing in the common opinion of
men: yet we shall not cease to be grounded upon this
promise: *That the greater shall serve the less and younger.* And
seeing it is so, let us not desire to be great after the world:
for although that we be contemptible and despised, yet this
hindereth us not from being the heirs of the world: although
we neither have lands nor possessions, yet do all things
belong unto us, and contrariwise the wicked have an
horrible and heavy account to make, for that they in such
sort devour God's benefits, and rejoice so much concerning
those riches which he hath given them, and yet glorify not
God in them. But they must pay full dearly for them: and
as for us, although we be stripped of all riches, that we be in
opprobry [*disgrace*] and reproach: to be short, that there is
nothing but poverty in us, yet seeing we know that he hath
his hand stretched out to uphold us, we may boast ourselves
against all our enemies. And in the meantime let us

remember that which is said in Esay†, that we are as a precious crown in the hand of the Lord, and as the ring of his finger, and as his seal, and that neither Egypt nor Africa: that is to say, the greatest Monarchies of the world, are so highly esteemed of him as we are: not for any value that is in us (as I have said already) but because it hath pleased him to choose us, and to reserve us in the number of those whom he will have to himself: and we know this, forasmuch as we see through faith and hope, that he hath drawn us from those gulfs, in which we were, to the end he might bring us to an everlasting inheritance.

Now let us fall down before the face of our good God, in acknowledging our offences, praying him, that he will in such sort make us to feel them, that it may be to spoil us of all wicked lusts and rebellions, and that we may be so renewed, that we may ratify our vocation in living holily and confirming ourselves wholly to his righteousness, and that he will so support us in our infirmities, that he suffer us not howsoever we be compassed about with so many enemies, that we never fail: but that he will supply all weaknesses, to the end that his election may declare his power even to the end, and that we may in such sort feel the fruit thereof, that we may have wherein to glorify him, both in life and death.

And so let us all say, O Almighty God and heavenly Father, we acknowledge and confess in ourselves as the truth is, that we are not worthy, etc.

---

† *Isaiah 62:3*

❧The fourth Sermon of

Jacob and Esau, Genesis 25.

24. *Therefore when the dayes of her deliueraunce was come, beholde twinnes were in her wombe.*

25. *So hee that came out firſte was redde, & hee was all ouer as a rough garmente, and they called his name Eſau.*

26. *And afterwarde came his brother out: and his hand held Eſau by the heele: therefore his name was called Iacob. Nowe Iſaack was threeſcore yeeres olde when Rebecca bare them.*

27. *And the boyes grewe, and Eſau was a cunning hunter, and was a man of labour: but Iacob was a ſimple man, and dwelled in tents.*

28. *And Iſaack loued Eſaw, for Veniſon was his meate, but Rebecca loued Iacob.*

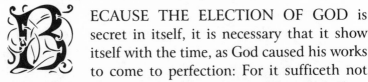ECAUSE THE ELECTION OF GOD is secret in itself, it is necessary that it show itself with the time, as God caused his works to come to perfection: For it sufficeth not that God have once chosen us, and that he have marked us, but he must also continue this to the end, and that he declare that his election is not in vain, but that he hath his strength and power to conduct us to salvation. Now he

doth this after divers sorts: For God is not bound to keep always one course: he hath his means, such as it pleaseth him to appoint. Sometimes he showeth his election very quickly: sometime he deferreth it for a long space: and they that think, that there is a certain seed, in all those whom God hath elected, so as men may discern them from other, because they are inclined to good, and have some affection to serve God: they foully overshoot themselves, and are also convinced by experience.

John Baptist was sanctified from the womb of his mother: but it is far otherwise in many others. For God suffereth his elect sometimes to be as scattered sheep, and they seem as though they were altogether lost: and this is to the end to give the greater glory to his grace. As we see now some sign in Jacob, that God had chosen him, and rejected his brother Esau. For Jacob held the heel of his brother, as if he had fought against him. And this came not to pass by chance, neither was it done by nature: but God showed as it were with the finger, that Esau was the firstborn, and yet was nevertheless put back: and Jacob, who was the inferior in his birth, should yet in time be preferred. Mark then what we have to learn upon this place: that is, that God will approve that which he hath pronounced as we saw yesterday: *That the greater shall serve the lesser*: and this hath already been showed in the birth of two infants. But of this example we have to gather in general, that those whom God hath chosen, he hath prevented [*preceded, anticipated*]: and by this means doth ratify his counsel and decree, when his execution appeareth. And so, though we cannot enter so far, to know who they are that were elected before the foundation of the world: notwithstanding our election shall be testified unto us, so far forth as shall be necessary: For if God (as a man would say) do keep the protocol or original draft thereof with himself, it followeth not but that he doth give us such testimony thereof, that we may be assured that he both is and will be a father unto us to the end: and that we should call upon him in this affiance. For it is not said here albeit there were a vocation (as the holy scripture speaketh) that is to say, that he had declared unto Jacob that he had elected him. This will come with the time: but it is said simply that God had showed it as it were to the eye, that the answer which he had given to Rebecca was not in vain. Why so? the effect appeared in this, that Jacob held the heel of his brother. But here by the way God would show by this figure, that his elect come not to their end without many combats. It is true that Jacob knew not what this meant, and his age also did not suffer it: but this notwithstanding must serve to teach us, and is set forth as it were to declare unto us, that God will have us to fight, howsoever he hath taken us into his custody, yea, though we be in his protection and conduction, and he will have us to hope for salvation from him, and that that which he hath begun shall be accomplished.

Although then that all this be true, yet will he not have us sluggish: but he will that everyone of us strive to the end, that we may be led to that end whereunto he hath called us. Mark then that which we have to learn of this which Moyses rehearseth, that Jacob held the heel of his brother. Now he addeth:

And the elder was called Esau, and the other Jacob.

As touching the second, it is as if a man should call him *Heelholder,* but of Esau it is said, that he came from the womb of this mother altogether rough and covered with hair, as if he had been a man already. See also from whence he took his name.

We see then the difference betwixt these two: that is, that a man would have said that Esau, was to be far advanced above his brother. For we see him thoroughly fashioned, he is big, and showeth great strength: To be short, he is not as a child, but as a man. But of Jacob, there is no other thing, but the hand that held him by the heel, and he was as a thing born before his time: and when they grew, he continued even so. For Esau was a Hunter, a man of travel: (as if a man would say) nothing but strength. Of Jacob it is very true that the name which Moyses useth, is taken in good part and signifieth sound or perfect: Howbeit it was a simplicity which was opposed against all that which was more apparent in Esau: and in very deed Moyses addeth, that he kept the house, that he was as it were a Cokes or Mieber [*cook*] always sitting in the Ashes. Mark then what we have to consider in Esau and Jacob.

Now this is an instruction to confirm that we have entreated of before: That is to say, that GOD hath not chosen men according to the outward show they may have: but contrariwise, that which is accounted most excellent, he forsaketh and despiseth: And that which is as rejected of men, that doth he advance. We see it always: but yet there is no doubt, but the holy Ghost meant to set forth this in the person of our father Jacob, to the end that we should learn to beat down all foolish presumption, and should not search in ourselves, why GOD doth choose us, why also he continueth his grace towards us: but that we should know that he would be glorified in our littleness: and we shall have well profited, when this doctrine shall be imprinted in our hearts.

For there is nothing that more turneth us away from God, than when we desire to have some virtue worthy of praise: but we must be utterly spoiled thereof, or else we shall be so puffed up, that the grace of GOD cannot enter into us: So much the more then it behooveth us to lay good hold upon this which is so necessary for us: that is to say, that when God chooseth us, that this is not (as men say) for our fair eyes. And finally, if we be despised of the world, let us not therefore be discouraged: as we have showed, that it ought thoroughly to content us that we be accepted of God, although the world disdain us: For we see what was in Jacob: one still sitting in the house, as if a man would say, a Do-nothing, or Idle-body. It is true that he was entire, but whence was it? Whence was this simplicity taken? did he any notable thing? had he any reputation? he had nothing at all. But see Esau, who was as it were above the clouds even from his birth, he was a man already, he had strength in himself: and further, when he grew he had great industry, so that it seemed that he was to work wonders. Very well, in this we are taught that all comes of God. For if we should seek the cause of election in men, it is certain that everyone would give his voice to Esau without doubt. But notwithstanding all this, God preferreth Jacob: and why so? This is quite contrary to that we imagine. So then we have to mark, that God hath in such sort dispensed his grace, that he would have men to know, that it was his only goodness that moved him to love Jacob. Now this doctrine is well worthy to be meditated upon, all the days of our life: and this is (as I have said) to beat down all overweening [*high opinions*] that men have in themselves, to the end that there be nothing but the mere mercy of God that may shine in this thing: and in the meantime let us know that the church was always small in her beginnings, yea, and that God, hath after such sort advanced it, that on men's parts their infirmity must appear, and that they must always acknowledge it, to the end men submit themselves to such a condition. And again, howsoever it be, let us know, that God will never forsake his own work, but will bring it to his right perfection, although it be not known of men at the first dash: For neither ought it to be so, neither is it profitable. Again, if God give any sign that he have chosen us unto himself, and that this be showed even from our infancy, we have so much the more, wherefore to glorify God: For the more his grace is enlarged, the more praise it deserveth: but if we remain for a time as rejected, and that God maketh no semblance of having any regard unto us: but rather that we be as it were forgotten, and in the end he calleth us back again, when we have for a long time gone astray: herein also shall we have a double occasion to praise him. To be short, howsoever he work in us, it behooveth that our mouth be always open to acknowledge his goodness and mercy. There be some which from their childhood will declare that GOD hath kept them, as if he had held them by the hand, and should bring them forth to say: These are mine, and indeed they have a good instruction from their infancy, and further it shall profit in them, in such sort as men shall say: Behold a seed of God.

Now these (as I have said) are deeply bound to

acknowledge that God had given them this privilege. For what have they more than others? we are altogether corrupted in Adam. So then, when God leadeth them as it were by a continual thread from their birth, even until their old age, so much the more are they bound unto him. But there are others, who are as poor and miserable creatures: whom men would say that God had wholly cast from him, and the one sort are lewd and dissolute in their youth, the other sort miserable Idolaters: and whatsoever devotion they have, yet nevertheless this is always to estrange them so much the more from God, and to provoke his wrath, yea sometimes they are enemies to all truth: as we may see in the example of Saint Paul, who was as an outrageous beast shedding innocent blood, and striving for nothing more as a ravening Wolf, than to scatter all the Churches. Again, see the Corinthians, who were whoremasters, and given to all kind of villainies, as Saint Paul declareth: And as much is said of the Romans. *Ye were* (saith he) *in times past, both whoremongers and proud persons, and given to all oppression and deceit, yielding all your members to evil, and to the service of sin.* And a little after he saith to the Ephesians: *Ye were in times past without God, without any hope of life, ye were altogether darkness, ye were in everlasting death.*

Now when our Lord, to the end to humble us, shall suffer us for a time to be so scattered, and then shall suddenly call us to himself: let us acknowledge and say alas we ought not only to magnify GOD for that he hath chosen us, as we see the fruit thereof: but also because he hath drawn us from this gulf, wherein we were. And so much the more must we strive and redeem the time past, as Saint

Paul speaketh[†] thereof, in that we have alleged: *Ye were sometimes darkness, but now you are light in the Lord* (saith he) *and therefore walk as Children of light.* And let us often remember that which our Lord Jesus Christ saith[††]. *There are many sheep that are not of this fold.* For he spake of the Gentiles, who were shut out from all hope of salvation. He calleth them sheep, not in respect of themselves: For they were savage beasts: but in respect of God's election: although they were a scattered people, yet he saith, that he would gather them together. Therefore when it pleaseth God to withdraw us from dissipation wherein we have been, let us learn to give ear to the voice of this great Pastor: not only by giving some outward sign that we do allow it: but that it be to follow him and obey him in all things.

Mark then what it is, that we have to learn out of this place. And farther let us not be ashamed, when the Lord shall not give unto his faithful and to his whole Church, such a goodly show amongst men, to the end to be had in reputation: Let us not be ashamed of our baseness, so that he be glorified. As now it seemeth that the Church must be trodden under feet: and we see also how profane people and the Children of this world, make no reckoning of those whom God hath gathered to himself.

Now let us bear this patiently, after the example of our father Jacob: and let it not trouble us, if the world (in a manner) do spit in our face, so that we be approved of

---

† *Ephesians 5:8*

†† *John 10:16*

GOD. Mark then, how everyone of us have to practice this doctrine in himself, and also in the whole body of the Church.

And again, although we be not esteemed of the world, and few do allow us and clap their hands at us, yet God worketh in such sort, that that which is most contemptible in the world, and in the outward show thereof, is more esteemed before, God than that which hath great show and setting out before men. And herein is that accomplished, which is spoken in Saint Luke. That that which is high and excellent here beneath, is not therefore esteemed of God, but much rather is sometime an abomination unto him: as it is certain that the virtues of Esau shall always be praised, if men were Judges: but yet Jacob's simplicity before God and his Angels, is in greater estimation.

Let us therefore march on as our Lord Jesus hath commanded us: and let it not grieve us, though there appear not in us at the first dash, these gifts which God hath put in us. As for example. There are many who are nothing worth in respect of God, yet they have a goodly show, and also there be occasion thereof. Men shall find great personages, of great estate and quality, who shall have great valor, and be in great authority: shall be in honor and dignity: and farther there shall be no extreme covetousness in them: to be short, there shall appear such an honesty in them, that you would think them Angels, and all men will extol them everywhere: and in the meantime there shall be poor handicraftsmen, husbandmen, and poor idiots, who have no opportunity to show themselves: For they shall be busied in their shop and small household: they must travel to nourish their poor children. A man shall hear no great fame of them, they are not eloquent, to show forth any great wisdom: and when a man shall hear them speak, he shall see nothing but folly, according to the common opinion: and yet GOD hath elected and chosen them. He alloweth that which seemeth to be of no value: For albeit it seem that these are base things, that a man sew or do some other thing, and take pain, yet this is a service that GOD more esteemeth of, than we can imagine.

So then, when we know that we are nothing in outward show, let us not think our state and condition to be the worse for it (and as I have said already) let us not be ashamed of our infirmity: and in the meantime, let us lift up our eyes on high, and though we lie in the ashes, let us know that as much happened to our father Jacob before, who was a figure of all the elect of God and of his children. Now it followeth,

That Jacob was loved of his mother, and Esau of his father.

And this serveth well to show that there was no such perfection in Isaack, as there ought to have been: For he was not ignorant of that which had been spoken: *That the greater should serve the lesser:* He knew full well, that so was the will of God, that Esau the elder should yield both the place and degree of honor unto his brother: and yet he loved Esau: it seemeth herein that he would resist the counsel of GOD. And what means he herein? When he will cast his whole love towards Esau: Yet God will reign in the end and his election must stand fast, yea though all the world should strive against it. Lo Isaack, who is very blockish: yet there is more: for it seemeth that he is led by a brutish affection. For why did he love Esau? Because that he brought him Venison. He loved him therefore for his tooths sake. Behold an ancient man: and who by reason of his age ought to have been stayed and settled: he should no more have been led of his foolish and inconstant affections, that for his tooth's sake and lickerishness [*keen appetite*], he should have forgotten that which God had pronounced, yea, by an unchangeable decree: that Jacob must govern, and that he should be heir of the promise: and yet that Isaack maketh no reckoning of it. But here we see that the Jews are too too blind, vaunting themselves in their fathers, as though the dignity which they sometimes had, came from the holiness and virtues of men. For it is certain that Isaack, as much as in him lay, overthrew the election of God: not that he had a will so to do. For if a man should have asked him, how now? Wilt thou resist God? wilt thou let, that he shall not put in execution, that which he hath pronounced? wilt thou alter that which he hath pronounced by his mouth? He would have said: No: and his intent was not such. But howsoever it be, he is driven and drawn that way.

So then we may not say, that Isaack went about to help the election, of God nor set it forward: but contrariwise he hindered it. Now by this we see, that all mouths must be shut, and that men pretend not to have had anything in their persons, to say that God should confirm unto them the blessings which he had already given them. To be short, we see hereby, that like as the election of God, is free and undeserved in his first beginning and foundation, and in full force, so also it behooveth that God show unto the end, that there is nothing but his only mercy and that all that is said on man's behalf, do cease and be abolished, and that this is not, either of the willer or of the runner (as Saint Paul saith) Rom. 9[†]. Mark then what we have to learn. Now in the meantime we see also the steadfastness which is in this counsel of God, whereby he choseth those, whom he thinketh good. So we have to resolve ourselves, although the whole world should labor to overthrow our salvation, that yet it will remain sure, so that we have our refuge always to that which hath been showed us before: that is to say, That our Lord Jesus Christ hath taken into his keeping all that the father hath given him, as being his own: and that nothing thereof shall perish, forasmuch as God is stronger than men: for it is thither that he doth lead us: *The father who hath given you unto me, is stronger than all.*

So then let us learn to stay ourselves wholly upon the invincible power of God, when there is any question of being assured that in calling upon him we shall be heard, and that we doubt not but that as he hath brought us into a good way, so he will give us perseverance: and although that we be weak and frail, yet he will not suffer us to fall: but we shall always be lead in such sort, that he will more and more increase his power in us. We must therefore come even thus far, namely that Jacob had not only those his enemies which had no fear of GOD, and were irreligious, but even his own father Isaack: yea who was then as chief in the Church: God had put him in trust as it were with his covenant, to the end that he should be the treasurer thereof, and dispense it: and yet nevertheless he (as it should seem)

[†] *Romans 9:16*

was an enemy to the election of Jacob. Wherefore if we see many contrarieties, and that it seemeth our salvation must be overthrown by many means, and that we see no issue, let us then know that God will be victorious in the end: and whatsoever weakness be found in us, nevertheless he will not cease to proceed, and although there be resistance and contradiction here beneath, yet nevertheless he will overcome all, and bring it well about. But by the way, we are here admonished by the example of Isaack, to hold ourselves under the bridle. For if this happened unto such a man as Isaack was, so excellent and of an Angelical holiness, that he resisted God, what shall become of us in comparison? It is certain, that we shall everyday be overtaken an hundred times, with some vain fantasy, that we shall rush against God, although we have no such purpose. We have great need therefore to distrust our own judgment, and to call upon God, to the end that he will govern us by his holy spirit: otherwise (as I have said) we are as wretched strays, and we shall go hither and thither at all adventures. And when we ween [*think*] to be very wise, there will be nothing but folly in us, yea rebellion, although it be not with our wills and knowledge. Mark this then for one lesson, But we must mark here the cause which is here noted by Moyses, when he saith that Isaack loved Esau: And wherefore did he love him? Because that Venison was his meat. Therefore let us take heed that we be not led by our carnal and earthly appetites, if we will keep our array towards God. It is true, that to eat and drink are not condemned. For God hath placed us in this world under that condition that we should enjoy his creatures: and seeing he hath ordained us to eat and to drink, it is certain that we offend him not: when we desire to have for our necessities, and search out also the use of those benefits, which he hath prepared for us. For it is said without cause, that we must do all things in his name, yea both in eating and drinking: but in that we be corrupted, it cannot be but there will be always excess in our appetites, and this excess maketh us to forget our duties towards God: so as we are altogether drawn away on every side: and when we think to do our duties we are far therefrom. But Isaack ought always to have had this before his eyes, yea and he ought to have had it engraven in his heart, this voice should have sounded in his ears, to wit, that the greater should serve the less: he ought without end, and without ceasing, thus to have thought: well, forasmuch as God will have his election to remain in Jacob, it behooveth that I agree unto it. But in the meantime his meat turneth him, and draweth him quite contrary. Let us therefore be well advised (as I have already said) on our parts, to repress our desires, yea though they be natural, and of themselves not unlawful. But to the end that there be no excess nor intemperance: Let us be advised (I say) to check and to tame them, in such sort that they never turn us away, or hinder us from ordering ourselves according to the will of God. Mark therefore briefly what we have to learn here.

But here also we see that Rebecca had an affection better guided then her husband. It is very true that always men shall see (or for the most part) that if the Father love one of his Children, the mother will set her love quite contrary: A man may see these contentions in most houses. Also it may be that Rebecca had conceived some kind of jealousy: forasmuch as she saw Esau preferred: and therefore she loved Jacob the better, forasmuch as he was not so acceptable to his father, nor had no such favor: but forasmuch (as we shall see hereafter) that she had regard unto God's election, and that she always held that which had been said, that Jacob must be preferred: we have here to judge that she was not passionate and affected, as women that would lightly set themselves against their husbands, when they see that some of their children, shall not be so much esteemed, they will the more set their affections upon them. But we cannot judge so of Rebecca: and why so? Because we see (as I have already said) that she always referred herself to God, and meant to obey that which he had pronounced. She would undoubtedly that both the children might have been reserved in the Church: but seeing she saw the one shut out, and that there was none but the lesser and inferior that God allowed of, she yielded thereto. Now here we see that our Lord sometimes will suffer those, which have the more virtues and greater gifts of the holy Ghost, yet nevertheless to fall: and that they who were not yet so advanced as they should outgo them, I mean in some respect. For if we make comparison of Isaack with Rebecca, it is certain that he having been brought up in the house of his father, and having received so great instruction in his youth, had generally a greater faith than Rebecca. But behold a particular action, wherein he faileth, and wherein his vice showeth itself. And yet Rebecca who lately crawled out of a den of idolatry: as we know that in her father's house, there was nothing but superstitions, the country was altogether corrupted: this poor woman, although she knew not God in her youth: yet notwithstanding she was so well taught and instructed of the holy Ghost, that she outwent

her husband. Now for this cause, they too whom God hath
reached out the hand betimes, and whom he hath lifted up,
to be as mirrors unto others: let them learn always to walk
with greater carefulness. And why so? For there needeth
but one wry step to make them to fall so grossly, that
everyone will be ashamed of them.

And therefore let us learn, that albeit our Lord have
generally framed and fashioned us by his holy spirit in such
sort, that everyone hath us in admiration, that yet in
particular cases, we may offend. Therefore let us always
stand upon our watch. Moreover, they which are the most
excellent, when they shall come to fail in some point, let
them not make a buckler of this, that they have done so
many good deeds, and worthy of praise: let them not allege
their valiant deeds (as they say) but let them acknowledge
themselves for such as they be, and say: Well, I perceive
that God would have me to acknowledge that I am a weak
man: and farther that I should acknowledge in general, that
it is not in men to uphold themselves: for there needeth but
one fault alone to cause us to be cut off from the church.
And when God hath cast us off, what shall become of us?
So let us learn all these things in the person of our father
Isaack, when we see that he was so blinded, and that he
never remembered, that he was as a rebel to God, in
esteeming that, which God had rejected, and despising his
younger son: to whom notwithstanding God had given this
testimony: That he must rule in his house. Now in the
meantime, although that Rebecca had been well guided in
her affection, and that she had sought to obey God: yet it
could not be but there must be some quarrel between them:
as oftentimes it falleth out. And this is that which Moyses

saith. *That Isaack loved Esau, and Rebecca loved Jacob:* and
when he speaketh so, it is as if he would show that there
was some strife in the house, and that they could not agree
together, to say, that the husband and the wife should love
their children alike, as by nature they ought to have been
inclined thereto: or rather that they knew that the will of
God was that they should have loved the younger. Now we
are warned in this behalf, that albeit our affections be well
grounded and tend to a good end, that notwithstanding
there be always crossings which are blameworthy. As for
example, I seek to follow God, and fully to conform myself
unto his will: but there are resistings, and it must needs be
that I must incur displeasure of the one, and purchase an
enemy of the other, if I discharge my duty. Likewise it is
true, that the beginning shall be good, when I shall desire to
do well, and that I shall only look unto God: but everanon
[*always after*] it will befall unto us, that in our good zeal we
shall be too excessive, and that we shall have carnal passions
in us: To be short: they which shall be the best guided, and
who have greatest perfection, it is very certain that they
shall yet pass measure in this place, and that they shall
show themselves men: and so much the more ought we to
suspect our passions, and albeit we see that the end be not
good, yet we shall not cease to fall therein. Again, we also
have a good warning to leave all contradictions: For it is not
without cause that the scripture exhorteth us so often unto
this union, to be of one mind, and of one mouth. And why
so? For when we agree in such sort, each one stirreth up his
neighbor, and helpeth to bring him unto God. But
contrariwise, when we are quarreling in contention and
strife, not only one letteth [*obstructeth*] and hindereth

another (as it is commonly said there needs but one restive [*balky, stubbornly resistive*] Horse to hinder the whole team:) but yet there is a worse matter: to wit, that when we strive for the service of GOD, we cease not to forget ourselves in some respects, and many things escape us, the which we would not let slip, if we were out of strife and contention. This therefore is the matter we have to learn. And these examples are daily seen amongst us in the church. For the best servants of God and they that are endued with most excellent graces, yea and who strive for the truth, yet nevertheless cannot always so bridle themselves, that they be not quarreling, and show themselves men, and yet God alloweth their zeal and that which they do. And why so? For because they have a good beginning, and they have a right end: but as I have said, there is always infirmity mingled therewith. Let us therefore (say I) always mark this, in this example of Isaack and Rebecca. Again, we have farther to note, that if sometimes we shall not agree so as we ought and as were meet and convenient and as we ought, to bend and enforce ourselves, that yet nevertheless we must make no divorce betwixt ourselves, neither be quite separated asunder. For although this was a notable vice, that Isaack and Rebecca were thus divided in the love, which they bare unto their children, yet they continued to serve God: and Isaack did never pretend to abolish this oracle: that is to say, this same answer which God had given, that Jacob must govern.

Now therefore we see here how the husband and the wife are at strife, and that in such a matter of importance, as whereupon depended the salvation of the world. For the question is here of the eternal election of God, the question is of the whole church of our Lord Jesus Christ, who is the head thereof: and behold some crooked controversies betwixt Isaack and his wife. Yet this meaneth not that Isaack meant to overthrow all: but he understood it not, and was confounded in himself. Likewise therefore, when through ignorance and error, it shall sometimes come to pass, that we shall be in trouble, and that the devil shall thrust in his foot, and that we shall not be able to speak with one and the same mouth: notwithstanding, we must always keep the principal: that is, we must always agree in this, that we hold God for our father: and that we know that there is no true holy unity, but in Jesus Christ: that we hold, I say the principles of our faith: and if we cannot comprehend all things so distinctly as were to be wished, let the ignorant and weak be humbled, and let them not be discouraged. Likewise let them that are more froward, bear with the weak, waiting when God will turn them, and take from them these opinions, wherein they are so troubled. This is that which Saint Paul saith unto the Philippians: For he showeth how we ought to be knit together, and what the knot of our concord and brotherhood is. Now having showed, that he concludeth, that therefore there should not be diversities of opinions amongst us, and that our speeches likewise should not be divers. But yet (saith he) If you cannot come to such perfection, and that some go as it were halting [*uncertain, lame*], and cannot overtake others, which are not so quick to comprehend all: *Wait* (saith he) *until God reveal it unto you.*

Mark then the first thing that we have to do, that is, to agree in the pure and simple truth of God. But forasmuch as it is not given to all at the first dash, to have certain understanding of all points of religion: very well, if there be any ignorance, let them reach out their hand to them who are so besotted, yea let them take heed that they be not willful on their parts. For sometimes, yea most commonly a man shall see, that the blindest are boldest and rashest: and further there will be such a willfulness, that a man can gain nothing of them. But Saint Paul to remedy this mischief, saith: *Wait till God reveal it unto you.* This then is that we have to learn: but let us also remember that which he setteth down: namely, that when we shall agree in our Lord Jesus Christ, and that we respect nothing but his glory, that always we keep our course, and if there be some little strife, that this separate us not one from another. For it shall be enough when we have this key, though in many other things we be not so resolved as were necessary: yet if we be not quite withdrawn and turned from our Lord Jesus Christ, it is enough. Besides when we shall tend to his glory, everyone shall know, yea the most froward, that they are yet far off. What is the cause that those which are learned and exercised in the scripture, do disdain their brethren when they see them ignorant? It is forasmuch as it seemeth unto them that there is nothing wanting [*lacking*] in themselves: but if we know what it is to aspire to our Lord Jesus Christ, and to come to the glory of his resurrection, we will say always with Saint Paul, that we have not attained unto it. When therefore everyone shall know, that there is yet something lacking in himself, it shall do us no hurt, and we shall not think it strange to call our brethren, although it be afar off. Go to let us go forward. It is true that there is great difference betwixt them that have the gift of interpreting the Scriptures, and those that are poor and simple idiots: they will know well that there is one God, who is their father by our Lord Jesus Christ, but yet they cannot expound a place of holy Scripture: and yet notwithstanding they cease not to walk on in one and the same path: and those which are the most forward, although they come sooner to the goal, yet they must always wait for the other. Mark then how we have to do, according as it is showed unto us, and how we may learn it, by the example which is here contained.

But now let us fall down before the majesty of our good God, in acknowledging of our faults, praying him that he will in such sort make us to feel them, that it may be to the end we may be displeased therewith, and that we always may have an eye to our condition which is so miserable, to the end to have our refuge to his mercy: and that it will please him to receive us to mercy, and so to govern us by his holy spirit that we may be rid of all earthly passions. And seeing there are so many vices hidden in us, that we may take the greater pain to examine ourselves to the end always to have recourse unto him, who is able to cleanse us: and that we may so fight, against whatsoever thing doth hinder us from dedicating ourselves wholly to his service, that in the meantime we know, that it is far off that our conflicts do deserve to be approved of him, but so far forth as he beareth with our weakness. And also that we may have recourse unto his power, knowing the need that we have to be succored [*help*] of him: and that by this means, we learn only to rejoice in him, and not to doubt but that as he hath once reached us the hand, he will likewise continue more and more to strengthen us, until that we have overcome both the Devil, and all the assaults, that he can assail us withal. That not only, etc.

The fifth Sermon of Jacob

and Esau, Genesis 25.

29. *Nowe as Iacob was ſeething Pottage: Eſau came out of the fielde and was hungry.*

30. *Wherefore Eſau ſayde vnto Iacob: Suffer mee to keeele foorth of this Pottage ſo red, for I am weary. Therefore euery one called his name Edome.*

31. *But Iacob annſweared, Sell mee now thy birthright.*

32. *And Eſau ſaid: Beholde I haſten too death: & what auayleth this birthright vnto me.*

33. *To whome Iacob ſayd: Sweare vnto me this day: who ſware vnto him. So hee ſolde his birthright vnto Iacob.*

34. *Then Iacob gaue Eſau breade and pottage of Lentills and he did eate and drinke and roſe vp, and went his way, and Eſau contemned his birthright.*

E SAID YESTERDAY that God approveth and ratifieth his election, when he governeth his Children by his holy spirit, and that he maketh them to strive up to the heavenly life, and giveth them an affection to despise the world, and to look up more high. Contrariwise, that he discovereth what man's nature is, when he letteth loose the bridle to those that are reprobates, so that they become as it were brute beasts, looking to nothing but this brickle and transitory life. We have the confirmation of this doctrine, in the history which Moyses here reciteth: For on the one side he setteth Esau before us, who returning out of the fields from hunting, was as a famished wolf: he desireth nothing but to eat, and moreover is content to sell his birthright with an oath and here he renounceth his birthright, so that he may have wherewith to fill his belly. He then esteemeth the Pottage so highly, that his birthright was nothing unto him in comparison thereof. Now let us mark (as it hath already been touched before, and as we shall see more fully) that this was not an earthly privilege, to wit, that he should have a double portion, and that he should be advanced in his father's house: but it was to be the chief of the Church of God, waiting till our Lord Jesus Christ should appear for the salvation of the world. Now although this was a thing of such importance: yet Esau preferreth his belly, and he careth for nothing, so that he may have meat. On the other side, Jacob although he had made ready his dinner, or his supper (albeit it were his resection,) and that he had an appetite to eat, yet, he chose rather to abstain and defraud himself, than to let slip the occasion of getting the birthright. We see then that Esau was but as a beastly man, who sought nothing but to be fed and nourished: yea and to be well frankt [*greedily fed*]. Jacob is a weak man, subject to hunger and thirst: yet he bridleth himself, and looketh up higher than to this world, and forgoeth bodily meat, to obtain a spiritual benefit, which was of more value than an hundred, yea than ten thousand lives. Mark briefly what we have to learn of this history.

Now it is very true that a man might think at the first blush, that this was but a Childish toy. For what hurt was it in Esau, after that he had labored and taken great pain, yea for to bring Venison unto his father, if he were weary, if he were an hungered and should demand to eat? It seemeth not that this should be imputed unto him for a fault. And again on the other side, some man might say, what cruelty was there in Jacob, seeing his brother in such want [*need*], not to succor [*help*] him, at the least with half of his repast? For he should not have tarried his brother's complaint, and till he had cried for hunger, but rather ought frankly to have offered him of that which he had prepared for himself. For if he had seen but a stranger to be so needy, so weary, and so weak, he must yet have given him some refreshing and alms.

But behold his own brother, for they were born both in one belly: yet he leaveth him in this case, and vouchsafeth [*allow*] not to give him one spoonful of his pottage. A man might say therefore that Jacob was too too uncourteous. And again. Why should he compel him to sell his birthright? For he put here the knife as it were to his throat, and we know that bargains are always of no force, when there shall be any violence offered: If men do anything by constraint, or if they promise anything by compulsion rashly, they are not bound to keep it. But see Esau, who was an hungered, he could do no more, he was so far past himself, that he knoweth not what his birthright meaneth. So then, besides the cruelty of Jacob, there was too gross an oversight: and when he bargained, what oath soever came between, yet this ought not in any case to hold, by any right or reason. Well, notwithstanding all this, this is not recited to reprove Jacob, as though he had committed any fault, or offended either God or his brother: But contrariwise the holy Ghost giveth him here testimony, that he showeth us the way how to search after Heavenly things, and that first of all we must seek the kingdom of God, and renounce our own desires, or else in suchwise captivate and bring them under, that they hinder us not from looking always to the principal.

And contrariwise the example of Esau is set before us (as the Apostle showeth[†]) to the end, *We should not be profane as he was:* that is to say, that we should not be given to the earth: but that we should think that this which is promised us, is belonging to eternal life. So then, we must not judge of this history after our natural opinion: but we must weigh to what end and purpose it is here rehearsed, to the end we may the better make our profit of it.

Now I have already said in the first place, that God would as it were seal his election here, in the person of Jacob: and that he hath showed also in the person of Esau, that he was of the number of those, that were cast off from him. It is very certain that if Jacob had not been governed by the spirit of GOD, he had been altogether like his brother Esau. But we must see how the spirit of God was rather given unto him than unto Esau: We shall not find this diversity, but in the only free goodness of God. So then, let us know that Jacob was led with an holy affection, forasmuch as God had holden him of the number and company of his Children: as also Saint Paul saith[††]: *That we are the workmanship of God, created to good works, the which he hath prepared.* He speaketh not there of all men in general.

[†] *Hebrews 12:16*

[††] *Ephesians 2:10*

It is true that God hath created us all without difference: but there is a new creation in those, whom God reformeth, and whom he purgeth from their wicked lusts, to the end that he may bring them to himself, and conform them to his righteousness, so that they desire nothing more than to honor and serve him purely. Mark therefore a second creation which God worketh in his Children. So then, let us know that if God reach out his hand unto us, to show us the way of salvation, if he give us courage cheerfully to march forwards, and strengthen us also to continue therein, that then he showeth that his election is not in vain and frivolous, but hath it full effect and virtue. To conclude, when he abandoneth us, and that we are as strays throughout all our life, that we forget the salvation of our souls: let us know that herein he declareth his curse upon us. And so let us learn to tremble, as often as we see men besotted in beastliness, so as they know not their own state and condition, neither to what end they were created, nor wherefore God hath placed them in the world: when we see this, it behooveth us (I say) to tremble and to pray unto God, that he will not suffer us so to be estranged from him: but that he will always hold us in, and keep us, and that he will imprint in our hearts, such an assurance of the hope which he hath given us, that we may bear therein the right mark of his election, as if men spread a little wax upon a seal, the form of the seal will remain perfect, but the wax hath the shape and image thereof. So, when our Lord engraveth his fear in our hearts by his holy spirit, and such an obedience towards him, as his Children ought to perform unto him, this is as if he should set upon us the seal of his election, and as if he should truly testify that he hath adopted us, and that he is a Father unto us: Forasmuch as we have the earnest of his free adoption: that is to say, the holy Ghost. But now let us come to that, which is here handled particularly. It is said:

> *That Esau being returned, he asked of his brother Jacob, that he would give him of that red Pottage, and of that meat:* He saith it, but this was as it were in contempt: and yet herein we see, that he was not so delicate and fine mouthed: but he could do no more, he was so weary, that he knew not what he did: and therefore he asketh nothing but to be satisfied. And hereupon he saith: *Give unto me:* as if he should say: It is all one unto me, whether I eat brown bread or white, so that I may fill my belly, admit it were but with Acorns, it is all one unto me. A man might here find some color to excuse Esau: and it seemeth that this might well have been pardoned him. But what? So much the more in this must we behold, that our desires how natural and lawful soever they be, are yet nevertheless to be repressed, when there is any question of the heavenly life: for then we must bring under every consideration, and rather loose life an hundred times, then go out of the path of salvation. It is not enough therefore that men abstain from those acts that are altogether dissolute and wicked, and whereof they may be ashamed, but yet whatsoever desire they shall have, yea permitted unto them of God, which is not altogether condemned, yet must they tame them, when there shall be any comparison with spiritual benefits. But hereof we shall yet entreat more at large. In the meantime it behooveth us to note this point, that Esau sought not after great dainties: he saw the Pottage, whereof mention is here made, and he

asketh nothing but to be satisfied therewith.

Now Jacob asketh of him his birthright in payment. If he had asked it of him through ambition, and that it had not belonged unto him, undoubtedly it had been no bargain: on the other side, the malice which he had, could by no means have been excused: and farther this had been to commit an outrageous and thievish act, so to hold his brother's throat shut up, as to say: if thou wilt not forgo unto me, all that belongeth to thee, I will not give thee one morsel to eat, rather thou shalt perish. And to what extremity would this grow? But Jacob demandeth nothing of Esau, but that which was before given him. For he was taught that before the two children were born, now already this sentence was pronounced, that God had declared, that it must needs be that the elder must serve the younger. Jacob then, in respect of God possessed already through faith the birthright: It is true that that stood him in no stead in the judgment of the world: but the question is here of the right title, that he knew that God had appointed him to be the firstborn, and had declared, that the birthright belonged unto him. So then, he robbeth not Esau of anything that was his, but he rather asketh again that which was his own: as if he should have said, Because thou art first come out of the womb, thou despisest the sentence that God hath given, both concerning me and thyself: but yet that must stand which God hath decreed, it cannot be called back again. For myself, I always remain in this hope, that I shall obtain, that which was promised unto me: but for thy part, this is to the end that thou shouldest understand that I set more store by the service of God than by mine own life: and therefore sell me thy birthright. We see here briefly, that Jacob would not get the good of another by deceit or malice, neither enforce his brother to spoil himself of that blessing which belonged unto him, but he demandeth, that that which God had given him, might be approved and ratified amongst men. Lo then the sum of that which is spoken here. And therefore they, who will use so great rigor, to get the substance of another, and to entice themselves with the loss of their neighbors, have not whereof to make them any buckler here: as we shall see very many, who will espy out occasions, that if a poor man, be in any extreme necessity, it must needs be that he be robbed. Lo then they will prey and violently grate upon him. For then they will bargain with him, when they see him in this case, and O say they (who live upon spoils, as Hawks do upon the prey) this man must pass through my hands. Lo then a poor man who shall have but one field or one meadow: if he be indebted or fail to find money to pay, if he come to some Usurer, he will say unto him, lo there is no remedy I must needs sell you such a piece, O I have no money (saith he) at this time, and yet in the meantime he will keep his money in his purse, watching that occasion, which is as a robbery, forasmuch as he seeketh the means to deceive his neighbor. This is commonly seen, that he that shall be pinched with any misery, he shall be eaten even to the bones, of such as only have the means to succor [*help*] those that are in necessity. But if such wicked wretches, (as I have said) will cloak their iniquity in the person of Jacob, it is too too vain a thing. For Jacob sucked not another man's good unto himself, nor he sought not to enlarge himself to the end to lessen his brother: but he remained in the possession of that which God had given him. The birthright was his own already, indeed not according to the order of nature, but because it so pleased God. Inasmuch therefore as he deceived none, did wrong to no man, neither used any rigor or excess to draw another's good unto himself, we must not take any pattern and patronage from hence of those same thieveries and oppressions which commonly are exercised amongst men. And forasmuch as the question is here of a spiritual benefit that Jacob seeketh not riches, he seeketh not his commodities, nor any earthly honor, to advance himself above his brother: he forsaketh all this, this is all one to him: but he would have that which God had promised him: that is, that though he be small in this world, though he be afflicted, tormented and devoured, and that men do him many injuries, it is all one unto him, so that this inestimable treasure be reserved unto him: that is to say, that of his race shall come the salvation of the world, and that withal he is made of the company and fellowship of God's children. Touching Esau his answer, we see already that which the Apostle saith, and that which we have also alleged: that he was altogether a profane man. *I haste to death, to what purpose* (saith he) *shall my birthright serve me.* In saying that he hasteth to death, and that his birthright served him to no purpose: we see that he was altogether dull and blockish, and that it was all one to him, so that he might pass this present life.

And lo also what this word, *Profane* importeth: for it is contrary to the word *Holy*. And what meaneth this word *Holy*? To be holy, is when we are separated and put apart to serve God: For all the world is full of filthiness and iniquity, as Saint Paul saith. And when we shall have our conversation here beneath after the common manner, this is to defile ourselves with all filthiness. But to the end we may be holden for the children of God, it behooveth that we be separated even as Saint Paul speaketh thereof, in the first chapter of the first Epistle to the Corinthians. It behooveth that God gather us unto himself. For if we walk among thorns, that is but to scratch us every minute. If we go through dirt and clay, that is to beray [*defile, disfigure*] us. It behooveth then that we be separated. But (as I have said) the word *Profane* is contrary and opposite unto this. What then must we do? This is it, that a man take good heed to himself: yea, even to his body. For even like as there are two parts in us, to wit, the body and the soul: so the spiritual life is, when we know whereunto God hath called us, and whereunto he daily biddeth us: to wit, that we should be heirs of the kingdom of heaven: See what it is to sanctify ourselves, as it is said *Purify yourselves, yea all you that bear the Lords vessels.* And Saint Paul alleging this place saith: *Having therefore such promises.* That is, that God accounteth us for his servants and children: Let us take heed that we cleanse ourselves from all filthiness, as well of the body as the soul. But behold Esau, who hath no care but for his belly, and that he showeth very well when he saith:

Behold I haste to death, and what shall this birthright avail me?

Yea, but it was for everlasting life, it was for an heavenly inheritance: he hath no regard to all this. So then we see, that he did eat as a Dog, or rather as a Hog that had his nose always in the swill trough, and sought for nothing but meat. Behold then the disposition of Esau, which is declared unto us in these words. And so the exhortation of the Apostle ought well to be practiced of us: when he saith[†], *Let us not be profane men as Esau was:* For see what is the cause that maketh us to forgo the hope of that salvation that God hath given us: when we are snared in our own sense, and in our carnal desires, it is certain, that we are quite out of taste with that which appertaineth to the salvation of our souls, that hath no favor with us: so that there is neither word of God, nor promise, nor anything, which we do not lightly esteem, when we are so profane.

Now then, let us take good heed, when we are provoked with some desire to think, Go to, God hath not placed us in this world, to perish as Asses and horses: he hath given us a soul, wherein he hath engraven his own image. So then, it behooveth us always to labor and to aspire unto this heavenly immortality, and specially to enforce ourselves to fight against all our affections, and not to be so holden here below, that we strive not always to break and undo these cords, that hinder us, that we cannot come directly unto God. Mark then what we have here to learn. That we be not like unto Esau, saying: *I haste to death and whereto shall my birthright serve me?* What? shall we do such dishonor unto the dignity and nobility, which God hath placed in us, forasmuch as he hath given us immortal souls: that we say we are not of this world, our place is above, and our right is above, and in the meanwhile, shall we rest and be entangled here? So then, though we should perish an hundred times, yet let us know, that God hath

---

† *Hebrews 12:16*

reserved a better life for us, and that there is our sovereign good that we ought to esteem: and albeit that we want [*lack*] and have need of transitory benefits, which only serve to maintain us here beneath, yet let us bear it patiently, and let us always mark, if I die, not to say I perish, or I am utterly lost and cast away: For this is but a passage by death, to go from one life to another. We must therefore look up thither. And this is the sum of that we have to mark here. But howsoever it be, we see here how God hath laid open the beastliness of Esau, and hath showed that he was already forsaken of him, and was not governed by his holy spirit: as the wisest of the world, albeit it seem they pierce through the clouds, yet are they so dull and blockish, that they regard nothing but that which is present unto them, and thereto they wholly give themselves. We shall see therefore they wittiest and those whom men so greatly magnify, which look to nothing but to build their houses. Now I say not only to build goodly palaces: but also to get great revenues for their children, to advance themselves, and to become great states, to live at ease, to be feared and honored, and that all the world may be constrained as it were to pass through their hands: and in the meantime: as for God, they do not much remember him, and they are in such sort unthankful, that it were much better to be a Hog or an Ass, than to be like unto them. And why so? A Hog hath but his natural appetites: when his belly is full he will sleep, or he will wallow in dung: and he is well contented with it. But men, what desires have they? It is certain that there can be found no greater grief to torment them withal more cruelly than their own appetites. So then for this cause, they are in continual vexation and torment, inasmuch as they respect nothing but this life: and if they once die, why with them as it seemeth, all is dead. Likewise we see in all the reprobate, that they have not any taste of the Heavenly life. And therefore we must so much the more pray unto God, that he will open our eyes, to the end we may always see beyond these present things, and that we may keep ourselves therein, in such sort, that we be not holden here beneath.

But Jacob contenteth not himself that Esau hath simply sold him his birthright: but he will have another. Esau sweareth: this is all one to him: and herein we see how God threw him under his feet. For although that hunger oppressed him so hardly, that he was constrained to renounce his birthright, yet when he came to swear, and that the name of God was taken to witness, and protested that God should be his judge and punish him, if he were forsworn and disobedient, and kept not his promise: when all this was done, and he not ignorant what his birthright was worth, it must needs be said, that the devil had altogether blinded him. But hereby we are admonished, that when we have once begun to start away and to turn our backs to God, it must needs be that so much the more we be indurate and hardened, to have no more understanding of God than brute beasts. And when we have after a sort renounced the inheritance of salvation, it shall come to pass that we shall renounce it an hundred and a thousand times, yea the devil will find an hundred means in one day, to plunge us in the gulf of perdition, whereout we shall never be able to help ourselves. Mark then what we have yet to observe upon this place: but by the way we have to consider Jacob's abstinence. Behold an example of true fast, and not as the Papists imagine. It is true, that fasts are commanded unto us in the holy scripture, for divers causes: For they serve to tame our carnal affections: and we must so cut off our drinking and our eating, that the temperance which God requireth of us, may be as a continual fast, for the whole time of our life: but yet it is oftentimes required, that we should lessen our portion. And why so? To the end we may be the better disposed to prayer. And again, when we are afflicted, there is no question then of banqueting and making great cheer: if God threaten us, and that he will show us some sign of his wrath (as he saith by his Prophet:) *I then call you to mourning and weeping:* and if we loose the reigns to our desires, it is as if we should bid him battle and despite him. Mark then how fasting serveth to humble us before God, and to make us as wretched malefactors acknowledging that we have offended him.

Moreover, the fast whereof mention is made here, is that which causeth a man to abstain, yea from eating and drinking, if the same hinder him from serving God, and which maketh him rather to forsake his own life, than to be turned way from God's will. For (as we have already said) Jacob suffered as much as his brother Esau: It is very true: that he had not traversed and run so far that day in the fields and woods: he had tarried in the house after his accustomed manner: but albeit that he had made ready his dinner: he was an hungered and had an appetite to eat, but howsoever it was, he liked better to abstain, and to captivate himself, and to renounce his dinner, and as it were his own life, than to lose this occasion, which he had, that his birthright might be confirmed unto him. So then, we have here to make comparison betwixt Jacob and Esau, and to make our profit of the exhortation which we have alleged: that is to say, that we be not profane. But contrariwise it is said of Esau:

That he did eat and drink, and rose up and went his way.

The speech here at the first sight is simple, but it carrieth much with it: For it was not enough that he had said that Esau, without any further thinking of the matter had emptied his dish and was gone: but Moyses saith, that he did eat and drink, that he took his refection [*nourishment*] wholly at his ease, and that he was well filled, as though his birthright had been nothing unto him. And this is the conclusion which he setteth down.

That he condemned his birthright.

But before we come to this, it is said that he did eat, that he drank, and rose up, and went his way: wherein it is showed that Esau was abashed at nothing, but he was as a Dog, that did nothing but shake his ear, after he had eaten and drunk. Then he went his way and pleaded not the matter against his brother, as they which repent themselves, and are better advised, when they have done any unadvised act. They consider, Alas what have I done? What shall become of me? How far have I overshot myself? Esau thinketh nothing of all this: but he leaveth his brother after he was full: he rose up, and had no care of anything. Now therefore we have here to behold how the Devil, when he hath taken possession of a man, maketh him so senseless and blockish, that he hath no feeling of sorrow in himself, no remorse nor scruple, although he see that he be as it were cut off and banished from the kingdom of God, yet he is no whit moved with it. But this which I have touched ere while is yet better expressed: that is, that always we fall from one evil to another: and when the devil hath gotten us into his snares, he so entangleth us in them, that we can never wind out. But we must gather this general doctrine of this history, that is, that we always think upon that which is said by our Lord Jesus Christ[†]: *That first of all we seek for the kingdom of God: and that the rest shall be cast unto us.* Now when he speaketh of the kingdom of God, this is not only to be understood of life everlasting, but this also is comprised in it. For the kingdom of God is, that God be glorified in us, that he be served and worshiped, that we be his people, as also he hath mutually sanctified us: as he hath spoken thereof by his Prophet Esay: *Sanctify the Lord of Hosts, and he will sanctify you, and will be your strength.* When we shall therefore seek that God may be honored, and that we labor to dedicate ourselves to him, and to be, as it were living sacrifices: then shall all other things be given unto us: that is to say (as Saint Paul also hath declared:) God will show himself a father as well of our bodies as of our souls. For he saith unto Timothy[††], that if we walk in the fear of God, thinking more upon Heaven than upon the earth: *We have the promises* (howsoever it be) *of this present life, as well as of the life to come.* It is very true that the promises belonging unto this present life are accessories, that is, no other than

---

† *Matthew 6:33*

†† *1 Timothy 4:8*

that which followeth and dependeth thereupon: but it is so much, that if we lean upon the bounty of GOD, and strive thither whether he hath called us: that is to say, to the salvation which he hath so dearly purchased for us, by our Lord Jesus Christ: God will not only become the father of our souls, but also of our bodies. We are thoroughly assured of this, and ought to be resolved in it. But now (howsoever it be) if we must be ready to renounce this present life, and all the commodities which are here. If we must renounce our own life, by a stronger reason we must renounce to live. Now we cannot live here without eating and drinking: but yet it behooveth that we be ready to suffer hunger and thirst, rather than to be turned away from our calling: and not only this, but when the question shall be of death, we must offer our lives to God, doing him this homage, and always desiring rather a precious and blessed death before him, than all the lives that might be imagined in this world, which he shall accurse. Behold then the rule that is given to all Christians, and whereby they are tried if they be the true children of God: and that is, when the world hindereth them not to serve God, but they always march on forwards by that path which is showed them by the holy Scripture. When I say that the world letteth [*hinders*] them not: I understand not only those wicked lusts as drunkenness, whoredom, covetousness, and such like: but also those desires that are not utterly condemned: as eating and drinking when it shall be permitted us of God, and yet if eating and drinking shall hinder us from serving God, then we must so strive, that our desires may be tamed. Now this may be better understood, by the common experience we have. There is a man which may live in delights and pleasures, he hath to eat to the full, yea of all manner of dainties and delicates, and exquisite meats: but he must hang his conscience (as they say) upon the rack, or rather be profaned with the wicked world. For there are a great many conditions offered to many, which are as the enticing baits of Satan. Thereupon they will think, O if I were in such a place, I might gather a great deal of good, and afterwards I should be in great honor, all the world would crouch unto me: In the mean season I should have my table well furnished, I should have wherewith to nourish me to my desire: yea and in mine old age, when I should have gathered together my livelode [*livelihood*] and rents, I should be assured to live at mine ease. But I cannot attain unto it. But whereto tendeth this? Even hitherto, that I cannot do this, without being in great danger, to bring myself to great wickedness, yea and without utter estranging myself from God: Howsoever it be, I cannot serve God purely as he hath commanded me. But if any man be tempted with this, it is certain that he is like unto Esau, if he make choice of this condition, which shall be more agreeable to the world, and in the meantime shall forsake the means he hath to serve God, and to live in the peace and tranquility of a good conscience. For he considereth not: I am a weak man, and have much ado to hold myself in the fear of GOD, although, I be every day exhorted unto it: yea, and though I do give myself wholly unto it, and enforce myself thereunto: and what shall become of me when I shall have no word of God, that I shall not be exhorted to do my duty, and that I shall be entangled with many business and affairs of the world? If a man think not of all this, and that be make choice of a good table, that is to say, if he rather

choose an estate whereby he may enrich himself, it is
certain that he shall be resembled unto Esau. Contrariwise,
when we shall think: Go to, it is true that we shall be at our
ease, if we will forsake God, or rather depart from him, and
will decline, be it never so little from a good way. But
what? The devil will by and by find new slights to bring us
wholly to wickedness, in such sort that we shall be as a
desperate people. But let us prevent such a danger, and
rather let us love hunger and thirst, yea and to feed
straightly, and not to have any great pomp and great
superfluity: Let us choose rather, I say, not to have so great
an estate, and hold ourselves in sobriety, than to be rich and
wealthy, and notwithstanding to forget ourselves, and to
have all our joy here beneath. When we shall so behave
ourselves herein: lo how we follow the example of our father
Jacob. But as I have said already, the question is not only
of forsaking our ease and commodity, but also, when need
shall be, of our own life. For if so be, we must die to make
confession of our faith, such as God requireth of us, and to
glorify the name of our Lord Jesus Christ, and must pass
that way: we must likewise also forsake our own life, and all
that belongeth unto it: and if we do it not, we show that we
know not, what it is to have tasted of spiritual blessings: but
that we have lost all taste of them, forasmuch as the devil
hath made us drunken with his poisons, and hath bewitched
us and made us senseless and blockish. We see here by the
way how profitable this history is unto us. For besides that
we have said already, that God hath ratified his election,
and hath discovered that which was in Esau and Jacob: here
our father Jacob reacheth out his hand unto us, and
showeth us that all the pleasures of this world, ought to be

nothing unto us, no not our very nourishment, when there
shall be any question: to be as poor starved people, that we
rather forsake to eat and drink, when all shall be made
ready, yea specially, when the smell shall have provoked us,
that we imagine to have the morsels already in our mouths,
and to have swallowed them down, when we shall be come
so far, nevertheless, that we enter into such a combat
against ourselves, that we renounce our natural inclination,
and specially that which is not utterly condemned amongst
men, if it let us from coming unto God, if it hinder us, or
entangle us here beneath in any corruptions. Behold what
we ought to do. And moreover that we take good heed on
the other side, that we be not like unto Esau, and that we
allege not this, and that as many say, O we must live. We
may well have our excuses before men: but when we shall
come to render a reckoning before that great Judge, who
hath declared unto us, that he will have us to set such price
upon the treasure of our salvation, that he hath offered us
in the Gospel, that we learn to withdraw ourselves from the
world, and that all that is in it be nothing in comparison of
it.   But this thing is practiced after sundry sorts and
manners: For when a Christian man shall have plenty, if he
be sober in eating and drinking, and do not so gorge
himself, that he loose both his sense and memory, but be
always disposed to praise GOD, to execute the charge
whereunto he is called, and to employ himself to that which
belongeth to his estate and vocation, if a man be so
temperate, he is like unto Jacob. For he forsaketh to eat
and drink, not because he useth not the benefits that God
hath put into his hand, but he forsaketh them, in bridling
his desires, to the end not to exceed measure: and after he

always lifteth up himself on high, regarding the service of GOD, and preferring it before any worldly thing. Again, if it be necessary that he which was rich, should be poor: and that he had rather be poor, yea if it were but to eat roots, if need should be, rather than to be alienated from GOD: and that always he remain steadfast in it, saying, forasmuch as I am an heir of the world: I ought to be well contented: and now if I endure hunger or thirst, if I bear any necessities and miseries, I will pray unto God that he will give me patience. And this is the reason, why Saint Paul also saith[†], that he had learned, in the school of our Lord Jesus Christ, to be hungry and to be full: that is to say, when he had enough, he left not to hold himself in: and when he had nothing he was patient in his necessity: he had recourse to God and chose rather to have many wants in respect of the world than to have wherewith to grow and enrich himself, and yet to be empty of heavenly benefits.

For it is certain that Esau had his soul buried in the pottage he saw there, he smelt them, and thereto he laid his snout. And wherefore? Because he had no other consideration than of this present life. Lo, his soul which was buried therein. Now we may be compassed round about, with all the goods of this world: but it behooveth that the smell do not so allure us, that we esteem not spiritual things far above them, and always to prefer them. Mark then briefly, how we ought to apply this doctrine unto our use.

And moreover let us mark well that which is spoken

---

† *Philippians 4:12*

here, that the wickedness of Esau was, because he made no account of his birthright. And therefore this is a sign that we contemn the graces of GOD, and as a man would say, cast them to the ground and tread them under our feet, when we are so much addicted, either to this life, or to our desires: and when we can endure and bear nothing: but will have all which is pleasant unto us after the flesh. When then we will in such sort hold our lusts, it is certain that we make light account of that heavenly inheritance. For how shall that be esteemed of us? It shall be esteemed of us (as I have said already) when the world shall be unto us, but as an accessory, and all that is in it, shall go as at the tail. But the gospel and the promises which are therein contained, whereby god testifieth unto us, how he hath adopted us, and likewise how he will have us to himself: this must mount up above them, and we must be ravished in them. And notwithstanding let us well advise ourselves. For if once the Devil gain this of us, that we become beastly in our pleasures, he will not put us in mind for nought, we shall seek after nothing but this transitory life, we shall do nothing but run up and down like poor beasts, and have no mark whereat to aim, as it fell out with Esau. I have said already that these words are not put in in vain. *He did eat, he drank, he rose up and went his way.* And what a company of such, and such like, do we see at this day? For they which have their delights after the manner of the world, will esteem us for beggarly mome [*fools, blockheads*]: and they deride our simplicity: Well, well, say they: let them have their Gospel, and notwithstanding die for hunger, and let them be such as have not a rag to hang on their tail, and have nothing to champ between their teeth, or rather let them droop and hang their wings, and be so miserable as none can be more: and let them rejoice in their Gospel, as much as they will, but we in the meantime will have our swing in this world, we will have all our desires, and our table well garnished. And above all these contemners of God, which are at this day advanced into states and dignities, it is well known how they flout us, and bleat out their tongue, if men speak unto them of the gospel and it seemeth to them, that we are as madmen, which cannot discern between good and evil. And why so? For they eat and drink they rise up, and go their way: yea the world doth so hold them, or rather Satan hath in such sort possessed them, that Heaven is nothing unto them, and they altogether forget everlasting life. We see this, and yet it is to no purpose to pursue it: For our Lord hath set before our eyes, that this is an horrible condemnation, when we fall into such blockishness, to prefer this life, which is nothing but a shadow before that eternity, to which God hath called us. For let us put the case, that we should live an hundred years after our death: and yet what is that? If we make comparison (as Saint Paul saith) with this world, it is but a minute *and a figure which passeth away,* and in sum, *but a moment.*

Now contrariwise of what weight ought our immortality to be with us, which is offered unto us in our Lord Jesus Christ, and whereof he hath so well certified us? And yet concerning this life, who is it that can promise us one day? For they who are well fed, they grow therein, and there cannot be a minute to uphold them: and specially intemperance choketh very many. And we see that men, the more they have wherewith to do well, they kill themselves. And yet in the mean season we cannot content ourselves, but (like poor beasts) we must seek for that which hath no certainty: and in the turning of a hand all is lost. We seek nevertheless for this, and hereunto we are given, yea wholly addicted, insomuch that we discern not betwixt that which is permanent, and that which flitteth away: For if we contemn that which is everlasting whither then go we? It is certain that the most wickedest themselves will say, that this is a madness: but after they have said it, they show that they are strayed, and that they do not greatly pass for it.

And this is so common a vice, that it behooveth that the most perfect especially fight against it. And the Apostle not without cause handling this matter saith: *Be not profane:* to the end to make us watchful: and to make us think who we are, and that we should not be so brutish, as to rest upon this present life. So then, let us go further, and that which is here given us, let us apply for our help, to make us run on the more swiftly: but if there be anything that hinder us, yea though it were our very eye (as our Lord Jesus Christ saith[†]) that our eye may rather be plucked out, and we rather desire to enter into the kingdom of Heaven blind, than having all our senses sound to go into everlasting destruction. So then to conclude, let us rather love hunger and thirst, than to cram and stuff our bellies, and in the meantime not to regard everlasting life: For we must not be so shared in these corruptible and transitory things, that we cannot always lift up our senses and affections on high, to

---

† *Matthew 5:29*

the end, through hope to be Citizens of the kingdom of heaven.

But now let us fall down before the majesty of our good God, in acknowledging our offences praying him that it will please him in such sort to make us to feel them, that it may serve to make us there to open them: and that we may learn in such sort to fight against all temptations, that if we must endure many poverties and miseries in his world (howsoever it be), that this do not turn us to wickedness and make us to decline from the right path: but that everyone may here resist both himself, as also all his desires, and all his passions: and that we may serve our GOD in such sort, that if it will please him to prove our patience in leaving us destitute of means, and of the commodities of this world: that we may bear all with a quiet and peaceable courage, until we be received into this blessed inheritance, where we shall not lack anything whatsoever it be: but there we shall have the fullness of all joy and happiness. That not only etc.

❧The sixth Sermon of Jacob

and Esau, Genesis 26.

1. *Now there was a great famine in that land, farre greater then that firſt famine, that was in the daies of Abraham: Wherefore Iſaack went vnto Abimelech the King of the Philiſtines into Gerar:*

2. *For the Lorde appearing vnto him had ſayde, Goe not downe into Egypt, but dwel in the land which I ſhall tel thee.*

3. *Be a ſtraunger in this land, and I will be with thee, and bleſſe thee: For to thee and thy ſeede, I will giue all theſe countryes, that I may eſtabliſh the othe which I haue ſworne to Abraham thy father.*

4. *I will multiply thy ſeede that it may bee infinite as the ſtarres of Heauen, and I will giue vnto thy ſeede all theſe Countryes: and all the nations of the Earth, ſhall repute them ſelues bleſſed in thy ſeede.*

5. *Becauſe that Abraham obeyed my voyce, and obſerued my ordinaunce, my commaundementes, my ſtatutes, and my lawes.*

 E SAW YESTERDAY HOW JACOB forsook his meat for that spiritual benefit which GOD had promised unto him: and hereby it appeareth that he had more care of his soul than of his body: Here we have an example, though not altogether like in Isaack his father, yet coming very near it. For we see how Isaack had more regard to the spiritual inheritance, than to all that concerned this brittle and transitory life. He was oppressed with famine: and there is no doubt, but that it was not his ease to go into Egypt. But when he was let by an express commandment, it was a sign, that his courage tended thitherwards: because his commodity likewise drew him: God stayeth his journey, and he obeyeth. We see then that Isaack left not only a mess of Pottage: but he seeing that he could endure much woe for a years space, notwithstanding he withheld himself, and sought no refuge in Egypt: and remained in the land of Gerar, which specially could not be altogether exempted from poverty, which was a part of that country: For it is impossible, when there is any famine, but that the neighbor and near places must also feel it: It may easily be gathered, that then there was no dearth in Egypt. So that Isaack here showeth us, that although temptations be great, if we be destitute of that which is necessary to maintain us, that yet notwithstanding we must always hold us to the will of God, and rather forget all our eases, and prepare ourselves patiently to suffer all want [*lack*] and necessity, than to seek our commodities, as it were, against the will of God. This is the first point that we have to mark in this history. Now it is said.

> *There was a great famine in the land, a greater than that former that was in the days of Abraham.*

For there had been two that Moyses already had rehearsed unto us. As soon as Abraham was arrived into the land of Canaan, he was fain to depart: and this was a very hard combat unto him, seeing that God had showed him that land, and that he had conceived great joy, for that he should be put in possession thereof: and now a little after he must be chased out, and become as it were a poor vagabond, and go down into Egypt, because he found not any succor [*help*] elsewhere. The second time he also withdrew himself into the land of the Philistines, which was of the very same country that was promised unto him, and under the King of Gerar: not he of whom now mention is made: for all called him Abimelech, which is as much to say, as *My father the king:* and this was not only an honorable title, but also expressed, that kings governed not by tyranny, and did devour up their subjects, but had a fatherly care over them whom God had committed to their charge. When then it is said that this famine came as the other, this is to show unto us, that altogether like as God had proved the faith of Abraham and his constancy: so likewise he would call his son to the like trial. For as Isaack was heir of the promise, so also must it needs be that he succeed his father in that which was promised to the children of God: For we must show by the effect that we so esteem heavenly benefits, to which God hath called us, that we pass through the world, and that we fail not, howsoever we be afflicted after divers and sundry manners. Mark then whereto Moyses has regard, when he compareth these two famines: that is, to show us that when Abraham was tempted, it was not only for his own cause: but his some also must be like him. But by the way we are called the sons of Abraham and of Isaack: it behooveth then that our faith be examined, as it shall seem good unto God. It is very true that we shall be more confounded: and that is because we have not received so great a measure of strength. Mark therefore the cause why God supporteth our infirmity: but yet this is not to the end that our faith should be idle. So then, we are here warned by the spirit of God, that being in this world, we must be subject to many miseries, and that we shall not have an earthly paradise, to the end to have all our desires, and to be so satisfied that we shall lack nothing: but that it shall oftentimes seem that god hath forgotten us, that he hath taken the bread out of our hand, and that we shall be in such case, as if he had condemned us to perish. When this shall come to pass, let us not think it strange, and likewise let us not be as young Novices: but let everyone of us think aforehand of that which may come upon us, and be prepared to suffer all things patiently. The promise is well given unto the faithful: *Although the Lions oftentimes seek their prey and find it not, and that they roar out for hunger, yet nothing shall be wanting to the Children of God.* Mark then how he hath spoken thereof, in the thirty and four Psalm[†].

And again in another place[††]: *All they which fear God, shall be satisfied with all good things.* But this is not therefore spoken as though God would fat up his own, and give them whatsoever they shall desire: but he nourisheth them after another manner. And when he speaketh of satisfying them, this meaneth not that he will always fill their bellies with exquisite meats: but we must yet have recourse to another

---

† *Psalm 34:10*

†† *Psalm 66:16*

place of the Psalm[†]: *That the poor of the Church shall be nourished.* Mark here a certain kind of contrariety, when God saith, that he will fill those of his church with bread, and notwithstanding, calleth them poor and needy. If they be poor and needy, where is this promise that God will fill them with bread and with all good things? But we must reconcile that which seemeth to disagree, and in such sort that we always depend upon the providence of God, to be as it were fed by him: In the meantime if he shall suffer that we endure hunger and thirst, that we do not therefore give over to hope, that he will be our good father to nourish us. And this is the cause why we do pray for our daily bread.

Now this opposeth itself against all those provisions, wherein the children of the world do put their trust: for they are never stayed unless *their barns and cellars be full*, as it is said in another Psalm[††]. And besides when they are well fraughted [*supplied, furnished*], they despite God as though they were without all danger as they think: But contrariwise, howsoever the faithful have wherewith to nourish themselves, yet must they every day open their mouth, as if God should put in bread by morsels: and when they have nothing, yet always they trust in him, and in his goodness, and hope that he can sustain them, with one crumb of bread, when it shall so please him: or rather, albeit they see no way how it should come, yet nevertheless, that God will find a means to maintain them.

When therefore it is said, that Isaack was driven out

---

† *Psalm 132:15*

†† *Psalm 144:13*

through famine, this is as much as if God would declare unto us, that when we shall fall into poverty and need, that we think not, that we are therefore forsaken of him, nor take it as a sign that he hateth us: or rather that we imagine not, that he thinketh no more of us: but that as our father Isaack endured hunger and thirst constantly, and in the end tried that God always had care of him, so we also acknowledge the like.   Mark this for one special lesson. And this is that also which is showed unto us by Saint Paul in the eighth chapter to the Romans[†] when he saith: *Shall hunger be able to separate us from the love that God beareth us in Christ Jesus our Lord.*   Saint Paul fighteth there, in the name of all the faithful, showing therein that if God should cut off our morsels, yea and that we should be deprived of all nourishment, as if it seemed that he would exclude us, from all the benefits that he hath created in the world, as though we were not worthy to be upon the earth: yet must we overcome this temptation there, and conclude, though it be in the midst of famine, that God will be our father, and we must content ourselves with this, rejoicing in our afflictions. But in the meanwhile we are also exhorted by the example of Isaack, not to be so grieved and vexed with famine, nor for other afflictions of what sort soever they be, to the end they make us to forsake God, or turn us out of the path wherein he hath set us: For as we have seen Jacob forsook his meat, to aspire to that spiritual inheritance, which had been promised unto him: So now likewise we see that Isaack had no regard to that which he might suffer in that length

---

† *Romans 8:35*

of time.   He saw Egypt which was a good refuge,
nevertheless he was turned from it. And why so? Because
God had forbidden him to go thither. So then, when we see
that Isaack was not overcome by famine, that he obeyed
God and forsook not to be guided by his hand: by this we
have also to learn, when our Lord will afflict us with poverty
and need, that we look not to unlawful means to relieve our
necessity. And above all, if Satan lay before us his baits to
entice us, that we rather choose to die of hunger (if need be)
than to withdraw ourselves from the conduction of God:
seeing that we cannot be nourished but by his blessings.
For when we shall have all the bread and meats in the
world, it is certain that the wind shall as well profit us for
our nourishment as these, and we shall think, that we grow,
and yet in the meantime we shall not be substantially fed:
For it is not bread (as it is said in Moyses[†]) *that nourisheth us,
but every word that proceedeth out of the mouth of God.* Now by
this word, he doth not understand the doctrine of salvation,
but that same virtue which God hath spread over all his
creatures. Mark then what it is that nourisheth us: I say not
only in respect of the soul but also in respect of this
transitory life. Which seeing it is so, let us take heed, that
we be not fed by that which the devil shall set before us,
when we are in necessity: and canst thou do this, and art
thou able to wind out from thence, and hast thou any such
help? yea if this be contrary to the will of God, that we
always remain steadfast, and that we wait till God shall
show himself pitiful towards us: as he that best knoweth the

---

† *Deuteronomy 8:3*

mean, although it be unknown to us. It is true that we shall have no such revelations as our father Isaack had, God will not appear unto us from heaven: but this ought to suffice us, that at this day the will of God is certain unto us: for GOD hath supplied that which was wanting [lacking] to our old fathers, when he appeared unto them: at this day we have the law, which is an infallible rule unto us: we have the prophets which are expositors thereof unto us, to the end that the shortness thereof be not obscure unto us: we have further more perfection in the gospel. Seeing God then hath revealed unto us that which is profitable for us to know, we must not desire visions at this day, but as often as we shall be in any perplexity or doubt, we must have recourse unto the Scriptures: and when we shall think upon the means, let us mark whether the same be permitted unto us, and whether God allow of them. And when we shall find that the means which shall come into our heads, be not agreeable to the will of God, according as it is contained in the law and in the Gospel, that we then forsake all. Mark how we have to follow our father Isaack, yea to overcome this temptation which is very heavy and troublesome: that is to say, when we have nothing wherewith to be nourished and fed, but a very small pittance. For oftentimes the unbelievers are found to have thirty times more than is necessary for them, likewise a man shall find prodigal and dissolute persons, that will waste and spend all the benefits of God: yea, and they will make havoc of them. But what of the poor faithful ones? having traveled for to maintain their life, yet scarcely do they find in the end, how to get their bread.

When therefore we see that God will oftentimes thus

prove those that are his, let everyone prepare himself thereto, and let us not be abashed, although that our Lord doth handle us with such rigor and severity: Nevertheless this is not to defeat us of that which he hath promised us, or not to hold us for his children: and let us acknowledge that the office of feeding and nourishing us appertaineth unto him, and that he will do it, although not according to our desires and fantasy. And moreover when we see that God presseth us not thereto, that hunger should drive us as they say from door to door, let us know that he bears so much with us, by reason of our weakness. This is the sum of that we have to learn, concerning the example of Isaack. But here a question might be asked. Why God permitteth of father Abraham to go into Egypt, and forbiddeth his son Isaack. But concerning this, we have to note that God knoweth who we are, what our strength is, and according to this also: *he suffereth us not to be tempted above our strength,* (as Saint Paul hath spoken[†]) *calling him faithful in this behalf.* God then knoweth that which he hath put into us, for that which is there of nature, shall always be to throw us down: but when he hath given unto us any power of his holy spirit, he knoweth whether it be in little or in great portion: and according to this also he exerciseth our faith and our patience, and when he seeth that we are weak, he suffereth us not to be tempted so strongly. Mark then how this came to pass: and this diversity which is here put between Abraham and Isaack, is to show that the faithful shall not always be alike handled of God, for this reason that I have

† *1 Corinthians 10:13*

alleged. Isaack was the successor of Abraham, he had the promise: and in this that he was tried and examined by divers afflictions, it is evidently seen that God made him to pass, by one and the self same path: but notwithstanding (as I have already said) it followeth not that he had one and the like rule in all points. For our Lord supporteth whom he will, and when he suffereth men to be more hardly entreated, by and by he likewise fortifieth and strengtheneth them.

Abraham forsook not to return to the country of Canaan, after he had dwelt in Egypt: but God also draweth him out of Egypt, as if he had held him by the hand. For he might long time have remained there, seeing himself rich there: but he might have been hated of the inhabitants: and therefore God draweth him from thence, he might likewise have done the like to Isaack, but we must not set him a law. If any man reply here, could not God have given as well an invincible constancy to Isaack, that he should not have slept there, and could he not have made as well him to have returned? Yes very well: but can we bind him to that. It behooveth that he govern us according to his infinite wisdom, and not according to our foolish dreams and fantasies. Let us mark well then, that when there is such a diversity in the tentations [*temptations*] of the faithful: it is because God knoweth what everyone will be able to bear. And always let us have recourse to this sentence of Saint Paul: *That we hope in him,* if he examine us, if he place us in the battle, if he try us with many griefs, that notwithstanding he will provide for this, that we shall not be altogether overcome or vanquished. Mark wherefore it was forbidden Isaack to go into Egypt. Now it is said unto him.

That he should dwell in the country of Canaan, and that God will always be with him, and that he will fulfill the oath which he had sworn unto his father Abraham.

This is to say, that he would multiply his seed as the stars of heaven, and that in his seed all the nations of the earth should be blessed. Here we see why god suffered not Isaack to go into Egypt: that is, that he might not forget the promise which had been given unto him concerning the land of Canaan, and likewise that he should content himself therein, and altogether rest himself there. Now if Isaack who was so excellent in the faith as we see by all his life, and to whom the holy Ghost hath given such a testimony, had such need nevertheless to be so bridled, what shall become of us? Even so we ought not to marvel, if our Lord do oftentimes hold us as it were chained in, and that he give us not license to rove here and there: for he knoweth that this shall be to cast us to utter confusion. So inasmuch as we have so slippery a memory, insomuch as there needeth nothing to cause us to stray, so as we know no more which shall be our right way: this is the cause why our Lord giveth us not so great liberty as we would. And likewise as often as we are holden within straighter bounds than our fantasy desireth, let us know that if our Father Isaack had such need thereof, we by greater reason, who are come nothing so near to such excellency of virtue as he, have greater need. Now in the meantime we see that in Isaack, which ere while was declared to be in Abraham, God saith unto him, that he will give him all those countries that he saw, and through which he walked: yea, but notwithstanding he saith unto him: *Thou shalt dwell there as a stranger.* Mark two things, which yet seem contrary. For if God will give him that land for a possession, why doth he not hasten it? Why doth he suffer him so to languish?

But there is no question of that which is past, but of that which was to come. *Thou shalt dwell there:* yea and the word which Moyses useth, signifieth to dwell as it were in a strange country, as one that were still going. Lo Isaack then who had a Lordship upon the earth: and yet had not one foot thereof, but must remain there by leave, and must be subject to many troubles and trials, which were bent towards him: and yet he had not one foot of land, unless it were the burying place whereof mention is made before. To be short, we have to gather here, that God would have Isaack wholly to rest upon his word: as likewise it is the foundation, whereupon we must build all the days of our life, yea and in death too. For if we should have all that we desire, what should we need anymore faith or hope? It behooveth therefore that the benefits which we wait for from God, that they be hidden from us, and notwithstanding that we behold them only by faith, and that we do God this honor, to account him sure in all that he hath spoken: although he show us not the effect and truth of his promises, which we apprehend not after our reason and carnal feeling: notwithstanding we must say, it sufficeth us that he hath spoken it, he will perform it: When therefore we can fetch all our contentment from the word of God only, then let us assure ourselves of a right trial of all that which we protest, that we believe in him: but if we

will always have a gauge, and have all that we desire, it is
certain that the word of God shall not be esteemed of us,
and we cannot exercise ourselves, sufficiently enough in this
meditation. And therefore as often as we see God to have
spoken to his servants, and not to have showed them the
accomplishment and execution of his word, let us know that
this is rehearsed unto us, to the end that we should learn to
call upon God, when he shall leave us in suspense, yea and
that we shall faint, and be stripped of that which should
have been in our hand: that we learn to say: O Lord seeing
we have thy promise, we shall not be frustrate in waiting for
it. When God promiseth Isaack to be with him, and that he
will give him the rest, this likewise is to show us, that the
principallest of all benefits that we can desire, is that God
have care over us, and that he think of our necessities, and
that we find him at hand when we call upon him. For
unless that we have him merciful unto us, although he give
us in all fullness and abundance, that we ask of him, yet it
should be nothing: but we must begin at this point: that is
to say, we must be well persuaded that God loveth us, and
that he is favorable unto us. When we have attained to this
to resolve ourselves, that GOD will always be merciful unto
us, and ready to succor [*help*] us when need shall require,
that he will never forsake us, then shall we easily wait for
the rest: but if we know not that he is with us: that is to say,
that he will make us feel his presence, and in feeling it, will
withdraw us from those dangers wherein we are, and in
withdrawing us, will lift us up when we shall be fallen, will
lead us there, whereas there is no path, and will there give
us an issue and way to escape, where there is nothing else
but confusion: If we have not (I say) attained to this, there

is no true foundation: but if we have once obtained it, we must stay thereupon and hope for the rest. For if God love us it is certain that he hath wherewith to succor [*aid*] and help us in all, and through all, and he will do it. And this is the cause why Moyses beginneth at this point.

I will be with thee.

And afterwards he saith: *That he will multiply his seed, that he will bless it, and that his seed shall be as the stars of Heaven.* It is true, that the benefits which God will bestow upon us, they shall not always fall out to our desires, as we have declared. For oftentimes we shall want [*lack*] them, to the end, we may be the more eager to pray: and also he will try us, and show us that we have no such affiance in him as we ought: and our unthankfulness many times depriveth us of that, that GOD otherwise was ready to bestow upon us: For we are not always capable to receive that which he offereth unto us. He hath an open hand, but we have a close mouth: that is to say, we are shut up in unbelief and distrust. And therefore see the cause why we must so oftentimes wait: but so much there is, that if we be resolved in this point, he is with us, and we are blessed of him in that which he knoweth to be expedient for us, and we shall lack nothing.

Touching this promise: *That all the nations of the earth shall be blessed in Isaack's seed,* this was special to him, as it was to Abraham: and this respecteth our Lord Jesus Christ, as it hath been expounded. For it was necessary that Jesus Christ should be the fountain of this blessing, the which should flow upon all the lineage of Abraham. It is true that the faithful which descended of him, were blessed and partakers of this promise: but this was by the power of our Lord Jesus Christ. So then, if he had been separated from the seed of Abraham, it is certain that he had been barren and dry, and that he should not have had one drop of the blessing. But at this day, forasmuch as God would by his infinite goodness, that his only begotten son should belong unto us, we were joined to the true natural Children of Abraham: and howsoever we were of the nations of the earth, who were then strayed from the Church of God, and who were altogether departed far from it, yet at this day we are blessed as well as they. For if it were said to him *I will bless thy seed*, and that God had added nothing, this had at this day been a very slender comfort unto us: But when he saith: *That all the nations of the earth should be blessed* in the seed of Abraham, we are of that number.

Mark then, wherein we have specially to rejoice, knowing that after our Lord Jesus Christ appeared unto us, this promise is to be applied unto us. It is true, that it is oftentimes said in the holy scripture, that men shall be blessed by men, as for example, when they shall set him before them for a pattern and example: and that men will say, desiring to be blessed, O that God would do unto me as he hath done unto this man here, or unto that man there: but the interpretation of Saint Paul showeth us, that that which was as well spoken to Abraham as to Isaack, was not only to be understood in that sense: but it is said elsewhere, that the faithful shall be blessed in God. So it is said now, that they shall be blessed in the seed of Abraham. But we have to search all our good and salvation in him alone, *who*

is the fountain thereof, as it is said in the thirty-sixth Psalm[†].
But because there is so great distance, and that we cannot
soar up so high, our Savior Christ hath approached near
unto us, and we have the living waters in him: there wants
[*lacks*] nothing, but that we come to drink, as he saith: *Come
unto me: and whosoever thirsteth, let him come unto me.*[††] For I
have the living waters, and whosoever shall drink thereof,
he shall not only have to quench his thirst, but also *living
waters shall flow out of his belly,*[†††] yea, and fountains of living
waters, that he may give thereof unto others.

When therefore we see that God will familiarly
communicate with us all his benefits, in the person of his
only begotten Son, so much the less excuse is there, if we
come not to receive part of this blessing the which is
provided unto us. Moreover, it is not only said that all
nations of the earth shall be blessed, but it is said, they are
blessed: not for that we can compass or attain to this
blessing of ourselves, or by our own power and diligence:
but it behooveth that everyone be blessed in Jesus Christ
through faith. For altogether like as he is presented unto us
by the gospel, so likewise we must accept him: and if we
remain unbelievers, this is because we shut the door as it
were, against all his graces. Then seeing it is so, that God
hath prepared all so longtime before, that belongeth to our

---

† *Psalm 36:9*

†† *Matthew 11:28*

††† *John 7:38*

salvation, and that *in the fullness of time* (as Saint Paul[†] calleth it) Jesus Christ hath appeared, and hath sufficiently witnessed, that he was that blessed seed, wherein we must seek all benefits: Let us likewise come with the like readiness of faith, and with such zeal, that we be not shut out through our own malice and unbelief, to the end God accomplish not that in us which is here pronounced, that we go not to him to have the ratification of his promise: let us, I say, take heed, that none hinder himself through his own fault and vice. Finally it is said:

> *That God will ratify his oath with Isaack,*
> *forasmuch as Abraham had obeyed the voice of*
> *God, and had kept his observations,*
> *commandments, statutes and laws.*

Here the oath is yet reiterated, for the greater and more sure confirmation of us all: For we cannot give any faith unto God, unless we have stoutly fought against distrust, to which we are so naturally inclined: and forasmuch as we are yet so fickle as is pitiful. For this cause God sweareth so much the more to assure us. But it is true (as hath been showed before) that this is worthy of great blame in us, that we should constrain God to swear. For we do not honor a mortal man, if we content not ourselves with the simple word that he shall speak, if we count him not for an honest man, contenting ourselves in that he shall have promised us: but when we say, I will that you swear unto

---

† *Galatians 4:4*

me herein. Behold this is a great sign of distrust, and will not be well borne amongst men. But if we shall notwithstanding do that dishonor to God, to require an oath of him besides his word, must it not needs be, that we be too too villainous? But if so be that God nevertheless do in this behalf take pity upon us, although it be an intolerable vice, that we would have him swear, farther than he hath pronounced: yet herein he doth apply himself unto us. What can we demand more?

And now what excuse shall there be, when we would yet say that his promises should be assured unto us by another? This word then of an oath, ought to pierce us to the very heart, as often as it offereth itself before us, yea and when there is any question of certifying us of the good will of GOD, and of that singular love which he beareth unto us. But let us come to that point where he saith:

That this was forasmuch as Abraham obeyed the voice of God.

It should seem here that GOD attributed the accomplishment of this promises to Abraham's virtue, and to his merits: but we have declared already that this could not be, neither ought so to be understood, as though the obedience which Abraham yielded to God had been the cause, why God should be bound unto him to perform that he had spoken: For we have showed already that this was altogether free in God. When Abraham was drawn out of the Idolatry wherein he was (as it is declared by Joshua[†]:)

---

† *Joshua 24:2*

What was it that moved him to do it?

Afterwards, when he kept Abraham to the end, this was not because he obeyed him: For contrariwise he had said unto him long before: *I will bless thee, I will be with thee, I will be thy large recompense: Thy seed shall be multiplied as the stars of heaven, and in it all nations of the Earth shall be blessed.* All this was spoken to Abraham before Isaack was born: and when Abraham would have sacrificed his son Isaack, it was said unto him: because thou hast not spared thy only Son: but wast ready to sacrifice him for the love of me, behold I will bless thee, and this was spoken to him long before: we see then, that that which is free in God, and that which he giveth us of his mere liberality, he attributeth to the service which we do unto him: not to minister unto us any matter of pride, but this is only so much the more to provoke and stir us up with cheerfulness and courage to serve him. Mark then the purpose of God: It is not to the end to rob himself of the praise which is due unto him, to the end men should usurp it: but it is because he knew that they have need of spurs, and must have aids, and helps to serve him, for otherwise we should be cold and dull. They therefore which seek here for merits, and would darken the mere praise of God's goodness to exalt men, as though they were the cause of their own salvation, it is certain they would overthrow all, yea and overturn the purpose of God as much as lieth in them. Likewise, let us learn that when it is said, that God will establish his covenant with Isaack, because Abraham had obeyed his voice, that it was not to note the cause why: but it was only to show that the service which Abraham yielded unto him was acceptable to him, to the end that Isaack should follow him and conform himself thereunto.

Hereby therefore we have to stir up ourselves, as often as we feel any slowness in ourselves, and when we shall not be so disposed as were requisite, to give ourselves fully to the obedience of God: and that we think, What? It is said that when we shall obey him, he will accept this *as a sacrifice of sweet smelling savor*: and yet notwithstanding all that we do is nothing, there is no strength in us: nevertheless if God will honor us so, without any worthiness of ours, must we therefore be sluggish, and not thoroughly employ all our powers to his service, especially according to that grace which he shall have given us, and according to our strength? and yet without all indenting or covenanting with him?

Mark then how the faithful ought to be provoked: and that this also is to teach us always to continue, to walk on in fear and carefulness, when our Lord showeth us that they whom he hath called, oftentimes make and show themselves unworthy of their calling. To the end therefore that we do not tempt him, and that we may be ready to receive that which he teacheth us, mark wherefore it is said that he rewardeth our services: not because we merit any reward. For (as I have already said) we must not here reason of that which we can do: For we can do nothing at all: and specially that which we have done by the grace of God deserveth no reward: For God can justly condemn it. But the question is, that God accepteth that which we do of his mere liberality, to the end to make us more courageous. And everyone ought to apply this to his profit, when we feel that we are slow to do well through our negligence and sloth. Lo then briefly what we have to learn here.

Now when it is said that Abraham obeyed the voice of God: this is to show us the true rule how to live well, to the end that everyone frame not unto himself devotions apart, as we are accustomed to do: For when men will serve God, what do they? They take liberty to live after their own device, and they contemn whatsoever God commandeth. What is that, that men may call the service of God in the papacy? That which men have devised of their own foolish brain. For when men shall have diligently gathered all their jugglings together, which they play there, if it be said that God be well served and honored, and yet they do nothing of all that God hath commanded, and that they do despise him: It falleth out thereupon, even as he himself complaineth thereof: to wit, that men for their traditions reject that which was ordained for them.

Seeing then, that so it is that we are so inclined to set out our own foolish imaginations, let us learn that when the holy Scripture speaketh unto us of living well and holily, when it speaketh of the perfection which GOD alloweth, that is to obey his voice: as also he showeth us by his Prophet[†], *Have I demanded you to offer me any sacrifice?*

Now it is very certain that GOD had required it: And why then doth Jeremiah speak thus? It is to show us that God resteth not there. Where then? *That we obey his voice*[††] saith he. Mark then the principal, and where we must begin, and which also is the end, whereto we must strive and contend: that is to say, that God hath authority to rule us, and that we be his subjects. But notwithstanding we shall find it strange, that is here spoken, that Abraham kept

---

† *Jeremiah 7:21*

†† *Jeremiah 7:23*

the Commandments, Statutes, Ordinances, and Laws of the
Lord. And yet he had not so much as one word of all the
Law in writing. For we know how long a time there was
betwixt the calling Abraham and the law: to wit, four
hundred and thirty years. How is it then that God now
saith, that Abraham kept his Commandments, statutes,
ordinances and laws? This is, as we have seen before in the
eighteenth Chapter: for albeit he had yet nothing written,
yet notwithstanding, Abraham was not ignorant of that
which God should afterwards teach his people. For he had
two manner of ways to govern his people: but yet this was
not for that in respect of himself he was changeable. God
therefore had not always one and the same way to teach the
faithful: but howsoever it was, yet the rule was one, whether
it were written, or inspired to them, whom he reserved to
himself.

So, howsoever Abraham had not yet the Law
written, yet he had sufficient instruction, to know how he
ought to serve GOD. This therefore is that we ought to
learn of this place.

But howsoever it be, GOD in the meanwhile,
showeth that if we be ready to obey him, and to be subject
unto him, that on his part he will never fail us to show us
the way wherein we ought to walk, and walking therein we
shall not be deceived. But if before there were ever any
scripture, Abraham had statutes, commandments, laws and
ordinances: at this day by a stronger reason, when God hath
declared himself so familiarly by Moyses, to whom he hath
further joined the Prophets, to the end they might there
have a more easy understanding of the law, and seeing he
hath spoken in the Gospel so clearly, shall we doubt that he

doth not the office of a good master, to show us all that is good, right and just? But what? The ingratitude of the world is such, that it will not be subject nor brought into order under him: and this is as much as if men would be more wise, than is permitted unto them, and would have a wisdom by themselves, as though it had never been said: *To God who is only wise, be honor and glory*†. When Saint Paul saith that God is only wise, this was not only for him, but this was to the end that we should search for all wisdom in him. For when we will not accept this for the only rule which he hath given us, this is as if we should say, God knew not all that was necessary for us, it must needs be that we invent of our own brain yet somewhat more: and say this will be better. And what blasphemy is this? O when we serve God after this sort, it is as a man would say to spit in God's face. So then let us note that when Moyses after he had spoken of the voice of God, addeth his commandments, his statutes, and his ordinances, it is to show us that God will not in any point fail all those, who shall be his disciples, and shall come to be ordered by him, to hearken to his voice. And indeed this is not only in this place, no nor in that we come to allege: but as it were through out all, where our Lord recommendeth his law unto us, and showeth us that it containeth all that is necessary to lead men rightly the way to salvation. And thus much concerning the words that are touched in this place. So then, when we will walk as it becometh us, let us mark that there is but one only Judge, to whom we have to render

---

† *1 Timothy 1:17*

account. But what is it that this Judge demandeth? Not that everyone should be driven by his own fantasy, or that our good devotions should be put in the place of his word: but that we should hearken unto the voice of our God, and then that we should be apt to learn, to bring us in order under him: and instead that men imagine, that they have done wonders to bind God unto them, by their virtues and merits, that we content ourselves to be approved before him and his Angels, although the world be not contented therewith.

But now let us fall down before the majesty of our good God, in acknowledging of our faults, praying him that it will please him to touch us to the quick, that we may more and more be brought both to repentance and to humility, continually to lament before him, and to pray him, that it will please him to cleanse us from all our vices, and to make us to walk in such integrity, that our life may be fully framed to his righteousness, and that by this means, his name may be glorified: when he shall have all the rule over us, and that we shall walk according as he hath taught us by his word, without adding anything thereto of our own: and that he will in such sort support us in our weaknesses, that we cease not always to continue in his holy vocation, albeit we go not on so swiftly, and run not with such zeal and fervency as we ought: and that in the meantime we may be armed (howsoever it fall out) with his power, to fight against all temptations, and never to decline out of the good way, albeit we have many occasions thereto. And that he may not only show us this favor, but also to all peoples and nations of the Earth etc.

❧The seventh Sermon of

Jacob and Esau, Genesis 26.

6.   *Iſaack therefore dwelt in Gerar:*

7.   *And when the men of that place aſked him concerning his wife, he ſaid it is my ſiſter, for he feared to ſay, it is my wife: For (ſaid he) I muſt take heeds leſt the men of this place kill me for Rebecca, becauſe ſhe was faire.*

8.   *Now it came to paſſe when he had remained there many dayes, that Abimilech the king of the Philiſtines looked out at a windowe, and as hee looked, Beholde Iſaack played with Rebecca his wife.*

9.   *Wherefore Abimelech called Iſaack and ſayd, ſurely beholde ſhe is thy wife: howe then ſaydeſt thou ſhee is my ſiſter? To whom Iſaack ſaide, becauſe I ſaid, I muſt take hede leſt I dye for her.*

10.   *Then ſaid Abimelech, what is this that thou haſt done vnto vs? It was not farre off that one of this people had not lien by her, ſo thou haddeſt brought ſinne vpon vs.*

E HAVE SEEN THE TEMPTATION which happened to Isaack, when he was so pressed with famine, that it enforced him to forsake the place of his habitation: For this should at the least have been, that God should have nourished and fed him in that country which he had assigned unto him for an inheritance: But if he would not accomplish his promise upon him, should he not have given him some little taste thereof? But now when famine driveth him away, this is, as if God had forsaken him there; and as though he had had no more care of him. Isaack therefore had here a great combat to endure, seeing he was as it were destitute of God's favor, which is common to all. For if he nourish the contemners of his majesty, and the wickedest of the world, making his sun to shine upon them, and causing the earth to bring forth fruit for their nourishment: what should he do for them whom he hath taken into his custody, and adopted for his children? But yet see a greater temptation, seeing Isaack was forbid to go into Egypt, and that God had showed him a certain place of rest, and would that he should dwell there, until he might return, and that the dearth were passed. When God then had led him thither as if he should say, behold a corner to rest in, which I do assign thee: and there farther, that he feareth lest he should be killed for his wife's sake: and after that he was taken and reproved: mark further these tokens of the wrath of god upon him, in such sort that he could not be but in an horrible perplexity. Now it is very true, that he was wonderful weak, as we shall see hereafter: but howsoever it was, the issue showeth, that God was not forgetful of him. And this is sufficient. For he will for a time keep himself secret, in such sort that the poor faithful ones shall be as it were lost: but this is enough, that after that he hath humbled them, after that he hath discovered their infirmities, that he showeth himself altogether to make them feel as it were by effect, that all this while that it seemed to them that they were quite abandoned from him, he yet in pity looked upon them. Mark then how it came to pass with Isaack.

Now in the first place it is said, that instead of confessing that Rebecca was his wife, he said she was his sister. We saw the like in Abraham: But this is marvelous, that Isaack had not learned this lesson, by the experience that was given to his father and mother: for they were both chastised for their overgreat fear. [And Isaack could not be ignorant of it.] There is no doubt but his father had such care (as we have seen) to teach his family, but that he had instructed his son herein: Take heed to thyself: For I have been tossed to and fro all my life long, the like may happen unto thee: For God hath yet set me four hundred years before we enter into the possession of that Country: it must needs be that thou go from one side to another. But I distrusted the protection of my God, and I have received my payment for it: yea I was chastised for it by a profane king, that had no fear of God: a poor blind wretch reproved me of my fault, and God made both me and thy mother ashamed thereof, when we were so corrected there. Therefore fortify thyself. There is no doubt, but that Isaack had received such instruction: but when he came to receive the blows, he had lost all, and was devoid both of reason and counsel, and there is no doubt, but he had some distrust in him. For faith will always minister unto us an invincible constancy, to attempt nothing, but that which God alloweth.

Mark wherein we may know whether we be well grounded in God, and stayed upon his promises: that is, when we shall be in any trouble, in any perplexity, and in any danger, if we walk on always in the path which GOD hath commanded us, and do not decline therefrom, then he will guide us in all our ways. If then we have this courage, only to repose ourselves upon God, and to hope that he will help us: then see an undoubted trial and proof of our faith. But if we decline either on the one side or on the other, it is very certain that our infidelity bewrayeth [*defile, disfigure*] itself, and that we show (not having any victory against temptations) that we are not sufficiently stayed, and that we have (as a man would say) our straggling thoughts. For we see that Isaack fell to a very unlawful thing, when to save his life, he cloaked the truth as we have seen.

This therefore is a token, that he had no perfect faith: but that he had some mistrust mingled with it. But in this he is not to be excused: and yet nevertheless he was a mirror of all holiness. So then we have all, good occasion to hang down our eyes, and to know that when we imagine that we have well profited in God's School, yet we shall be far off from our mark. And indeed it shall be a very easy matter unto us, when we are far off from all combats, to be the valiantest in the world: but when they shall approach to buckle with us, than behold us all afraid. Thus then let us know, that there is not one that hath not need to pray daily, that God will increase his faith, correcting the remnant of his unbelief. Mark this for one lesson. Now hereupon we have one good advertisement: and that is, that when any danger befalleth us, or that we fear to fall into any evil: that this is as it were a cloud to dazzle our eyes, in such sort that we know not what will become of us, we have no certain counsel, and the wisest are overtaken therein: Let us not presume to be subtle or sharp and to have such promptitude, to esteem that we shall always be strong and mighty, that we shall have light hearts, and shall find remedies in our brain when any trouble shall come upon us, let us keep ourselves from such arrogance: but let us rather acknowledge that God hath in himself the spirit of wisdom and of counsel, and let us run unto him. And when we shall be as it were oppressed and that we cannot at the first resolve ourselves, let us not be as those that always forge and coin new discoveries: but let us go unto God, and pray him to shine unto us in the midst of darkness: yea and specially let us wait that we be not altogether pressed down: but let us acknowledge the ignorance that is in us. And forasmuch, as we have not by a great deal so much staidness as were requisite, let us both morning and evening pray unto God that he will guide us, and show us what we have to do. Mark then that which we have to learn by the example of Isaack. But here a question might be asked, whether he committed so great a fault, seeing he lied not: For we have seen before, that Rebecca was his Cousin. He might then say she is my sister: For the word in that language importeth as much as of my blood or kindred. There is no question here neither of the first nor second degree. So Isaack lied not in saying that Rebecca was his sister. And yet notwithstanding all this, he faulted, yea indeed: For God is no Sophister, and doth not stay upon a word as we have declared before: but he regardeth the intent.

When therefore we shall have well painted our words, and that there shall be some goodly color and fair show to acquit us before men, all this is nothing: For GOD soundeth the heart. And though men can find nothing to say against our excuses, yet this proveth not that GOD is content therewith. And this which is here, is a very good and profitable admonition. For how do men commonly jest with God? It is true, that we will confess that it belongeth to him to search into our secret thoughts, and that nothing is hidden from him: but yet so it is, that we deal with him after the manner of men: and which is worse, we will altogether go beyond him, and we will blear his eyes: and we will jest more boldly with him than with men. For although we have many starting holes, which might discharge us of blame, yet so much there is that we have some remorse, knowing other men will not judge so thereof, this man is no beast, he may know my craft. When therefore we have thus disguised our words, yet we shall be always in doubt, whether men be satisfied or not. But when the matter is of God, we do nothing but writhe [*twist*] our mouth, or rather mow and snuff at God: For we are as brute beasts, yea and worse too in this point. But so much the more ought we to learn this doctrine: that is to say, that God careth not for all our goodly colors: for they are nothing else but breeches of leaves, and this excused not our father Adam, that he came not out to make his account. What must we then do? We must so acknowledge our faults in simplicity, that we be first our own judges: and when we shall once have found out, that there was some crooked and indirect dealing, we must acknowledge that it displeased God. For mark Isaack's intention, it was to hide his marriage. It is true that the words which he useth are not such as for which he should be called a liar: but yet for all that there was some leasing [*falsehood*] in him. And why so? Because he would not confess his marriage: but would that it should be unknown, and that men should not think that Rebecca was his wife. Mark then in sum the thing we have to learn: That is, that whatsoever words we have in our mouth, nothing can justify us, unless that our affection be pure and right, and that we go not in any bypaths, to stray here and there. And when Saint Paul condemneth lying: he addeth *that everyone speak in truth to his neighbors*[†]. When we shall have proceeded thus far herein, see how we shall be holden and reputed true before God. But if there be any slights or crafts, and that we endeavor to speak so, that it cannot be understood what we say, and that it be so wrested and turned, as if our tongue were double, in this we are already condemned for liars. This then in sum is that which we have to learn upon this point. Now when it is said, *That Isaack feared lest he should have been killed for his wife's sake:*

There is no doubt, but that he might thereby also have taken occasion, seeing (as Abraham his father alleged) that there was no fear of God in the country: not for that there was so outrageous impiety, that neither good nor evil was known there. For we see how the King of the Country spake: but forasmuch as the true religion ruled not there, and because there was nothing but Idolatry, it seemed rather to Isaack that all was confused. For indeed we shall never have a sure rule, to walk in equity and right, unless we have the majesty of God present, and that we be holden in with that, as it were a bridle. Now when we know not what God is, and that we have nothing but confuse speculations,

---

[†] *Ephesians 4:25*

albeit that we have some honesty, and though we have the discerning of good and evil, and that we are not given to hurt, nor to commit wrong and violence, yet so it is that there is not staidness in us. For (as I have said) we cannot build upon any other foundation, to have a firm and stable building, but upon the fear of God going before. Isaack therefore might have some occasion to fear and to prevent danger: but in the meanwhile he ought to have known, of what force God his safeguard was, even such as it had been before by experience declared unto him: For if he had been well advised, he would not but have understood that God had his arm stretched out, for to have succored [*helped*] him, and that in visible manner: For he had said unto him: *Fear not, for I am with thee: I am thy very large reward:*† It is true that this was not spoken expressly to him: but that which was spoken to his father, was as well spoken for him. For he was the heir of that promise.

Seeing then he waited not upon God, herein he is reproved of infidelity. It is true that Faith letteth [*hindereth*] not but that we may apprehend those dangers, wherewith we are beset round about: For Faith serveth not to make us insensible. And this should be no virtue, to us to call upon God: unless we were provoked, seeing that we cannot escape danger without his aid: but there is a great difference, whether our fear be such as maketh us to go out of the right path: or rather be as a spur unto us to provoke us to go unto God. If Isaack had thought thus with himself, it behooveth that I return me to my God: For I have no other refuge, but

---

† *Genesis 15:1*

to have had recourse to his help: he hath promised it me, yea and I have already experience thereof in my need. It must therefore needs be that his truth do yet declare and show itself towards me. If Isaack had been come thus far, it is certain, that his faith had been so much the better tried: and his fear had showed, as if he had been strengthened in God, being weak in himself: but when he is overcome with fear, and farther taketh such counsel as God condemneth: therein he frameth [*proceedeth, disposeth*] not himself to the duty of a faithful man. When Isaack went thus, herein he showeth he feareth, inasmuch as he was not sufficiently given to the word of God, and that his faith was not well resolved: but in that he wavereth and varieth, hereby he showeth that he did not steadfastly trust in God as he should.

But now we see Isaack's fault, we must so much the rather be warned (as we have already said) that in all the objects which we shall have to make us afraid, that we always do God this honor, that there is sufficient in him to remedy it, that if we call upon him, and after that we use the means that he hath left unto us, and which he alloweth, without going beyond our bounds either to the right hand or to the left. Isaack therefore did no wrong at all to them of that country, but to God, which is much more. And moreover, he is not wholly to be excused, seeing he conceived such a judgment of his own head: For although there were no fear of God in that place, nor true Religion in that country, yet so it is that true charity is not suspicious. None had yet done him any scathe or injury, ought he then at the first dash to have condemned them? For this cause God suffered this evil to come upon him: and yet showeth him singular mercy: For his wife might have been ravished, as also might have come to pass to his father.

Behold a king which is of the country of Gerar, and yet God bridleth him from doing any hurt to Isaack, yea knowing well that he had no such virtue in himself, as was in his father Abraham, like as we have showed already: and mark also wherefore God preventeth [*precedes, anticipates*] him, when he had determined to go into Egypt he withdraweth him: as it were by force, and forbiddeth him to go out of the land which he had promised him. We have showed already that God according to the measure he hath given us, doth also prove us. He worketh therefore in all men, as in sundry shops and by instruments which are not of the same power. And so, mark Isaack who was spared for once: but also we see how pitiful and kind the Lord was unto him, when he loosed not the bridle to King Abimelech to do that unto him which was done unto Abraham his father. For if we demand, why it fell out at one time, and not at another. It is certain that God governed this by his wonderful counsel: For after he once looseth the reins unto men, it is certain that they pass their bounds. And it is said expressly that he *holdeth the hearts of Kings in his hand*, and that he turneth them hither and thither as he thinketh good. So then it behooveth us to conclude, that the heart of the king of Gerar was holden that it desired not Rebecca: otherwise he had been subject to that concupiscence, that poor Isaack should have been thereby tormented even unto the uttermost and had been swallowed up with terrible distress: but (as we have said) God who is faithful spareth his own, or trieth them more to the quick, according to the power that he knoweth to be in them.

Moreover when we shall be so fearful and so weak, that with much ado, we shall be scarce able (as a man would say) to bear one fillip [*blow, buffeting*]: yet let us trust that God will give us strength, when it shall please him to draw us out to a more hard trial: but notwithstanding this ought not to make us careless. If I feel myself feeble, and that I say, O, God will spare me, for, he knoweth that I can bear nothing: it is certain, that I shall be punished for my unthankfulness. And why so? So far forth as we are weak we must run unto him, who hath all power to supply our wants [*lack*]. And therefore let us learn when it is said that God will help us, and that he will give us strength to endure all the combats, which shall be directed against us, this is to the end we should learn to exercise ourselves in prayer day by day. And therefore let us not be sluggish, because it is said that God strengtheneth his, all after as it shall please him to draw them into trial: but let this serve to make us always to look more nearly unto ourselves: and after we know our miseries, that we should seek for remedy, and pray him that it would please him never to suffer us to fall in any sort whatsoever, but that he will support us, or else when he will that we shall fight more courageously, that he will give us wherewithal that we may be armed from above, as he knoweth best always how to give victory to those that trust in him, and who fight not but under his banner. Mark then concerning the diversity we read betwixt Abraham and Isaack. Now it is said:

That the King saw Isaack sporting himself with Rebecca his wife, and that afterwards he called him, and said unto him: For a truth that is thy wife.

By this we may see that there was a great deal more integrity at that time, than there is at this day, and that whoredoms and dissolute lives were not so common. For some men at the first dash would have set up a sinister judgment against Isaack. It must needs be therefore, that men had more honesty, than is to be seen in our time. And seeing there is no doubt, that Isaack getting this reputation amongst all, that he was no villain nor whoremonger, that under color of saying she was his sister carried a whore after him. There is no doubt (I say) but when both he and his manner of life was known, but that everyone was persuaded, that he was an holy man, and fearing God, and that he was not given to any such vices and enormities.

And this is a point which we ought well to mark: For there is no man that would not be counted an honest man: and so soon as men do conceive any evil of us: we think that they do us great wrong: and yet in the meanwhile we regard not to use the means, that should not cause us to be ill thought of, and how to avoid that men should not charge us with blames and faults. The means were so to bear and order ourselves, that all might have their mouths stopped: that first of all the fear of God bear rule in us, and next that we have our conversation with men, in love and in uprightness, even as God hath commanded us the same. If we have this, it is certain that we shall stop up many wicked mouths. But it is very true, that the holiest and godliest, men cannot many times let the wicked to speak evil of them: For was not the Son of GOD himself subject unto slanders and opprobries [*reproaches, disgrace*]? Was it not upbraid him, that he blasphemed against GOD his father. But yet for all this, the Scripture saith not without cause, that then we stop the mouths of the wicked, when we shun all offences, and when we do not only labor to abstain *from evil*, but also from *all show of evil*.

Wherefore they that have so great care of their credit and reputation, that they cannot abide to be abased either in one respect or other, let them have regard to the means: that is to say, let them prevent that they be not justly blamed, and herein they follow the example of Isaack. For we see that being a stranger in a barbarous Country, where there was nothing but Idolatry: nevertheless so it is that he is yet esteemed for a man fearing God, and that they could not raise up an evil judgment of him. And why so? Because they were convinced of the contrary by his good life and honesty: Let us do the like, and it is certain, that we shall stop many slanders and many reproaches. But yet we have further to note, that then there was such honesty amongst men, that if a man sported familiarly with his wife, it was in marriage. But nowadays all is so overflowed, that a man must shut his eyes against the greatest villains of the world. Let a man go into Courts, O, it is certain that therein the wickednesses are so unruly, as a man can behold nothing more. And especially if a husband see his wife to be allured with another man's eye, and that some do abuse her thereby as though she were an harlot, he must set a good countenance upon it: for if he show any sign, that he is grieved therewith, and that he do not laugh at it, as others do, O, say they, he is a jealous fool and a dizzard [*jester, fool*]. Lo how it is in this case: For men are come even to the heap of iniquity, insomuch that they have lost all shamefacedness, because they are given to such beastly liberty, that there is no more honesty amongst them. And I would to God this mischief were in no place else but in these courts: But it is even a deluge or flood, which a man shall see in all estates, yea even to the least, such gestures of incontinency, and dissolute wantonness, that it is pity to behold. But let us mark how far off we be from these men which were as it were miserable blind ones having no knowledge of God, having no law written, no nor yet any revelation: and yet notwithstanding they had this honesty, that none ticked nor toyed overfamiliarly with another man's wife, nor had any gestures whereby any evil might be suspected, as we see here. *For truth* (saith he) *this is thy wife.* And whereupon doth he conclude it? It is because that vice was not accustomed there: and it was not come in use nor in possession amongst men, in such sort but that they might easily discern betwixt marriage and whoredom.

Now this teacheth us so to behave ourselves each towards others, that there be no unchaste looks, no vicious gestures: but that we be in such sort pure from all evil, that even before men we give no occasion to speak evil, nor yet to think evil of us. It is true that he speaketh here of some gesture which was overfamiliar to a strange man: For it needeth not that we should be so austere, that we cannot live together, without giving occasion of evil: and yet in the meantime living in familiarity, yea and sporting ourselves with all honesty, showing that we have chaste hearts, chaste eyes, and all our senses chaste.

But when Isaack played thus with his wife, he made some sign of a husband to his wife: so that it might be judged either this man is a whoremonger, or else he must needs be her husband. Now to think him a whoremonger, they could not, because he had behaved himself honestly in the fear of God, and with the good will of everyone in the country of Gerar: he must therefore be esteemed for her husband. But hereupon Isaack confesseth his fault: but he confesseth it alleging that he feared, lest he should have been killed. Here things are rehearsed more briefly, than we have seen before. For Abraham was rebuked more sharply: and likewise he maketh a more long excuse thereof. *I did know* (saith he) *that there was no fear of God in this Country.* Only Isaack saith, *I feared lest they would kill me.*

Now he showeth here that although Rebecca were his sister, nevertheless seeing that his purpose was to cloak the truth: it was to be condemned. So likewise, when we will be very subtle for a time, let us not be so obstinate as altogether to maintain all that we have said and done (although there be some fault in us:) but let us frankly acknowledge it. For Isaack might have said, yea, she is my sister. But notwithstanding that which he had said, he addeth that he was to be blamed, as also Abimelech did: For he saw just cause to condemn Isaack, and therefore he saith unto him,

Wherefore hast thou done this thing?

Now we have to note on the one side, that which was alleged before: that is to say, that God had reproved and chastised the kings because of his servants, albeit they were but a few in number, albeit they were as poor wandering people in the land of Canaan. And seeing GOD maintained their quarrel, and set himself against all the violence and evil that could be done unto them: hereby he showeth the singular favor that he did bear unto them. And also the Prophet addeth, that for this cause he saith: *Touch not mine anointed, and do my Prophets no harm.*

It is true that there was in Abraham and Isaack excellent virtue and holiness: but howsoever it be, yet so it is that we at this day are also anointed to be under the keeping of God, and we succeed to all the promises which were given unto them. So then, though we shall be never so small a number, and as a poor despised people, as Sheep in the throat of Wolves, yet let us not doubt, but that GOD hath wherewith to defend us, and that he will display his power, as much as shall be necessary, yea and that against the mightiest Kings of the world. For sometimes God hath indeed suffered that those of the meaner and common sort of people have vexed and molested his servants, as we shall see hereafter, and that very shortly. Which whatsoever it be, when he hath declared that he foreseeth the war, and that he setteth himself in order against the Kings: Hereby he hath showed that the life of his servants is dear and precious unto him. Let us therefore hope the like, and we shall not be deceived. And when we shall see the mightiest of the world to be our enemies, and shall daily hear rumors of many tumults and troubles: let us not doubt, but that our Lord will remedy all, and will always be our buckler to put back all our blows, when it shall be most like that they must fall upon our heads. Lo what we have to put in practice by the example of Isaack. And although here God afflicted not Abimelech as before, and that he reproved him not as he had done the king of Egypt: nevertheless he keepeth him bridled, and holdeth him as it were in fear: so that although

Rebecca were fair, yet it fell so out: that the king of the country desired her not, no albeit he imagined that it had been lawful for him to have taken her to wife. Lo then on the one side what we have to mark: on the other this, that nevertheless God humbled Isaack and suffered not his infidelity to remain altogether unpunished: yet the punishment is very gentle. But howsoever it was, he was reformed. Now if nothing had happened unto Isaack, and that it had not been perceived that Rebecca had been his wife, he had not returned from it, neither had he ever remembered his fault which he had committed: and specially he had pleased himself herein, because the event was good and as he would have wished, and therefore he would have thought that God would have allowed it. For men when their faults are not showed them, flatter and harden themselves in them. But God worketh our good and salvation when he maketh us to feel our sins, and correcteth us in such sort, that we are even compelled to think upon them. Mark then how it fell out herein to Isaack. It is very true that God did bear with him very much, when he suffered nothing to be attempted against his wife, that the very king of the country called so gently for him, and complained to him as to his equal and companion. Lo a wonderful support: and hereby we see that God hath pity upon his, not trying them further than they are able to bear. But whatsoever it is, yet so it is that Isaack cometh to acknowledge his sin. And who is judge thereof? Even a poor painim [*pagan, heathen*], an Idolater. God might rather have sent an Angel from heaven, or else have given him some revelation to have said unto him, what dost thou? But he leaveth him there: For he was not worthy to be taught so honorably, but the blind ones must discover his evil and condemn him.

Lo then, the shame that was done unto him, to the end that he might be the more humbled thereby, and to the end that he might learn forever after, better to trust in God, and no more to fall into that fault. This is that we have to mark. And withal let us take good heed unto ourselves, and let us not care that men reprove us: but let us take in good part all corrections that God sendeth us by his word. For what honor doth he unto us, when he provoketh us to come unto him, and when with doctrine he joineth exhortations? And after, when he seeth that we are too slow, and besides that we are as it were incorrigible, he useth more sharp reprehensions. But whatsoever it be, all this is done in his name, that when we read in the holy Scripture, and that we come to the Sermon, and that there he summoneth us, he is always our Judge.

And lo, also why our Lord Jesus Christ speaking of the preaching of the Gospel saith[†]: *When the holy Ghost shall come, he shall judge the world.* The spirit of God therefore exerciseth his jurisdiction upon us: and to what end? It is to the end that when we have been condemned, so that we do pass willing condemnation, and that we be apt to learn, and that we ask pardon, he is ready to give us. So then, seeing that GOD hath done us this honor to judge us as it were in his house, and privately by ourselves: when he showeth us our faults, are not we overmuch hardened, if we do not bow down our neck, and become apt to learn, and be

---

† *John 14:26*

ready to be reformed by him? For if we will rebel so against him, God will suffer that we come to another school, and that even the wicked and unbelievers condemn us. We shall find very many even in this case, that fret themselves and gnash their teeth, if a man scratch their scabs and rub them on the gall, when they come to the Sermon. For see their replies: was the Scripture made to spur poor people in such sort? and is this the manner to teach, to cry out after such a fashion? It seemeth that he would lighten against us. But in the end God teacheth them after another sort: that is, that his trumpet must sound, and that their shame must be published in every place, and in the end they must go to the school of the Gibbet. And moreover when we make not our profit of the corrections which are daily set before us, it must needs be that we be condemned an hundred miles off, and that by good right. But if herein we suffered alone, there were no danger: the worst is that the name of God is blasphemed through our wickedness.

So then, let us learn by this example to become so tractable and apt to be taught and wrought upon, that when GOD shall reprove us, we willingly suffer ourselves to be condemned of him, and that we be ashamed of ourselves: to the end that our shame and infamy be not discovered and laid open to the whole world. Lo then what we have farther to learn of this place. But it is said that Abimelech complaining to Isaack added,

> *It was not far off, that some of the people had not lain by thy wife: and thou caused great evil to come upon us.*

Concerning the first point, here Isaack is reproved, of his inconsideration and folly. For that as much as was in him, he laid his wife open to be defiled. And why so? We have seen before that the husband ought to be as a veil or coverture to his wife. When a woman shall be married, and that her husband shall live with her doing his duty, this is to the end, she may be there as it were in safeguard, and that none come to deceive nor defile her. Now therefore Isaack, for the discharging of his duty, ought to have been as a veil or coverture to his wife: that is to say, under the name of a husband and of marriage: he ought to have let that none should have attempted to withdraw her, whether it were to have her to wife, or after any other manner: For marriage is as a safeguard, (as we have said) and God would have it honored in all ages. And although adulterers would abandon it, as Swine and Asses: yet notwithstanding they have always had remorse in it: and evermore even amongst the Painims [*pagans, heathen*], adulterers went not unpunished. It is known that if ever anything in this world was privileged, it was marriage: yea, and thefts and other crimes ought a great deal rather to be borne with, than such enormities: to wit, when the covenant and company which God hath dedicated in his name, to the end it should be holy, as it were separated from profanation, is violated.

When therefore this was violated, the Painims [*pagans, heathen*] knew that it was so great an abomination, that in no wise it ought to be borne with. Now therefore by the way, Abimelech findeth fault with Isaack concerning this, that he had thus prostituted his wife, as much as lay in him. And we are taught by this doctrine to meet with dangers aforehand, and not to tempt God by our rashness and folly. Let us take good heed therefore how we cloak evil, and (as a man would say) shut the door against God: so that through our rashness and unadvisedness God be offended. Lo then the wisdom which we ought to have: and therefore because we have it not, we must ask it of God. But now for the second matter Abimelech saith:

Thou hadest made great evil to come upon us.

And how? When any of the people had committed adultery, and that he had so offended, what grief soever it had been, he should only have deserved to be punished: and ought then a whole country to have answered it? Now we see here that a miserable heathen, and unbeliever, and a poor blind person, knew that the land should be defiled by an adulterer: and that if this remained unpunished, notwithstanding before God, lo an whole people culpable therein, in respect of the temporal punishment. It is true that God knoweth how to turn the chastisements that he sendeth to them that are innocent from that fault to their profit: For if they suffer, which consented not unto the evil, this shall not be altogether as if they had been faulty: But God turneth this to their salvation. In the meanwhile so it is that he never chastiseth them without cause: if we see it not now with our eye, yet when all those registers shall be opened, then we shall find, that God hath not gone (as they say) indirectly and awry. And when he sendeth general punishments upon a whole people, for one particular fault as it seemeth, nevertheless he knoweth well that all be not innocent therein, as it is expressly said here, and as also Abimelech understood. For when adulteries are committed, and be not punished, lo an infection which creepeth over the whole land: but shall we yet say that a man is innocent therein, when we close our eyes, and when we suffer all this to overflow? Although a man be no judge but a private person, yet he ought to oppose himself as much as lieth in him.

Now on the other side there is not anyone, but he spreadeth the sail instead that he should let the evil: if we had the courage and zeal of God, we would procure that he might be served and honored, as he is worthy. But this we do not: there is a certain faintness and sluggishness in all. To be short, vices never reigned, and had sway in any Country, but both great and small were partakers therein, by reason of their too much patience or dissimulation or coldness. Mark then why God punisheth sins not without cause.

But moreover concerning adultery, we see what a miserable Heathen hath pronounced. Let us therefore be ashamed when such a great evil shall reign in the midst of us: and let us know, that there shall need no other judge to condemn us, us (I say) that have been baptized in the name of our Lord Jesus Christ, when we shall maintain such filthinesses and infections, seeing a poor miserable blind Heathen, knew well what heinous enormity there was in such a vice. Lo then what we have to learn, that we may make our profit of this place. And farther, let us learn to honor Marriage, seeing God hath dedicated it, and that it is a covenant which he hath consecrated in his name: that also it be maintained in his honor and dignity, and that both Husbands and Wives dwell in such honesty one with the other, that each one may govern their houses in peace and quietness, and that there be no looseness amongst us: but that we know that we have better profited in the School of GOD, than our Father Isaack had done in this point, forasmuch as he declined therein.

But now let us prostrate ourselves before the high majesty of our good God, in acknowledging our offences, praying him that it will please him, to make us feel the infirmities and vices that are in us, to the end that we may be displeased therewith, in such sort, that we may fight against them, and not to give ourselves any liberty therein: and when we have offended, that we may be touched with such repentance, that we may return to him, and mourn for them, until he have reformed us by his holy spirit, and have drawn us into a good way, after that we shall have strayed from it. And that withal he would in the meanwhile so support us in our weakness, that we never leave to be his Children, albeit we honor him not as our father, as were meet. And that he will not only show us this favor, but also to all peoples and nations of the earth etc.

❧The eighth Sermon of Jacob

and Esau, Genesis 26.

11.   *And Abimelech commaunded all his people ſaying, He that ſhall touch this man or his wife, he ſhall vndoutedly dye the death.*

12.   *Now Iſaack, ſowing in that lande, he got euery yeere an hundred meaſures: ſo did Iehoua bleſſe him.*

13.   *So did that man increaſe, and growe on with a continual increaſe, euen vntill he was very rich.*

14.   *For hee had great poſſeſſion of flockes, and poſſesſion of droues, and ſo great a familie, that the Philiſtians inuied him:*

15.   *And they dammed vp all the Welles, which his fathers ſeruantes had digged in the time of his father Abraham filling them vp with earth.*

16.   *So as Abimilech ſaid vnto Iſaack, Departe from vs, for thou art made more mightier then we.*

17.   *Therefore Iſaack departed from thence, and pitching his tentes in the valley of Gerar, he ſetled there,*

18.   *(For Iſaack had digged againe the wels of water, which they had digged in the time of Abraham his father, and which the Philiſtines had dammed vp after the death of Abraham: & he had giuen them names, according to the names which his father had giuen them.)*

19. *And the ſeruants of Iſaack digging in the ſame valey,*
    they found there a well of liuing waters.

20. *Now the Shepheards of Gerar, contended with Iſaacks*
    ſhepheardes ſaying: Theſe waters are ours: Wherefore
    they called the name of that wel Heſek, becauſe they
    had mooued ſtrife with them of their owne accorde.

21. *Afterwards when they had digged another Wel, they*
    contended alſo for that: Wherfore he called the name
    of that Sitnah.

E HAVE SEEN HOW GOD HAD PITY
upon Isaack, although he was worthy to have
been forsaken in the time of his necessity: For
this was a singular favor, that Rebecca's
chastity was kept: because Isaack had given it over, and as
much as was in him forsaken it, for the safeguard of his own
life. Lo a distrust which deserved rather severe
chastisement: but yet would God support him, and be the
protector of his wife, who otherwise was forsaken. Now it
is said here, that God stretched out his mercy farther: that
is to say, that he would have Isaack to be in safety for the
time to come, and that none should molest him either in his
own person, or concerning his wife. And in very deed it
must needs be that this provision was freely given him: For
it might have been laid in his dish that he had not greatly
passed that his wife had been put to shame and reproach.
And this was to cause him every day to have many quarrels.
But herein God trieth him: and yet he useth the King of the
country, to the end he might be in rest, to the end that

none should come to assail him. It is therefore ordained that none shall touch him upon pain of death. Now this was done by special privilege according to that we have alleged out of the Psalm. That God for the favor he did bear to Abraham and Isaack, *even chastised Kings and rebuked peoples*: but yet so much as we may gather that Abimelech, being seized with fear, made a decree the which was very right. And why was not this law perpetual? Because that men who have not the lively root of the fear of God, do nothing but by force and violence, there is no hold nor constancy in them, as we shall find oftentimes. But inasmuch then as Abimelech perceived, that if Isaack were offended or that any did him any wrong, that this should not remain unpunished, and that God would take vengeance of it: Lo why he was thus bridled.

Now this is rehearsed unto us above all, to the end we might know, how God hath kept his own, though they have dwelt amongst wicked and cruel people, as it were amongst savage beasts: nevertheless he hath maintained them by his power: and this is to the end that we likewise should trust in him. For the goodness of God, which he used towards our old fathers, is not only rehearsed unto us, to the end that we should know that he was then pitiful towards them which trusted in him: but that we should not doubt, that he will suffer us to be molested at this day, so that we have our refuge unto him: and when we know that he will be on our side, that we be also certain that he will maintain our part, and that his protection will be enough for us, against whatsoever, men shall be able to attempt or devise against us.

When therefore we shall have such an affiance, the

example of Isaack which is here rehearsed unto us, ought to serve us for an instruction, as if God should show us his hand stretched out, to help and succor [*aid*] us in our need. And specially when our enemies shall be strong and mighty, and that nothing shall be able to let them here below, from oppressing us, then let us know that God will not cease to put to his helping hand. For we know what he hath said by his Prophet Esay[†] touching his Church, that it is more precious unto him, than all the Realms and Empires of this world.

Now admit we be never so much despised of worldlings, that we seem not worthy to them (as a man would say) to be cast to the Dogs: Yet howsoever it be, forasmuch as God hath once declared that we are his flock, and that he hath taken us into his charge, let us assure ourselves, that he will not fail us, when we shall be assaulted of them who torment us, and to whom it seemeth, that God must not touch them. But moreover Moyses addeth:

That Isaack sowing, he gathered an hundred measures.

That is to say, an hundred times as much as he sowed. Here a question might be asked, seeing Isaack had not one foot of land, how he could sow. But some imagine that he had purchased some there: but this were against all reason. For it must be that the fathers content themselves, with the promise which was given them, and that they dwell in the land of promise as strangers. And indeed, it is said

---

† *Isaiah 62:3*

soon after, that Isaack pitched his tents, to declare that he had no certain house nor building. We see therefore that he was a vagabond in earth, as was his father Abraham: but he might well hire some land to sow therein: For he had a great family: as we saw Abraham himself had, who gathered out of his house more than four hundred chosen men, to enter into battle. Isaack had not much diminished it as we see: likewise it must be that he could not be much increased, especially dwelling in a strange country: he had hired some farm or taken some land to sow therein: according as we know that the ancient fathers, although God had enriched them, yet they ceased not to give themselves to labor both they and their household. For although they had both riches and commodities, yet they abused not those benefits that God had so bountifully bestowed upon them, in pomps nor in Idleness to become Kings: but to maintain always themselves in the mean estate. Mark then briefly that we have to learn, when Isaack having hired some possession sowed therein. And this is rehearsed of Moyses because he addeth, that GOD blessed him therein, and made him so to prosper, that he gathered in an hundredfold. But we shall find it strange in this country, which was so hungry and as it were barren in comparison of Judea and Syria, and of those Countries thereabouts: especially when he spake of an hundredfold, forasmuch as the thing may seem incredible unto us: because we esteem that which is spoken unto us according to that we have seen.

But it is not without cause that our Lord Jesus Christ, declareth this unto us by a similitude, taken from the seed which is sown: although he spake to another purpose: but notwithstanding he saith that when men shall

sow, one part falleth into the path, and the fowls of the air
devour it: another shall fall among stones, and this shall
take no root: for it hath no nourishment: The other part
shall be choked among bushes and thorns: *But that which*
falleth into good ground (saith he[†]) *shall bring fruit, one thirty,*
the other sixty, and the last an hundredfold.

When we come thus far (as I have said) we cannot
be persuaded therein, unless the son of God had spoken it.
But the ancient fathers, who have written of the land of
Chaldea, and especially have been in the same place, and
know it thoroughly, they say that the ordinary increase was
eighty and an hundred. But here because he spake of the
country of the Philistines which was fertile, but not as
Chaldea, therefore Moyses rehearseth that, for a singular
gift which God gave unto Isaack, that he gathereth an
hundredfold. Lo here a sign of the blessing of God upon
Isaack, yea concerning that, which belonged unto this
transitory life. For although the ancient fathers always
respected the heavenly inheritance, and bent all their
affections thitherward: yet notwithstanding being mortal
men, they needed that God should give them some taste of
his goodness in this world. For that which Saint Paul
saith[††], hath always place here: *That the fear of God hath the*
promises not only of everlasting life, but also of this present life.
While we are in this life God will not give us the fullness of
those blessings he promiseth us: For in very deed, we would
have our paradise here, and would cast our eyes no further

---

† *Matthew 13:23*

†† *1 Timothy 4:8*

but all our senses would be clean glutted, if GOD should give us in all respects such abundance as we require, and therefore he giveth us only a little taste of his goodness, to the end to draw us on further. But what though? yet can we but in part acknowledge that God is our father not only by the testimony that we have thereof from his mouth, but also by those blessings which he liberally bestoweth upon us. And here we behold both these things, in this history which Moyses setteth down: that is to say, that God blesseth his own, in such sort, that they have occasion to rejoice in him: and yet in that he divideth their morsels in such a portion, that they be always in mourning whilst they are in this world, and thereby are occasioned to cast their eyes farther. For mark our father Isaack, he prospereth, he increaseth, and becometh mighty, so saith Moyses: and he saith not only that God blessed him at once: but that he multiplied him in such sort that he always grew and waxed richer and richer. But on the other side he addeth:

That the Philistines envied him.

We see that Isaack had such cause to rejoice in God for the prosperity which was given unto him, that yet notwithstanding God awakened him, and mixed his sweet meat with some sour sauce. This was a great cause of joy unto him, when GOD did so sensibly multiply him. It was as it were a looking glass to all the Philistines, wherein to behold what it was to serve god: yet notwithstanding this turneth to his trouble and causeth him to be molested. We see then how God tempereth his benefits which he bestoweth liberally upon his children (I say, the temporal

benefits which concern this life) that they can never settle
themselves and rest therein. But yet here further a question
might be asked, why God caused Isaack so to prosper, that
the inhabitants of the country should rise up against him.
Had it not been much better for him that he had continued
in a mean estate, and had lived quiet under his tent than to
be so enriched that everyone should war against him, and
that they could not abide him, fearing lest he would become
Lord over them, and tread them under his feet? If GOD
had kept such a means, it seemeth that it had been more
profitable to Isaack. Wherefore then is it that he doth
multiply him, and that this is the cause that he is pursued,
yea, and that he hath no water for himself neither for his
family or for his cattle? But God is so wise in disposing all
things, that if he make his servants to prosper, he showeth
them that they ought to keep themselves fast unto him, and
that they have occasion to bless him. And yet
notwithstanding: when he layeth them open to troubles and
vexations, he turneth this also to their good. So then we
must mark this for a rule, That all the graces which we
receive from the hand of God in this world, they are joined
with some miseries, and that our honey is never pure, but
always there is some vinegar mixed with it: God could well
take another course, if it had pleased him: but we must be
subject unto him, and be content with that, that he doth,
although that our senses and the lusts of our flesh resist
against it. And true it is that a man which were well
advised, would never seek to be rich or wealthy: and so that
he might have competent for meat and drink and clothing:
he would seek for no other state or condition. Yet
notwithstanding it pleaseth God to exercise one sort with

poverty, and to be bountiful towards others: and both poor and rich may be faithful, and both two the children of God. I speak not of all in general: but we see that there are some fearing God, who are not all of like estate, and condition. Some of them have wealth enough for their maintenance, yea and that to make them live with some credit and countenance amongst men: others some have scarcely a morsel of bread to eat.

Now if it were in us to order this matter, we would that God should use rather an equal and like measure: yea, but he knoweth wherefore, he choseth rather such a diversity. And therefore (as I have said) it is for us to content ourselves with his pleasure. And so when it pleaseth him to make his servants to prosper in such sort, that we may know for a surety that his blessing resteth in their persons, it is a testimony of his goodness: and hereof they ought to make their profit. But when there is any sourness mingled with it, they ought to think, GOD would not that I should sleep here, nor rest myself so upon these earthly benefits, that they should make me to forget everlasting life. It behooveth therefore that the faithful have this wisdom and consideration in them, that always they know how to make their profit, of those benefits that God bestoweth upon them: and in the meantime that they forget not the favor that he hath showed unto them? although that they have many cares, griefs, troubles and wrongs, which shall be done unto them by men. And namely here both the rich and poor, are taught their duty. When a man shall be afflicted with poverty and need, yet in the meantime god will not suffer him to be so destitute and forsaken, but that always he shall have some little portion, to the end he may feel that God hath care of him. And therefore when the faithful have not all that they desire: but God leaveth them there as if he forsook them: they must not therefore murmur against him nor think that he hath cast them off: but how little so ever it be, that he hath given them (yea be it never so little) they must apply it to taste the goodness of God, so that they may call upon him as their father, and put their trust in him, and patiently bear their condition, which otherwise would be hard and miserable unto them. And as for the rich, when they shall have more wealth than they have need of, if this breed them any care, and bring some griefs as the common Proverb is: *He that hath land, hath war at hand.* If a man have but an Acre of ground, he shall either be drawn into suit of law, or else he shall have some other trouble about it. As for the rich (I say) when they see these things, that they cannot possess their goods with peace and quietness, but that they shall always have some trouble and disquietness withal: let them know that for all this, they must not be distasted, and that the blessing of god always giveth them courage to trust in him: and that they be not led to unthankfulness and forgetfulness: but that always they bless his name. And this is it that we have to note out of this place where it is said, that God make Isaack to prosper, and that this was the cause that moved the inhabitants of the country to envy him, who therefore did drive him out from amongst them. Now it is said expressly:

> *That the king of Gerar sent unto him saying, we cannot suffer thee to tarry amongst us, for thou art mightier than we.*

Here we see more clearly that which erst I touched: to wit, that they that are not well rooted in the fear of God may do virtuous acts: but this is as it were by blasts and they do not continue, there is no perseverance unless it be in them whom God governeth, and whom he hath so reformed by his holy spirit, and that his fear and obedience that they follow on their course till they come to the goal: yet notwithstanding even the faithful themselves are not so constant in well doing, but many times they tread awry and go out of the way: but God correcteth them, and when they are strayed here and there, he bringeth them back into the good way.   But as for them whom he hath not yet regenerated and born anew, and who keep their natural inclination, although it seem oftentimes that they will do marvels, yet lo in the turning of a hand they are changed. We see this in the king of Gerar, ere while he was as an Angel: for when he spake of abusing another man's wife, he said that it was to infect the whole country, and to cause the vengeance of God to come upon great and small. Behold, a divine sentence, it seemeth that God spake by his mouth, and indeed there is no doubt but that this confession was wrung from him both against himself, and against all those, who esteemed this (as a man should say) for a venial sin.

Behold then Abimelech who showeth that God had even enforced him and inflamed him with such a zeal, that he had this fault in great detestation, for he knew that it was displeasing to God.   And thereupon he caused his Proclamation to be made, that no man should touch Isaack nor his wife, upon pain of death.   This is yet another commendable point: It seemeth therefore that Abimelech was wholly become fearing GOD: but straightway after he saith unto Isaack, Away, *get thee hence*. He driveth out Isaack: he knoweth that Isaack is under the protection of God: and when he attempteth anything against him, is it not as it were to despite God, and to break the safeguard which he hath set upon his servant?

Let us learn therefore, that seeing it is so, to be so conversant amongst those which have no fear of God, as that, if they be gentle and courteous for a time unto us, and afterwards be changed, that we bear it with patience, and that we be ready to suffer injury of them, after they have done us good. Moreover let us know that unless God have imprinted his fear in us, and given us a lively root of it, we should never have any constancy or staidness in us. Let us pray unto him that it would please him to show unto us by effect, that he hath truly renewed us by his holy spirit: and that we have not a zeal like unto a fire of stubble which quickly goeth out: but that we may desire always to march on forwards in his obedience and to continue therein: and although that we sometimes slide from it, as we are very weak, notwithstanding that we be not clean misled and carried away from him, but that we may follow on our course even unto the end. And so we have to beseech him from day to day, that he will increase in us the graces of his holy spirit: for were our desire never so good, it is certain that we should be quickly cold: and as our nature is unconstant, we should from this day ere tomorrow be changed, were it not that God continued to govern us. This is it in sum that we have to mark. Now the reason that is here brought by Abimelech, is taken from common experience: For we know that rich men despise the poor, and he that hath much, thinketh that others are not equal unto him: thereupon is he by and by puffed up with pride and boldness, and cruelty followeth: as it is said, Men are like unto horses, when they are well fed, they are wanton and untamed, they kick, they bite: to be short, they will not be ridden. And thus fareth it most commonly with men. So then, when a man cometh to be of great substance and wealth, it is certain that by nature he will be bent to advance himself, and pride will bear sway in him. And so is it expressly said of Sodom, That when they had great abundance of wealth, they became proud, and afterwards followed cruelty, so that they had no pity upon their poor neighbors to help them. And this is as it were almost an ordinary matter.

So then, when Abimelech saith unto Isaack: *Thou art stronger than we: depart therefore and get thee hence.* This is because men do abuse the graces of God, and cannot content themselves with sobriety nor modesty, when God doth advance us.

Now we know hereby, how perverse we be: for in that God showeth himself liberal towards us, it is certain that he draweth near unto us, and draweth us near unto him: and this should give us an occasion to humble ourselves so much the more. For there is nothing that ought more to bring us into order, and to do our duty, than when God showeth himself on this sort unto us, and that we walk as it were in his sight. But if we abuse his graces, and (as I have already said) if riches engender [*beget*] in us both pride and presumption, and thereupon contempt of those which are our inferiors, and afterwards cruelty, so as we torment one and molest another: we devour this man here and that man there, is not this to turn light into darkness? So then we have to know the perversity which is in us, and whereunto we are not only inclined, but also given, unless that God do withdraw us from it. Now when God dealeth well with his children, it is certain that he doth correct this vice in them, that they have no lust to advance themselves, to put out their horns, and to show forth their jollities, and to tread under their feet those which are not equal unto them: and we have already declared, that there is always mingled a certain cooling, to the end they should not glory and flatter themselves too much in their felicity. Howsoever it be, it must be that he work herein by his holy spirit, for there will never be any modesty in us, whensoever any occasion is offered unto us to advance ourselves: the peel of an Onion (as the common Proverb saith) is enough to make us to forget from whence we are, and to make us drunken with arrogance, and to despise all other.

But Isaack was not so given to pride and presumption: and Abimelech doth him wrong. But (as I have said) he measured it according to the common Ell, because that the fashion of men is always to oppress the least, when they can do it, and to take, leave according to their might to hurt.

And therefore it is that Abimelech saith: *Thou are more strong than we.* And hereupon we have to note that God admonisheth us by this common example, to carry ourselves peaceably and modestly: when we have any occasion offered us to make any account of ourselves: that we lay it aside, and be so much the more careful to keep ourselves in our degree, yea in the basest, and in the meanwhile, if it please him to bring us down and to hold us in a low and despised condition, let us know that he doth if for our good, and that it is as a preservative medicine: and let us know, that if we were advanced to any high place or honor, that it would be to make us stark blind.

And this is it that we have to bear away in this place, Now it is said afterwards:

That Isaack came in to valley of Gerar.

He went not quite out of the country: but he went apart, to the end not to be anymore in their sight, and to take away all occasion of malice, from all the inhabitants of Gerar: for we know what manner of people the Philistines were. Here we see in the first place the patience of Isaack: who not only replied not: but to purchase peace and rest, trussed [*secured, bound*] up his baggage and went his way, to pitch his tent elsewhere, and herein he hath showed his humility. It is true that he went not quite out of the country: but yet notwithstanding he might have made some resistance, for to have tarried in that place, where he had as it were taken a Farm. We have seen that his father Abraham had as it were prepared a little army in his house: he might have therefore done the like, and so might have withstood the wrong which was done unto him. But he is so far off from this, that he is as it were a Lamb: and Moyses saith not, that he moved any great contention, or that he skirmished, though he were chased from them and that wrongfully, after they had received him, and after they had showed him some sign of courtesy: but he leaveth all. So then we are taught when we shall be oppressed, to bear our wrongs patiently, and not to take the sword in hand, to work our revenge, when it shall seem that we have a just cause before men. For we know what is commanded us: to wit, to give place unto wrath: that is, to suffer that God revenge for us, and so let us follow our father Isaack, in that that he suffered himself, to be wickedly driven out of the country, where he had so behaved himself, that he ought rather to have been beloved of all. For what occasion had they given them that they should suspect any evil in him? And yet notwithstanding they cast him out, and say that he is too strong, as though he had abused his greatness. So this is one lesson touching this retreat of Isaack, where it is said that he came into the valley of Gerar.

Now Moyses addeth another temptation, which was very hard unto him: and that was that he had digged the wells that his father Abraham had digged in his lifetime, and that he kept the same names that was given unto them. Here we see in the first place the malice of the Philistines, although that Abraham had lived very courteously amongst them: yea and that Abimelech this man's predecessor, had made a league with him, and came to seek him, and Abraham in way of homage, had given him one of the Wells that he had digged, which he had bought again, and had presented the homage unto him as we have seen: yet notwithstanding all this, that they came to dam up these wells. They knew that Abraham was the servant of God and a Prophet: God had maintained his quarrel, and they had a visible testimony thereof: for even the house of Abimelech had been beaten, and GOD had scourged it: and therefore they might have been moved thereby to have suffered him: and albeit they had not for a time been well advised, seeing that Abraham had protested that he would not do wrong nor hurt any, as he had been sworn to Abimelech: they should have contented themselves herewith: they had known the man to be very loyal, and keeping his promise where he had made it: notwithstanding to the end he should never return again, they dammed up the Wells which he had digged: for there is no doubt, but this was done to the end to shut him out from coming anymore amongst them: For as he was a stranger, he might have sought out a place fit for him to dwell in: as if you would say, at the leastwise I shall have Water, and again there is some pasture for my Cattle. So then, he might have returned back again: but what do they? O when the water shall be taken away from him, he shall be constrained to seek pasture elsewhere: he can never return hither again. See here a vile and mischievous malice: but let us know that it is God's will, that his children should be so molested, to prove their patience. And again, let us note that all falleth out to the confusion of the wicked, when they are so unkind against the servants of God: For it is certain that if Abraham had dwelt there, the blessing of God had rested in that Country. And when it is here rehearsed of Isaack, that he gathered in an hundredth fold so much as he sowed, there is no doubt but that the land was fertile, and that all his neighbors tasted of the favor of God. To be short, the children of God always give some sweet savor of his mercy: and we have seen that which was said of Sodom and Gomorrhe, that if God could only have but found one ten, the City had not been sunk.

But see the contemners of GOD and the unfaithful, who drive out the faithful from amongst them, and cannot abide them: and this shall always turn to their own confusion. In the meanwhile God will have pity upon his own, and howsoever they be thrust out of the world, are persecuted, and have not where to set their foot, yet will he always find some refuge and shadow for them: but yet we must be armed with great patience, when men are so cruel unto us, that we can find no equity amongst them, that they are as mad beasts: yet must we endure all this, that we may be armed with the spirit of God, which is the spirit of lenity. For certain it is that we need nothing to make us to cast out our poison: For we are so delicate and nice, that we can suffer nothing, and we are always ready to revenge our own quarrels. We shall therefore never be so gentle, to bear the wrongs that are done unto us, unless that GOD govern us by his holy Spirit: but howsoever it be, the example of the fathers is here set before us, to the end we should learn, not to vex and disquiet ourselves too much, when men torment us in any manner of sort whatsoever.

Moreover it is said here expressly, that *Isaack kept the names of the Wells*, as we have seen of Beersheba, which was the Well of the oath, inasmuch as Abimelech had there sworn with Abraham. Now this was to maintain possession: For this was as much as a public instrument or Indenture, or rather more. Abimelech had made a league there with Abraham: Lo, a promise made with a solemn ceremony, Abraham had acknowledged homage unto him for the Wells: the name testifieth the same. So that Isaack pretendeth that the inhabitants knew, that this was a parcel of the inheritance which his father had purchased, for him, and therefore that it was his own by law. But all this prevaileth nothing, what just title so ever he had, yet notwithstanding they cease not to quarrel against him.

Thus we see, howsoever the children of God seek nothing else, but to enjoy that which is their own, and which it is lawful for them to use: notwithstanding they shall be thrust from it. For the contemners of God are impudent: and whatsoever men allege unto them, yet neither reason nor equity can prevail with them, and be made account of. When we shall see the like at this day, let us not think it a new and strange thing. There was more simplicity in that time then, and yet nevertheless we see that Isaack must be thrust from all that which he pretended is justly to be his, as was possible.

Now thereupon it is said, that he gave names to these two Wells which were taken from him, that is to say, for which he was drawn into law: that is to say, from which he was put: For it booted him not to plead, as at this day: but by violence he is driven out of possession. Now there is no doubt when he gave these names of strife and brabble [*obstinate disputing*], or contention, but that this was done, as if he made his complaint to God, when he saw that men's ears were deaf, and all reasons excluded: he hath no other way, but this to set up a memorial, to the end God might have pity upon him. Now therefore let us learn, when we can gain nothing by bringing forth our titles and right to keep that which is ours, and that which is given us: that yet notwithstanding we leave not off to trust that in the end God will have pity upon us. Lo then what we have to do: That is, that as much as lieth in us, we endeavor that men may leave us peace, and that they come not to devour us. This shall always be lawful to the children of God: For howsoever we be commanded to be as sheep amongst Wolves, yet hath God permitted unto us a peaceable defense, inasmuch as he hath taken us into his hands.

We must endeavor therefore, as much as lieth in us, to repel all violences, wrongs, outrages and riots, that shall be done unto us, and all molestations that can be devised against us. Have we done this? If we gain nothing, and that men be so obstinately bent to mischief, and specially if they be possessed with such fury, that all reason be trodden under foot amongst them, let us have recourse unto God, and pray him that it will please him to take our cause into his own hands: and doubt we not, when men shall become so uncourteous, that they shall deride at whatsoever we can allege, that in the end God will take order with them. Lo then what we have to bear away of the example of Isaack, when he named the wells. Strife, debate and contention. For this was not of Choler, or of the Spleen: as there are very many which will revenge themselves, and cast out some injurious word: but Isaack commended his cause to God: as also we are exhorted by Saint Peter, that if we be envied of men and can find no remedy at their hands, that then we wait when God will put to his hand, as surely he will.

Now in the end it is said, that Isaack having digged a Well for which he was not assailed, that he named it *Rehoboth* as if he should say, *Largesses*: and specially he putteth it in the plural number: and contenteth not himself to say. Lo a *Largesse* but he saith, behold the *Largesses* which God hath bestowed upon us. We yet see more plainly that which I have touched before: That is, when Isaack was in so great distress that he had no water to drink, that men were so cruel unto him that he could not drink of the water which he had digged by his own labor, and by the hands of his family, that he remitteth this matter to GOD, who is the just Judge.

But contrariwise, when God had compassion upon him, and that men came no more to torment him, and that he had water to drink for himself, and for all his company: Oh well saith he. This is God that hath bestowed this upon me. He saith not O: in the end yet I have obtained my purpose, These wicked ones have let me alone at the length: now let us take our ease? He speaketh not so simply, as a profane man would have done, but he would have a memorial of thanksgiving unto God, as he had set up memorials of his complaint to draw the Lord to have mercy upon him.

Likewise his mind is, now that this benefit of God should be as it were engraven there, and that men should speak of it, not only for three days, but after his death: and that they should acknowledge that Well a sign of the favor that God had showed him.   And let us note this circumstance: For he ceaseth not to give GOD thanks with a quiet heart, though he had become a long time afflicted. When we have endured long the like troubles, the graces of God are wont to be darkened by that feeling of our evil: and if GOD suffer us to languish for a time, although afterwards he reach out his hand unto us, yet we think it is not from him: but we attribute this to fortune.

But Isaack did not so: but although he was driven out, and that he had endured this for a longtime, yet so soon as God had given him release, he blesseth his name, and saith, God hath enlarged me. Lo (saith he) the *largesses* or *bounties* of GOD, which I behold in this Well. But now in the end we have to note the patience of Isaack, when we preach nowadays of patience, hardly can we get this point, that if we have to endure never so little, we be not by and by hot and angry: and when it seemeth that we are very patient, yet there will always be some grudging, unless God even at the first push comfort us: and in the mean season, what suffer we? Surely in a manner nothing. If we endure but a fillip, O, it is so hard as nothing can be harder: and moreover if men go on to do us wrong, O, we suffer too much. But we are far off from this lenity and softness, which is here showed us in our father Isaack. We will say I cannot bear it. If any man wrong us, but the value of three halfpence, or of some small portion of our good: O I cannot endure it: this is too much. Yea but Isaack strived for water (I say strived,) he took not a sword to fight: but he suffered wrong: although he had digged the wells, and his father had purchased them with his own proper good, and that the King had made him a grantee, and that he had digged them again, and taken a great deal of travel to have water to drink, notwithstanding all this, we see his patience. And so when God shall afflict us, and shall loose the bridle to the wicked, that we shall be pilled and polled of them, let us yet know that we are not come to that extremity, not to have a drop of water, and to have those elements taken from us, which God would have common amongst men. For every man will have his portion apart, both of corn, and of wine, of flesh, and such like things, and of moveable and possessions: everyone will have his own: but as for water, it is an Element which GOD hath ordained for all men.

When there are Rivers, Wells, and fountains in any highway: why should they be taken away from those that are the creatures of God? But howsoever it be, yet it fell out that our fathers were brought to such extremity. And this (as I have already touched) serveth to this purpose that we should learn to be patient, not only to suffer some one little injury, or two or three: but that in all respects we should be so meek and soft natured: that if it were in a matter of life and death (as they say) we put our hope in God, that he will show himself pitiful towards us. And therefore let us not double our evil, let us not make of one devil two, when the wicked and ungodly persecute us unjustly: but let us labor to soften their hearts, and to assuage the malice which they use against us. If we do so, it is certain, that howsoever we be for a time in extreme anguish, yet in the end God will so enlarge us, that we shall have good cause to bless his holy name with full mouth.

But now let us fall down before the majesty of our good God, in acknowledging our sins, praying him that it will please him in such sort to make us to feel them, that it may be to make us to be displeased with ourselves for them: and that we may learn more and more to conform ourselves to his holy will, renouncing ourselves. And that it will please him in such sort to bear with us in our weaknesses and vices, that we do not therewith nourish them: but that he will more and more purge us until he have stripped us of all carnal affections, and clothed us anew with the affections of his holy spirit: to the end we may so behave ourselves with men, that whatsoever yet we have whereof to advance ourselves, we cease not to lowly and humble. And when we be oppressed that therefore we give not over to be courageous, always to submit ourselves to him which is able to help us: and that he will not only show us this grace, but also to all peoples and nations of the Earth etc.

❧The ninth Sermon of Jacob

and Esau, Genesis 26.

23. *Afterwards he went vp into Beer-ſcheba.*

24. *And Iehouah appeared vnto him in the ſame night, ſaying, I am the God of Abraham thy father: Feare not, for I am with thee, & I wil bleſſe thee, & will multiply thy ſeede, for Abraham my ſeruants ſake.*

25. *Therfore he hauing builded an Altar there, he called vpon the name of Iehovah: & there he pitched his tent: & there the ſeruants of Iſaack digged a Well.*

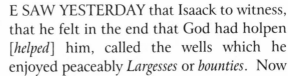E SAW YESTERDAY that Isaack to witness, that he felt in the end that God had holpen [*helped*] him, called the wells which he enjoyed peaceably *Largesses* or *bounties*. Now by that which Moyses addeth, it appeareth that he enjoyed not this very long. For it is said, that he withdrew himself into *Beerscheba*, the place where Abraham his father had dwelt before. We know that if he had not been constrained, he would not have gone from the place where he had commodity: for there was no such nimbleness in him to cause him to trot up and down hither and thither, but that necessity constrained him so to do. We have therefore to bear away, that GOD would always exercise him: and that he was not contented that he should dwell in the land of Canaan as a stranger, without one foot of ground in

possession: but moreover he led him up and down, as we have seen heretofore. Wherein we are taught always to be (as is said) as a bird upon a sprig, that know not which way to fly. And if God maintained us in that case for our infirmity, that we dwell in a certain place, and rest there: yet must we not there so nestle ourselves, as if our assured rest were there: but we must learn in this point to be fleeting as Saint Paul also used the same word. For howsoever Christians that must have their foundation and seat so stable that amidst all storms and tempest they never change and vary: yet notwithstanding as concerning their dwelling, they must be flitting and have no resting place, unless they be lodged from day to day (as it were) by the hand of GOD, and in the mean season, that they prepare themselves to wander and go from place to place, after the example of their fathers, who learned by experience not to have their inheritance here beneath upon earth, and confessed themselves to be Pilgrims, as we shall see hereafter that Jacob answered Pharaoh. In the meantime we may see also the malice of all those near neighbors thereabouts: For the Wells especially, which Abraham had bought, were taken from him after his death, to the end that his successors and Children might have no use of them. But it is said that Isaack yet digged a Well there: for he could not be without water, both for the family he had, which was great, as for his Cattle: but he went very far to seek water, until GOD restored him to that which was wrongfully taken from him. He dwelleth therefore in *Beerscheba* for a time without water, unless he borrow or buy it: but afterwards he findeth his Well again, and so is at some better ease than before, and God suffereth them not that would as it were have made them to die of thirst to use their malice and to come to their purpose. But howsoever it be, God heard him not at the first dash. We have then to learn here, that which was touched yesterday: that is, that we learn to endure need, yea in the need of water, and that we think it not strange which our fathers have tried. For it is no reason that we should be more privileged than they. And if God spare us, that we acknowledge his goodness in this point: and if he afflict us in any other sort, that we be so much the more framed to patience. But yet it is said:

> *That God appeared unto him, the very first night*
> *that he went to Beerscheba.*

Here we must note that which we have handled before in the life of Abraham: that is, that God appeared unto him, forasmuch as he had need to be aided and comforted, by reason of his great heaviness and troubles, which he had suffered before. This circumstance then is worthy to be noted: and that is, that God seeing his servant to be afflicted even to extremity, he would give him some ease: as at this day, although we have no such visions, GOD nevertheless ceaseth not to show himself unto us, when he seeth that we can bear no more, and that we were like to fail unless he reach forth his helping hand to sustain us. How oft soever we are in distress, we think that God hath estranged himself from us, and we imagine that he hath utterly forgotten us. But contrariwise, when he maketh us to taste his favor, in what sort soever it be, or rather that he doth strengthen us, and that we fight valiantly against all temptations, or rather that he delivereth us from the wrongs and vexations that are done unto us, or that he doth assist us as it were, after some visible manner: then lo his presence, and then we see that he hath care over us. So let us note, that when God appeared to Isaack, that it must needs be that he had been in some great necessity: For this happened not every day: and thereupon let us learn to hold ourselves contented, when God after that he hath suffered us to be tormented, to be disquieted, troubled, and molested, that in the end he showeth himself to be father unto us. And if this fall not out so soon, let us wait upon him, as we see Isaack did, who had not always a certain sign that GOD would assist him: but contrariwise he then seeth himself quite destitute of all succor [*help*], and that for a longtime: and after one misery was come, behold another followeth as thick as might be: and yet notwithstanding he quailed not: And therefore let us follow that path. And in the mean season let us mark also that one only word which God shall speak unto us, to witness the love which he beareth unto us, will be better worth unto us, than all the goods which we can have, yea if we had to eat and drink our fill, and that in all delicacy, though there were no man to trouble us, though we rest on every side: To be short, though we had all at our hearts desire: If the world went thus with us, it is certain that we ought not to esteem so much of it, as to have this testimony, that GOD is merciful unto us. For let us put the case, that a man did swim in all pleasures and had all the ease in the world and wanted [*lacked*] nothing: yet notwithstanding, if he know not, how it standeth betwixt GOD and him, if he have no doctrine, no promise, he shall be always as it were in doubt whether his ease will last or no: and if he become so drunken therewith, that he think that his prosperity shall yet continue with him, what may it be to have after this sort all his felicity in this world? How long endures this life?

So then all the blessings that may happen unto us, are nothing, neither can they have any good favor, unless we be assured of the favor of GOD: but on the other side, when it pleaseth God to declare unto us that he loveth us, and that we are in his protection, that we cannot perish, that he holdeth us by the hand, and that we are kept and guarded by him. This is it then that ought to content us, though all the rest did fail us. So then, howsoever God gave some sign unto Isaack, that he had looked upon him in pity: this was nothing in comparison of that which Moyses rehearseth now, which was *that God appeared unto him*, to the end to continue his covenant towards him, and to ratify it so much the more, and that he was altogether resolved therein, in such sort that he was a Buckler unto him, to break all temptations. But we have here in the first place to note, that this was a vision to prepare Isaack, to the end that the word which must be given unto him, might be received with the greater reverence and authority.

Now this vision was a sign that God spake: and this hath always been very necessary: For we know how the devil laboreth to seduce us by illusions and vain fantasies. When therefore the fathers were taught, to the end they might have a full assurance of their faith, the majesty of God manifested itself unto them, whereof they had some infallible impression: For if the word only had come unto them, it had been as a sound in the air without all steadiness. This therefore is no superfluous thing, when Moyses saith, that God showed and declared himself unto

Isaack: For it was necessary that Isaack should know and be thoroughly persuaded, that the word which he heard, proceeded from heaven, and that he might rest therein, that it was an undoubted truth, in which he could not be abused. It is true that God is invisible, and cannot be comprehended: and so far is it off, that we can comprehend him with the eye, that if we do apply all our senses thereto, it is certain that we shall never attain to his high majesty. The Essence of God therefore, in that it is infinite, cannot be seen of men, but this letteth [*preventeth*] not but that he may show himself so far forth as is expedient for us, and according to that small measure that is in us. Thus as often as we read that God appeared unto the ancient Fathers, this showeth not that they comprehended all his essence and majesty: For that had been a thing impossible: Man's spirit is very rude: but he so showed himself, as they were able to bear: that is to say, so far forth as he saw it to be profitable for them. Yea and if God should lay open his glory unto us, it would by and by overwhelm us: I say if we had a great deal more understanding than we have, and that our spirit could comprehend an hundred times more than it doth: yet should we be so astonished at the glory of God, that we should therein be altogether confounded. It behooveth therefore that God have regard what we are able to bear, when it pleaseth him to appear unto us. And so let us mark, how the word which Moyses useth here is to be taken, that is, that Isaack, to the end that he might be more assured of the promise which was made unto him, and that he might hold it as an authentical promise, and in no wise doubt but that it was god that had spoken unto him, he had some sign and mark, whereby he felt that he could not be deceived, that it was no fancy or some light imagination: but that God would give him a sure hold to lean upon, that he would give him such a rest, as he might by virtue of the word, which shall afterwards be added, fight against whatsoever evil might happen unto him. Now it is said, that God exhorted him, that he should not fear, and he giveth him a reason why:

I am (saith he) with thee, yea I, the God of Abraham thy father.

When he saith, *Fear not*: we have expounded this already before, that God meaneth not to exempt those to whom he speaketh, from all fear: For howsoever the fathers were Conquerors against all the defiances, which could be made against them, yet were they not insensible. Abraham was tempted: but he was not overcome. Therefore we must remember this point, that they that became Conquerors through the power of the spirit of GOD, fought notwithstanding.

Now what strife or combat can there be, unless there be some feeling of it? For if Abraham had not felt this in himself, See I am in danger, he would never have called upon GOD, and he would never have had recourse unto him: if he had not been pressed with the griefs which he endured, he would not have made his requests and complaints unto God, to be eased and lightened of them. So then we may not think, that God would have them to be without all feeling to whom he hath said, Fear not: but it was, to hold them so fast unto himself, that they should not be unmeasurably afraid as we used to be, unless we have our rest upon God: For the least blast of wind in the world is

enough to shake us, and to make us so at our wits end, that
we cannot tell which way to turn us: as it is said of Achas,
that he was afraid, and shook as a leaf of a tree: and Esay to
remedy this evil, saith: *Hush, hold thy peace before God.* And
this is the common style of the holy scripture. So then
mark what this word importeth, where it is said, *Fear not:*
that is to say, howsoever we have occasion to fear, and to be
astonished, yet let us resist , and wait with patience till god
shall succor [*help*] us: and let not this fear oppress us, and
quite stifle us: but let us endeavor to recover ourselves and
keep the right path. And albeit we be disquieted and tossed
hither and thither, let us always remain fast upon our feet,
seeing we are grounded upon the promise of God. But it is
said expressly: *I am with thee:* to show that when we have
God on our side, this ought to suffice us, though all the
world mischievously practice our ruin, that look how many
men, so many enemies there are: yea and that it seemeth
that all creatures have conspired against us, notwithstanding
so that God take our part, it shall make us to overcome all
fear. And indeed we see how the Prophet David[†] did
practice this doctrine, and Saint Paul also giveth us example
thereof: *Seeing God* (saith he) *is for me, I will not fear though I
were compassed about with an hundred thousand men:* when I
shall see all the deaths in the world, I will assure myself
upon God's shepherds crook. Lo how he speaketh in the
three and twenty Psalm[††], O Lord thy hook, that is to say,
the staff which thou erectest, as a shepherd, (For he taketh

---

† *Psalm 3:6,7*

†† *Psalm 23*

a similitude from the shepherd, who will have his staff or his hook to lead his sheep:) Lord (saith he) so that I may have some sign to assure me, that thou accomptest [*accountest*] me one of thy flock, I will walk in the shadow of death, and yet I will comfort myself: For I will accompt [*account*] myself enough comforted, so that I may be grounded upon thy grace. And afterwards in another place, *seeing that God is with me*: I defy all those which shall come to assail me. What is that that flesh shall do unto me, so that God take my part (saith he?) He scorneth there the weakness of men, showing that God blowing upon them, he can overthrow them all, and bring them to nothing: and notwithstanding if he be armed with strength from above, all the threats which the Devil shall be able to bend against him, shall be nothing. And this is it that Saint Paul teacheth[†] us: *If God be with us, who shall be against us?* Not that we shall not have many things against us, albeit that God be the keeper of our life: but notwithstanding we may boast ourselves against all our enemies, and against all that the Devil shall devise against us, so that God be favorable unto us. So, that it is not without cause that this word is couched in, to take away all fear, when he saith: *I am with thee, Fear not therefore.* Now altogether like as we are taught to rest ourselves upon the only goodness of God, and in his fatherly favor: so contrariwise we have to mark, that without it, we are always as a people that are even sowning [*swooning*]. And this also is that we have touched erewhile [*heretofore*] to wit, that if God do not testify unto us the love that he beareth us,

---

† *Romans 8:31*

though we should be in an earthly paradise, we should be in
a hell: and contrariwise, though we were in some hell, that
is to say, in some gulf, so that we feel that God is merciful
unto us, and that in the end he will take pity upon us, and
that we be assured of his aid, and hell will always fall out to
be a paradise. And this is the thing we have to observe in
this place: That when a man knoweth not how it standeth
with him in respect of God, that is to say, he cannot assure
himself, that God beareth a fatherly affection unto him: he
must needs tremble, and be always shaken on every side,
and have many pricks to vex and torment him, without
knowing any cause why: and that very often, he shall be in
great perplexity. Lo then in what case the unbelievers are:
not that they are not bold enough, yea even to despite God:
For it seemeth to them that they are escaped his hand, and
that if he should thunder from heaven, that he cannot touch
them. The wicked then and those that are contemners of
God will indeed be so far bold in their pride: but
notwithstanding God giveth them pricks within, so that
they have, as a man would say, blind assaults, that they
know not from whence they come: and nevertheless it is
God that maketh war against them with their own unbelief.
And this is the reward of all those, that rest not only in
God, and know not that all our safety, all our joy and
felicity is to be in his keeping. All they therefore that
presume of their own strength and virtues, all they that so
occupy their minds in these earthly creatures, they must in
the end be paid home with their own foolish presumption,
because they have not given unto God that honor that
belongeth unto him: that is, they must find themselves as
poor sowning [*swooning*] people. And therefore let us learn,

albeit that God give us our desires and all the pleasures that
are possible to be wished for, that we do not such sort rest
upon them, that we turn away from him: but rather let us
learn to keep ourselves in that favor and testimony that we
have, that in that he hath adopted us for his children, he
will always show himself a father towards us. When then
we shall be thus thoroughly persuaded, it is certain that we
shall overcome all fears: but contrariwise, when we shall
imagine to be assured without the protection of God, it
must needs be that he show us what our folly and
overweening [*high opinion*] is. And this briefly is that we
have to bear away in this place. And so let us join these two
things together as inseparable and not to be sundered: That
GOD is with us, and that we are well assured against all
evil: For if he be far from us, Alas, we are more than
miserable, albeit we were in a paradise, as I have said
already: but when he is with us, though we walk in the
shadow and darkness of death, and that it seems we must
perish every minute of an hour, yet we leave not off to
comfort ourselves, knowing well that death shall be turned
to us into life, and that all shall fall out to our salvation.
Again, we have to note this, that he saith, *That he is the God
of Abraham*: For by this word he calleth to Isaack's
remembrance all the promises, the which he had learned of
his father. If he had not been instructed, and that Abraham
had not done his duty to say unto him: My Son, GOD hath
given me this privilege above all men, that he hath declared
unto me and said unto me, that my stock shall be as his
heritage, and that he will bless us, and we shall be separated
and sanctified from all the rest of the world: but yet mark
how it behooveth us to worship him, mark how we must call

upon him, See how we must serve him.   If therefore
Abraham had not faithfully taught his son Isaack: this word
should have been of no force: *I am the God of Abraham*, and
indeed it had imported nothing but superstition.   And so,
let us mark well that by this word, God would give a
confirmation to Isaack of that which he had learned before
of his father.   The Papists make a buckler of this when they
will keep themselves to their filthinesses and errors: For
they have that from other fathers and ancestors which they
follow, they have not invented it at this day: it seemeth
therefore unto them, that this is enough to beat back, yea
even whatsoever god himself hath showed by his word so
that they follow their fathers and elders.   Well, but when
god is named the God of Abraham, he presupposed this one
thing, to wit, that Abraham had a faith ruled by the
doctrine, which had been taught him.   And wherefore is it
that he nameth not himself the god of Nachor?   And why is
it that he calleth not himself, the God of Thare?   For this
had been somewhat more.   The Papists will not say, It is an
hundred years since that that which we call the service of
God amongst us, was used amongst men: but they will say:
What?   There is a thousand years, since the world was so
governed.   Lo then themselves in possession to despite God,
as seemeth unto them, when they allege a thousand years.

   Now then if the question were simply of Antiquity,
he must have said, I am thy god of Thare and of Nachor, or
rather he must have gone further, until he had come to
those that went before.   But there is no question of speaking
in that sort.   God had called Abraham, and Abraham was
dead of late, the others had been a great deal more ancient:
what distinction shall we make here?   We must not forge it

according to our own brain: but we must look unto that mark, whereunto God would direct Isaack: There is no doubt but this was, because Abraham (as we have said already) had a full certainty of faith, that he had not an opinion only as had the rest of the world, to say, I imagine so, I think so, but he was fully certified that God had spoken unto him. Lo then in what respect and for what cause it is now said, *I am the God of Abraham, thy father.* And so, let us well mark what fathers we ought to follow, that we be not deceived therein. For if our fathers had been duly taught, and that they had been framed unto the truth of God, it had now been a good help unto our faith; For when we have guides to show us the way, this is much to our advantage, and we ought not to despise it: but if we have had fathers who were not the children of God, (whereupon all paternity and parentage dependeth, as Saint Paul saith) then must we shut our eyes. For when God hath not his sovereign degree of being the father, and everything be not referred to him, then woe upon all parentages and bonds which we shall have in this world: for they are so many nets of Satan. So, let us mark well that as it is said in this place, that God is the God of Abraham, Isaack's father: so it is said on the contrary by the Prophet Ezechiel[†]: *Walk not in the righteousness of your fathers.* And why so? These fathers followed not Abraham's steps, but departed therefrom: and therefore they were no longer worthy of so honorable a title of fathers, forasmuch as they were not (at a very word) the children of God. And so let us fear, lest that be spoken

---

† *Ezekiel 20:18*

unto us (that Saint Stephen hath spoken[†],) *Ye uncircumcised of heart, ye have always resisted God and his holy spirit, as did your fathers also.* But if there were any ignorance or rebellion in our fathers, let us forsake it, to the end wholly to resign up ourselves to our heavenly father: and notwithstanding, whereas the Papists cry, *The fathers, fathers*, let us learn to discern, and let us not be beasts as they are, to take our fathers from some stews (Spittle house) [*brothel*]: as they take all those for their fathers, who have perverted and corrupted the simplicity both of the Law and the Gospel: to wit, these Dotards [*foolish talkers, imbeciles*] and rabble of Friars and Monks, who have been the falsifiers of the holy Scripture. To the end therefore we be not in suchwise bereaved and spoiled of our senses, let us know that our fathers must be the children of God, of whom dependeth all parentage, as we have alleged out of Saint Paul. Lo then shortly what we have to learn out of this place: that is to say, that Isaack was admonished, to acknowledge and call to his remembrance, whatsoever he had learned before, and that this was for to confirm his faith, when GOD said, that he had manifested himself unto his father Abraham. And now at this day we have to put this doctrine in practice, as often as we shall have need to assure ourselves, or rather when our spirit is troubled, and we tossed with some wavering and uncertainty, we must have our recourse thither: That is to follow our father Abraham, to conform ourselves to follow that rule, which he hath showed unto us. And why so? For we are certain, that GOD was manifested

---

† *Acts 7:51*

unto him. Lo then a good direction, and which shall not turn us out of the path of our salvation: when we shall be conformed and fashioned to our father Abraham, who was adopted of GOD, and who received the pledge of our salvation: that is to say, all these promises whereupon we ought at this day to be grounded. And such accompt [*account*] ought we to make of all the rest of the faithful. For although they no whit appertain unto us, concerning the flesh, yet notwithstanding we cease not to be their children. And therefore it is not without cause that the apostle in the eleventh Chapter to the Hebrews† setteth before us, this thick cloud of witnesses, when as he would show us, that we are very unkind, if we follow not those, whom GOD hath set forth unto us for an example, *Lo* (saith he) *a great and thick cloud of witnesses who calls us to GOD*, that would seem, (as if a man would say) to stop up our eyes. We will be offended with a man, when he shall seduce us, we will imagine to be excused by saying, O, he did therein as much as I: we need no more but a small fly to make us to turn away from the fear of God and his obedience: and notwithstanding that GOD shall set before us so many witnesses, to prove our faith, that we ought therewith be satisfied, yet we come not to him. And if this profit us nothing, and we be not confirmed thereby, what is the cause thereof, but our own unthankfulness? And so then so often as our faith shall be weak, that we shall have overthwartings of ignorance, as it were storms, let us think. And what? hath God begun but yesterday and today to speak? Spake

---

† *Hebrews 12:1*

he not unto Abraham? And was not his truth certain from
that time forward? and besides all the faithful which came
afterwards, all the holy kings and prophets, and others, are
they not so many witnesses, whom God showed unto us?
Let us therefore join them to this holy assembly now. For
how often soever the Gospel hath been preached unto us
(according as the Apostle hath entreated thereof) it is not
only to gather us together with all the faithful, which are
living at this day, but also into the fellowship and company
of all the holy spirits, whom GOD hath taken out of this
world. We are therefore at this day joined in fellowship
with all the holy Patriarchs and Prophets, as often as GOD
speaketh unto us. But we shall be so much the more
without excuse, because we know not how to make our
profit of all this: seeing that GOD hath yet revealed it more
clearly unto us, and in a more familiar sort in the person of
his only begotten Son. For he is not only named at this day
the GOD of Abraham, but also the father of our Lord Jesus
Christ. Inasmuch therefore as we have the full and perfect
revelation of whatsoever is profitable unto us for our
salvation in this lively image in whom GOD set forth: it is
certain that we have no color, that we can allege, why we
should not have such a certainty of faith, that we should
never stray hither and thither: and when the world changeth
itself an hundred thousand times, yet nevertheless, that we
should remain steadfast in that we have received of God,
knowing that his truth is unchangeable. This therefore
shortly is that which we have to bear away concerning this
text.

And further, let us likewise note that word of the

Lord Jesus Christ, when he saith[†]: *I go to my God and to your God, to my Father and to your Father.* See the Son of God, who is the everlasting, God, nevertheless to the end to gather us unto himself, and to keep us sure there, in such sort that we should never be seduced from that foundation which he hath given unto us of his truth, he saith, that we have one God together with him, inasmuch as he is man, and in that he is our brother: that we have the same God who is his God, and the same father who is his father. When we hear these things, is there any farther cause for us to doubt, or to be shaken? As there are many who will say at this day: O, I know not what to hold: there are so many sundry opinions, that I am confounded: and likewise I can believe nothing, I know not what to follow. But it cannot be chosen, but that such people are possessed of the Devil, when they tread under their feet the truth of God, which is as a most undoubted light to guide us, and to show us the way of salvation. So then, seeing God hath showed himself since Abraham and Noah, and appointed Moyses to be the conductor of his Church, and that he hath knit us altogether, when in the end he sent his only begotten Son, in whose person he hath gathered us all to himself: let us learn to keep ourselves in that unity of faith which he hath given us, and let us not doubt, but that he will always avow us for his children. Now we have to note that which God saith, *That he will bless Isaack and will multiply his seed*: For this serveth to show that the favor which god beareth to those whom he hath called to himself, is not vain nor idle:

---

† *John 20:17*

but that it bringeth forth his fruit and effect in time. It is therefore very certain, that when God shall be merciful unto us, he will give us so many good things, as he knoweth to be good for us: it is true that this shall not be according to our desire, but howsoever it be, prosperity shall always be coupled with the favor and love of God. Now we know that he hath all in his hand, and he is no niggard [*covetor, stingy*], that he will not give to his children whatsoever he knoweth to be meet for them. Let us learn therefore to wait for all prosperity, and free favor of our God, when it shall please him to testify unto us that he loveth us, and that he is with us (as I have said already:) and in the meanwhile notwithstanding, although that we have many adversities, which trouble and molest us, and that they be hard and bitter unto us, yet let us never give over to hold us fast unto his promise. And when we receive any grace from the hand of God, let us apply the same always, to strengthen our faith, and to have this undoubted persuasion, that we shall try that to be true which is spoken here: *I will be with thee, and I will bless thee.* And certain it is, that if we would consider well the benefits of God, that we daily receive from him, and that they were valued of us as they ought, we should have always good cause to honor him and to rejoice ourselves in him: but alack we devour up the benefits that he bestoweth upon us: and in the meanwhile we move at them and never think upon them. And we may see, that this is the cause that we are so given to murmur, to fret and to discontent ourselves. And who so? For the benefits of God, ought to suffice to satisfy us in him: but (as I have said) we despise and set light by them. And so we are not worthy to taste, what this promise is worth: *I am with thee, and will bless thee.* Now it is said a little after:

> *That Isaack erected an altar, and that he called*
> *upon the name of the Lord in that place.*

We have seen already why altars were erected by the holy fathers, and to what intent: but yet we must here speak somewhat of it, even as the place requireth. The altar which Isaack erected, was to this end, that he might make profession of his faith. Thus much concerning the first point. For if we pray unto God, we have no need to erect an altar unto him: the service of God is, of itself, spiritual. Isaack therefore erected not an altar that he might only invocate and call upon the name of God, or make his prayers and supplications unto him: but to the intent that his faith might be known, and that God might be glorified before men. For although we ought to serve God in spirit, and inwardly in our heart: yet notwithstanding this letteth [*hindereth*] not also, but that we must give him that praise which he deserveth before men, and that we protest as much as lieth in us, that we are wholly his, both body and soul.

Here therefore we are instructed, that the faithful after they have put their trust in God, and shall have called upon him, and given unto him the praise of all his benefits that they must yet further make a confession of their faith before men, to the intent they may wholly (as also all is his) dedicate themselves to him. There is also a second reason: And that is that by reason of our sloth and slackness, we have need every manner of way to be pricked forwards, to the end to stir us up, to march cheerfully forwards in the

service of God. How so? It is true, that when we pray unto
God he embusieth himself with no ceremonies: and yet for
all that, we bow our knees, we hold up our hands towards
heaven, and uncover our head. And why so? First of all, in
respect of men. For (as I have already said) it must needs
be that we do homage unto God with our bodies, which he
hath created, and which he hath appointed to his glory, and
to the crown of immortality. But, howsoever it be,
forasmuch as we are slack, it behooveth us that these means
stand us instead to provoke us to have a more fervent zeal
to pray unto God, and with a more hearty affection. Lo
then, why it is meet for us to have our joined hands lifted
up, to kneel upon our knees, and have our head uncovered:
For it is to show, that we present ourselves before God as if
we should say: And poor wretch, who art thou? with what
lowliness oughtest thou to come before him, who hath
created and fashioned thee, and to whom thou hast to
render an account of thy whole life? And again this also, is
to this end, that we should bereave ourselves of all vain
fantasies, that make us to stray here and there: and that we
should wholly rest upon him. So then, the Altar that Isaack
erected, served to this purpose: to wit, that by this means he
might be the more provoked, and have his heart so much
the more inflamed to serve God. And on the other side, he
made a confession before men, to give example to his
family, and to testify that he mingled not himself with the
superstitions of the Painims [*pagans, heathen*]: but had a
pure and undefiled religion, inasmuch as he was ruled by his
word. And thus much concerning the Altar. And by the
way we have also to learn here this thing which was
declared before, that the prayers of the holy fathers, and the

confession which they made of their faith, was not joined with the sacrifices, for no other end but to lead them unto our Lord Jesus Christ: For they were continually taught, that they could have no access unto God, but by the favor of a mediator, who was not yet sent into the world: but yet so it is that they rested there. But now that our Lord Jesus Christ is come down, and that he hath taken our nature upon him, and hath said unto us[†], *That he is the light of the world, that he is the way, the truth, and the life, that he is our advocate to God his father, and that through him we must have entrance into Heaven.* Seeing therefore we have all this, must we not be so much the more assured, when there is any question of calling upon him, that we know that our requests shall be heard of him, and the gate shall be open for us, and that we shall always find him ready and favorable to help and succor [*assist*] us? Now howsoever it be let us mark, that Altars in old time, and specially in the time of the law, were always erected to this end, that the faithful might know that they were not worthy to pray unto God, nor to call upon him in their own name: but that always they must come to him by the means our Lord Jesus Christ, and by the virtue of that sacrifice which he must offer up to his father, for the reconciliation of the world. And indeed we must not think that Abraham and Isaack devised Altars according to their own fantasies: For their sacrifices were never acceptable but through faith as the Apostle showeth. Now they could never have been grounded in Faith, unless the word of god had gone before

---

† *John 8:12 & 14:6 & 1 John 2:1 & John 14:6*

to enlighten them. Let us know then, that Isaack offered not up a sacrifice, at all adventures, as if he had thought, O this shall be found good: but he was taught, that he being a wretched sinner, he must not presume to call upon the name of God, unless he put his whole trust in him, who must be sent to make satisfaction and to purge the sins of the world. The Painims [*pagans, heathen*] had indeed their Altars, and sacrificed, as did the holy fathers: but they wanted [*lacked*] the principal. They were wholly occupied in the ceremony, which of itself was frivolous: because they looked not up to that heavenly pattern, whereof mention is made in Leviticus. So then we have to learn, that when our father Isaack would call upon the name of god, he had an Altar to witness that he could not be received but in the name and favor of our Lord Jesus Christ. And therefore at this day, as often as we will pray unto God, let us learn to wash our Prayers with the blood of our Lord Jesus Christ: for otherwise they shall be but profane and defiled: but when the blood of our Lord Jesus Christ shall be applied therein, certainly our Prayers shall be pure, they shall be consecrated, in such sort, that God will accept of them. And when we shall call upon God, everyone in the secret of his own heart, let us labor also to draw our neighbors thereto, to the intent that he may be glorified in the midst of us with one accord. And as we ought to be knit together in one Faith, so also let us have but one mouth to protest that we hold him for our father and Savior, and that we are wholly his.

But now we will fall down before the majesty of our good God, in the acknowledgment of our faults, praying that it will please him, in such sort to make us feel them, that it may be to make us to be displeased with ourselves for them, and to make us to lament before his judgment seat, to the intent we may be absolved through his mercy: forasmuch as we should justly be condemned by his judgment. And that it will please him to strengthen us, so as we faint not, whatsoever miseries we have to suffer in this world: but we may meditate in his word in such sort, that the only promise which he hath given unto us, to hold us for his children, may content us, and that we may be armed therewith to the end to submit ourselves to his will peaceably to bear all afflictions, that he shall send us: and that we may glorify him also in our hearts, without any feigning [*pretending*] or hypocrisy: and that we may labor also to show the fruits of our faith before men, and that by this means he may be honored of all, both of small and great. And that he will not only show us this grace, but also to all peoples and nations of the Earth, etc.

The tenth Sermon of Jacob

and Esau, Genesis 26.

26. *Nowe Abimilech comming vnto him to Gerar, with Achuzath his friende, and Picol the Captaine of his hoaſt:*

27. *Iſaack ſayth vnto them, why came you vnto me: ſeeing you hated me, and haue ſent me away from you?*

28. *Who ſaide vnto him vve ſavv for aſuretie, that Iehouah was with thee, therefore we ſayd: Let there be an othe betweene vs, that is, betvvene vs & thee, Let vs therfore ſtrike a couenant with thee.*

29. *Aſke vengeance vpon thy ſelfe, if thou ſhalt hurt vs, like as vve haue not touched thee, and like as wee haue don thee good, and haue ſente thee away vvith peace: Doe thou conſent now, thou bleſſed of the Lord.*

30. *When therefore he had made them a feast, they did eate and drinke. And ryſing in the morning, they ſvvore either to other: And Isaack led them foorth, and they vvent from him vvith peace.*

31. *And it came to paſſe that the ſelfe ſame day, Iſaacks ſeruantes comming vnto him, ſhewed him concerning that wel which they had digged, and ſaid vnto him we haue found waters.*

32. *And he called the ſame Sohibbah, therefore the name of the Citie is Beer-ſchebah euen vntill this day.*

Chapter 27. verse 1

1. *Now when Esau was fortie yeeres olde, he maryed a wife named Iudith the daughter of Beer the Chithite, and Basmatha the daughter of Elon the Chithite.*
2. *Who were a greese of minde to Isaack and Rebecca.*

OWSOEVER MEN LIVING in this world are subject to many miseries and afflictions, yet nevertheless the most part of the evils that they endure, proceed from themselves, everyone of them being as a Wolf to his companion. We are compassed about with savage beasts, who are altogether our enemies: there is neither Heaven nor earth, nor other elements, that do not bring with them a thousand hurts. We know not how to go upon the water, but we must be, within half a foot of our death: There needs but one torment to swallow up a people: The earth also hath many annoyances, as if God had threatened us on every side. But when we shall make comparison, there are no wild beasts, nor heaven, nor earth, nor anything whatsoever, which so much annoyeth men, as each one annoyeth his neighbor. Now for this cause we ought to think it a singular benefit of God bestowed upon us, when he giveth us peace and that we are not oppressed and wronged on every side, when no mischief is devised against us, no hurt nor damage done unto us: It must needs be that the protection of God have a hand in it, seeing that every man will always be as a Wolf unto his neighbors, as we have said. And this is the mark whereunto this present story tendeth: For Moyses would show that after God had appeared to Isaack, he yet farther declareth his favor unto him, in that the King of Gerar came unto him, and sought his amity and friendship, and hereby was Isaack honored, and specially it was unto him a great advantage, because he might always have been in doubt, inasmuch as he had been greatly envied in the country, and had been constrained to depart from thence, notwithstanding he had lived amongst them, in all humanity and courtesy. He might therefore have been always in great suspense, fearing the rage of his neighbors. But God made them to come unto him of their own accord, and not only to show themselves friends: but they flatter him, and fear that he will hurt them, and therefore they demand a covenant to be made between them with a solemn oath. Now we have to note here first of all, that God hath the hearts of men in his own hand to mollify their hardness, when it pleaseth him, and to abate all their rage, and to turn them to courtesy and kindness: for certainly the king of Gear had not changed his nature, when he came to Isaack: and on the other side if he feared Isaack, he might have conspired with his subjects and neighbors, and so have set upon him altogether. On the other side, he had given no occasion to doubt of him, inasmuch as Isaack had not given him any argument of distrusting him: he rather had behaved himself in such sort, that he plainly declared that he desired not to grieve any, no not so much as his presence: For we have seen how he departed from their company.

It must needs be therefore that God stirred up these profane people, to cause them to come unto Isaack, and to submit themselves, as they do with such humility, that they entreat a poor man, a stranger, who had no great credit amongst them, nor had any but his own family, which he kept apart, without giving any token of attempting any such matter. Before God had laid the bridle in their neck, but this was to prove the patience of his servant. For when he was denied water, and that in the end it was said unto him, that he was stronger than they, and that he could be no longer suffered, there is no doubt but that God then exercised him to the end he might try what patience there was in him. And so Isaack knew, that if it had pleased God to give him peaceable dwelling in that Country where he was, that he should not have been driven thence: but inasmuch as he saw men perk up against him, he knew that it was as a passport from God for him to depart.

Now on the contrary we must also note, that god moved them upon the suddaine [*sudden*] to come towards Isaack, and to appease and abolish all enmities and quarrels, which might yet be moved either on the one side or on the other. Let us mark well then, when any outrage is done against us, and there, where, we shall have endeavored to do pleasure and service to everyone, that we shall be wonderfully pricked and tormented, that this should be done by God's appointment, who willeth us to strive, not in doing evil, or requiting evil for evil, but by possessing our souls in patience, as also our Lord Jesus Christ hath thereto exhorted us. And likewise on the contrary, when we shall see men to be favorable unto us, and to intend no evil quarrel, or riot against us, let us know that God hath pity upon us, and that he governeth his creatures, and directeth them to such purpose as he seeth good. And likewise let us beseech God, as often as our enemies shall use any cruelty against us, and that we cannot win them by any means, nor by any moderation that we can use, that it will please him to put to his hand, knowing that he can turn when it shall please him, those that are Wolves into Sheep. This is, that we have to learn first of all by this History. But it is said that Isaack at their first coming spake bluntly enough on this wise:

> *Why are you come unto me? Seeing you hated me,*
> *and draw me out from amongst you?*

We shall see by the sequel of the matter, that Isaack nourished no spite nor bitterness, nor any desire of revengement in his heart: For he was quickly appeased: and when he upbraided Abimelech and all his company, that they had hated and persecuted him: it was not in manner, of any injury, so as we are accustomed to do. For if any spite be done unto us, or any wrong, we sharpen our tongues to speak evil and to slander: there is nothing but hatreds, contentions and wranglings: to be short, if we could tear them in pieces, that have hurt us, we would willingly do it.

And this is it that Solomon saith[†]: *That hatred discovereth reproaches, faults and injuries.* When the hearts then are thus set on fire, it is not possible but that the tongues also must overflow to outrage one against the other. But Isaack took no such course: but we have to note, that whensoever we shall be patient that this letteth [*hindereth*]

---

† *Proverbs 18:2,3*

not, but that we use our liberty, to show them that have faulted, the wrong that they have done unto us, and so make them to understand their offence: to the end all may profit them.

It is true that in this case we must thoroughly examine our affection: for it is a very hard and rare thing, that a man who shall have been provoked and offended, that he should not be moved with some passion, and so always pursue his own particular cause. And therefore I have said that we must enter into ourselves, and diligently mark, if we be not moved with some desire of revenge, or tainted with some hatred or rancor: when we shall have thoroughly known this, and find ourselves clear, then we may have an open mouth to show them their offence, that shall have wronged us, not to be revenged in condemning of them: but to the end that they flatter not themselves in their sins, as this is a very common evil against men. Lo then a point which we have diligently to mark: that is, that the patience of the faithful is not without all touch of any passion, neither is it against this, that we frankly show them: ye have done me wrong, and ye have offended GOD, and ye have had no occasion to do so: and yet: that they always have special regard unto the salvation of those, who have persecuted them, and have been their enemies. For this that Isaack nippeth them withal, was undoubtedly as an admonition, whereby he sought the good and salvation of them, to whom he spake so bluntly: For if had dissembled it, what profit might come to him thereby? The others would have thought it deep hypocrisy, if he had made show to have been contented and well pleased with them, and that he had nothing but honey in his mouth, and have said:

Lo it is even so: Abimelech knowing himself to be faulty would have thought, See, a double man and a liar. Lo what they gain that dissemble so much, and set such a fair countenance upon it. So then, although the Children of God be patient, and that they be always ready to forgive all wrongs committed against them, and have not any manner of ways cankered hearts against their enemies, yet they cease not oftentimes to say, See wherein you have done me wrong: and this is to show that they walk in all roundness and simplicity. And this end ought always to be kept: that is to say, when we shall be grieved, or any wrong or extortion shall be done unto us, that yet we procure always the good of our enemies, and that the reproofs and accusations that we make unto them, be so many advertisements or warnings to draw them to the right way, and to touch them: to the intent they be not hardened and made obstinate, and that they may be better advised in time to come, and that they fight not against God, thinking they have to do with men: as it is very likely that Isaack did here, who would likewise provide for the time to come. For this shall be very lawful for us, when we shall have suffered any wrong, to do as much as lieth in us, to rid ourselves from it. For although our Lord Jesus Christ commandeth us to be ready, when we shall have received one blow upon the one cheek to turn the other: Yet it meaneth not that we should go and provoke our enemies, and give them occasion to use us. We ought to avoid this as much as is possible for us: and by all good and loving means we ought to stop their malice who have no fear of God in them. Isaack then had respect to himself in this case: But it was not to the end to be avenged, nor to render like for like: He only contented himself to have set a bar against all those which had entreated him evil and dealt unjustly with him before time: to the end they might be stayed, and might surcease from such wrongs.

This briefly is that we have to learn out of this place. And this rule is very necessary: For oftentimes when men are reconciled one to the other, they must be silent and then there shall need none other means: and he yet who shall have sustained the greatest wrong, he shall have more liberty and more boldness to justify himself, against them that would make us believe that the Lamb hath troubled the water. Let us mark well therefore, that when any shall have done wrong to his neighbor, if he come not to pursue his particular quarrels so stoutly, that he rest thereupon, that it shall be good that each one be advertised, and that he which hath done the wrong, notwithstanding know it, confess it, and be humbled in it: but we see that this greatly profited not: so far off was it that Isaack pursued not the matter to the uttermost, although he saw that his admonition was not received, and that it touched not their hearts, to whom he had spoken: howsoever it was, he dealt not spitefully against them. Notwithstanding mark Abimelech who saith:

> Like as we have been friendly unto thee, and have done thee no hurt, so swear unto us that thou wilt attempt nothing against us.

Abimelech not only hideth the evil which he hath committed, and would excuse it: but he boasteth that he hath done his duty wonderful well towards Isaack: and this is the common manner, as we have said: For there is nothing more hard for a man than to condemn himself: although he feel himself faulty. Men will be drawn sooner to anything than to this lowliness, which yet notwithstanding is a token necessarily required to true repentance. For if a man feel that he have faulted, and have true repentance, he must needs confess himself guilty before God, and likewise towards his neighbor, when it shall be requisite. And therefore our Savior Christ also exhorteth us, that if we have any quarrel against our neighbors, that is to say, if we have offended them, that rather we should leave our sacrifices at the altar, to the end to seek agreement, than to flatter ourselves, and to harden our hearts, despising those to whom we are bound. Now he speaketh of that time of the sacrifices: but that was as much as if he should have said, that we cannot pray unto God, nor do anything that shall be acceptable unto him, as long as we disdain to repair the faults which we have committed. Now although God command us never so straightly to humble ourselves, when we have offended, yet can none attain unto this way: and that is here sufficiently taught us in the person of Abimelech and of his companions. For men are so blinded both with selflove, pride and arrogance, that they cannot in any case be brought to this, to say: I have offended: for they are always ashamed to confess their fault: and yet notwithstanding are not ashamed to be condemned before God and his Angels: and yet when they have remorse in themselves, they must condemn themselves in spite of their teeth. They can trimly trace out all the ways that can be to maintain their corruption, they have their goodly starting holes, to uphold themselves in their mischievous cause: but when they shall have won both great and small, whether it be through corruption or favor, or by any other means, and all the world stand for them, yet must they in the end come to the judgment of their own conscience which they cannot abide: and as I have said, there they shall find themselves to have gotten nothing by all their fetches and starting holes: For maugre [*in spite of*] their beards will they [*willingly*], nil they [*unwillingly*], they must feel themselves guilty before God. Now when this is set before us, it is not to the end that we should sleep in any such vice: but to the intent, that we knowing ourselves to be subject unto it, should the rather seek for remedy. When Moyses saith therefore that Abimelech made as if he had well acquitted himself towards Isaack (and we know the contrary by that which hath been rehearsed) it was not only to show that Abimelech was an hypocrite and a double man: but it was also to set a looking glass before our eyes, to the end we might know that there is not anyone amongst us, which is not inclined to flatter himself, and who is not bent to bolster out an ill cause: although he were sufficiently convinced to have offended, that yet nevertheless pride would not suffer us to submit ourselves. Lo then Moyses purpose and drift. So then, what have we to do? that everyone gage and sound himself to the bottom to find what is in him: and after we have duly examined ourselves, we shall find that there is not anyone of us that would not hide his faults, and that would not wrong his adversary, when we have any quarrel: and hereupon it is that we seek out goodly colors to excuse ourselves, and starting holes and delays: and turn (as they say) black to white, and white into black, that we might justify ourselves. Seeing therefore that we are subject to such an evil, let us fight against it. For it is not enough for us to feel our vice, but we must forsake it, and in forsaking it, we must yet resist it, albeit we cannot altogether get the upper hand of it. And when we shall come to put this in practice, and shall have offended this man here, and that man there, let us not look upon men to blear our eyes: but let every man withdraw himself into his own secret, and say, Go to, what can I do now? It is true that I might justly do wrong unto mine adversary: for he hath offended me thus and thus: but notwithstanding am I innocent before God and his Angels? It is meet that I begin to judge myself. For although that I be a poor blind wretch, yet for all that I feel in myself that I have offended, and I cannot lie unto myself: and in the meanwhile will God be deceived? When I have cunningly dissembled, will not he find out the least drop for all that.

So then there is no other means to be absolved and released before God, but this, that I condemn myself. Mark then, I say, how we ought to practice this doctrine, and to apply it to our use and commodity. And to be short, how often soever we offend, let us note that repentance containeth in it confession, not to go and whisper in the ear of a Priest, as was done in the Papacy: but a confession to give glory to God, and likewise to make amends for the fault which was committed against our neighbors. And therefore, they who committed any wrong or outrage against another, it behooved them to labor the amendment thereof, in humbling themselves, and howsoever it was not to be ashamed to say, I have offended you: I pray you forgive me. For mark also how we shall obtain favor and forgiveness before God, and by what means those wrongs we have done to our neighbors shall not cry out for vengeance against us:

For undoubtedly, although they to whom we have done the wrong, content themselves, and think no more of it, yet the evil shall be enrolled before God, and cry more loud before his majesty, than if all men were armed and set themselves against us. So then, to the end our faults may be blotted out and defaced before God, and that there be no cry that may hasten the Lord to judgment against us, by reason of the offences that we have committed, let us learn in such sort to appease all strifes and quarrels that everyone may prevent it by humbling himself with an upright and pure confession. This is that we have to mark upon this point. Now on the other side, we see as I have already touched, that Isaack had not as a man would say, an heart puffed up, neither that nourished any manner of rancor against such as had been his enemies: for he pursued them not, he had indeed special cause against Abimelech and his company: For as Saint Paul saith, they which are not of the flock and body of the church, we cannot judge them, to the end to bring them to repentance, as we may those which make profession of Christianity, who ought out of hand (as much as lieth in them) to receive admonition of their faults. For this is the order which GOD hath set amongst all those that are his, that we should be subject to receive admonition both from great and small.

So that there is, as it were, a mutual jurisdiction without the sword, and without authority, if we do our duty. For everyone having the word of God in his mouth is as a Judge, to show his neighbor the faults which he hath committed. He shall be a judge in one respect and he shall suffer himself to be judged in another. Mark then, how we judge these that are of the household, as Saint Paul saith, that is to say, such as are of our body, and of the Religion of the faithful, and of the children of God. But those that are without, although we condemn them, yet cannot we call them so familiarly, to say, Thou hast offended. For they have no such acquaintance with us, and there is no such mutual right, as there is amongst the members of the body of the church. And this is the cause why Isaack dealeth not so earnestly with Abimelech and his people, as if they had been knit together in one faith, and worshiped the same God, and had been of one Church, and had had one and the selfsame order established amongst them. It is very likely that Isaack would not have passed this over to have said unto him: What? Come you hither with your brags, making as though you were my good friends, and had used nothing but courtesy towards me? And what courtesy was that to deny me water, yea and to dam up the wells that I had digged by mine own labor and the sweat of those that were mine? And this could bring you no loss or hindrance: and yet through malice you have gone about to put out mine eyes: and in the end you have driven me out and have not suffered me to dwell amongst you. And what friendship was this? Isaack therefore might have stood to have maintained his cause, if Abimelech had been capable to have received such reproof: but it was enough for him freely to have laid open his affection. For seeing Abimelech would not be corrected, neither had any such repentance as was requisite for him: thereupon he leaveth him. So then, when we shall have labored to bring those to repentance that have offended, if we see them obstinate, we can no further press or urge them. It is true that if they be members of the Church, we must follow them, to the end they continue not obstinate, and if they will not endeavor to open themselves, and that we see they will not be displeased with their faults, that yet nevertheless we hold them as vanquished. For mark how it behooveth us to handle them who are so wild and hard hearted. My friend, now thou showest thy impudence: before I well perceived that thou wast strayed out of the right path: but now I see that thou art altogether desperate and without hope: For thou doest manifestly despite God. And what gettest thou either in this or in that? For thine offence is well known. And thus we may very well beat them down, who imagine through toughness and stubbornness to win their cause. But if we have to do with those, which have no acquaintance with us, and are not our brethren, let it suffice us to have showed them the truth in one word: For this shall be dearly enough bought of them, if they think not better upon it to humble themselves. And for our part when we shall be reproved for any offence, let us not wait for any long process and such great inquests to be convinced as it were by fine force of many witnesses: but let us receive correction patiently as soon as it shall be offered us, and not be like to those that throw up an handful of ashes, to take away the clear light: let us therefore confess our faults: for this is the only remedy, except we will resist god: and let us know that when any warning or admonition shall be given us, that then God would have his grace felt of us, and that he is careful to draw us back, to the end we should not perish, that we should not remain obstinate, and that Satan should not take possession of us. Let us know this, to the end we may come to repentance and true lowliness. Now Isaack showeth yet better, that he keepeth no mind of revengement or enmity, although they had offended him: For he prepareth a banquet, and they eat and drink together. Lo here a point which we have well to meditate upon. For this also showeth, how that we must fight against our passion, all the time of our life: so that this is as it were the ABC of Christians, not to requite evil for evil: but contrariwise to render good for evil, and to get the victory in this matter: the which cannot enter into our fancy. This I say, is as it were our ABC: and there is no such perfection in us, but that we should begin here: That so soon as we desire and have a will to serve God, it behooveth that we be spoiled of all bitterness, hatred, and rancor, of all desire to revenge, not only to forgive our enemies without procuring of their hurt: but also that we be ready to do them good. But now who is he that dischargeth himself herein of the hundredth part? But we shall find, albeit it seemeth that many are (as they say) petty Angels, and have nothing but a fervent desire to serve god, and to honor him, yea and there is nothing in them but love, and they are therein resolute and settled: yet as soon as they be provoked, the poison so breaketh forth and afterwards dwelleth so long in them, that they keep the remembrance of some small offence, in their hearts all the time of their life. When we see therefore that we cannot be purged at the first day, nor the first year, of this cursed affection of revenge, so much the more we must apply this remedy, to the end we may be ordered and governed by the spirit of God: not to remain asleep in enmities and rancors [*bitterness, deep-seated ill will*]: but willingly to forgive them, and to be thoroughly patient in all things. And so, we shall have well profited all the time of our life, when we shall have learned, to what use this history of Isaack is rehearsed unto us: that is, that he prepared a banquet for his enemies, not in a ceremony, or for fashion sake only, but to show that he was pure and clean from all malice, and that he had forgotten and buried all the offences, whereat they might pick any quarrels, Now it is said a little after:

That they made a Covenant together, and swear each to other.

It is true that Isaack had the hurt, when the other demanded of him, that he would promise and swear unto them not to wrong them nor hurt them: For they had had sufficient proof, that they had not found him a violent man, nor one given to do any harm. Wherefore come they then to disquiet him farther? He might have put all this back: but he doth yield something of his right: as when we would purchase peace amongst men, we must always have this means, not to give it them wholly, who have done us wrong: but for all that, not to too extremely to challenge and hold whatsoever belongeth unto us, without yielding unto them one crumb, (as they say) thereof. For if every man should be so given to his own particular right, men could never be united and knit together: and although they were, they could never cease from day to day to have new occasions to devour and eat up one another. There is therefore but one way to nourish peace and concord: and that is, that no man seek that which is his own: as also Saint Paul maketh mention thereof, speaking unto us of Charity, 1 Corinthians the thirteenth Chapter, where he saith[†] expressly, That Charity hath this property, *Not to seek her own.* And further, when he exhorteth us to live peaceably, and that we should love brotherly fellowship, and that none of us should give himself to ambition, nor have a desire to be more, greater, and higher, and to have the upper hand: For the word which he useth, meaneth, there should be no desire of superiority or having the upper hand. Now, as long as we shall have this desire (as I have said), Lo as it were a fire blowed up and kindled: there are a thousand ways which Satan will find to set us at such discord, at war, dissention, and such contention, that it should seem we would overthrow all. So, let us mark well, to the end that we may dwell in friendship and brotherly concord with our neighbors, it behooveth everyone that he forsake and yield of his own right, and that everyone keep not this extremity, to say, I will keep whatsoever is mine, and will pursue it, and forgo nothing by no manner of means whatsoever. When we shall deal thus, certainly the Devil will always find some cunning, to kindle the fire of discord and strife of words, and in the end of war. This therefore is that which we have to learn concerning this text. But here by the way we see that it is lawful for the children of God to enter into league and friendship with heathen people, and such as profess nothing but false religion: as long as it is not to join ourselves with them, nor to draw in the same yoke. For we must mark well, that admonition of Paul, who saith[††]: *Take heed that you draw not*

---

† *1 Corinthians 13:5*

†† *2 Corinthians 6:14*

in the yoke together with unbelievers: For he speaketh this by way of comparison, as if two oxen were coupled together, to draw in one yoke, they must one answer the other: and though they be wild and sometimes straggle, yet being tied together by the necks with the yoke, they must follow the same train. Saint Paul would show us, that we must not be coupled with unbelievers, in such sort, that we be holden with their chains, and that we be so entangled with them, that we consent unto evil, neither in any respect to be tied therein: but only for to nourish peace, to stop outrages and violences, it shall always be lawful for us to enter into league with them. Let us take heed therefore that we be separated from all their malice, and therein that we have no acquaintance with them, and especially that we condemn their iniquity as much as lieth in us, so as we be not so much as companions and brethren with the wicked, no not complices [*associates*]: as it is said, specially in the fifteenth Psalm[†], that we must hate them. But nevertheless, to stop their rage, and to take away all occasion of hurt, and to shut the door against them, to the end they put not in practice their lewd enterprises, we may well meet with their evil by making league with them, to the end they may not flow to all licentiousness of evil, when we shall have put such a bar first before them. Yea we see that God hath showed us this favor and grace, that we should take his name to witness, to the end we might be assured either of other: whereby he showeth, how acceptable a thing Concord amongst men is unto him, and in what detestation he hath all quarrels,

---

† *Psalm 15*

wars, wrongs, hurts, outrages, and oppressions, which men shall do each unto other. For this is no small matter, that God giveth his own name so to be used, and as it were, pawneth it. And when a Prince must give some of his children for hostage, he will do it with great difficulty and much ado: but our Lord giveth his own Name for hostage, when there is cause of nourishing peace amongst us, yea and when the matter stands so, that Concord must be had with infidels, to the end they may leave off to rage against us, and not hurt us. Seeing then God hath vouchsafed [*permitted*] to lend his own Name to this purpose, so much the more ought we to be bent, to seek by all the means that can be, that men may be peaceable, and that we have no quarrels with them, yea that we seek to appease them that are raised up: we must (as much as lieth in us) prevent them: but yet if we cannot altogether perform it, when we shall see any quarrels begun, we should endeavor to kill it: yea by the means that I have already spoken of: that is to say, by forgoing outright, as much as shall be possible for us. This then is the sum of that we have to learn. Now it is not said in this place, in what form they swear: but we shall find afterwards, that Isaack always made his oath unto the living and everlasting God, rendering honor unto him to whom it belonged, albeit he had to do with heathen people, who had forged idols and corrupted the true service of GOD through their own superstitions: yet continued he in his own soundness. Thereupon it is said, that his servants being returned, (as we expounded yesterday) they said unto him: We have found living water. And after he addeth concerning Esau:

*That he took a wife from among the Hethites, yea
two wives: which were bitter to the souls of Isaack
and Rebecca.*

Here we see on the one side, how God would
comfort his servant every way: For it was not only showed
him that he should be assured from thenceforth that none
should hurt him: seeing the king himself of the country was
come to seek to him: but also he had water given him,
which he might enjoy peaceably and quietly as his own.
When therefore our Lord showeth this great favor towards
Isaack, let us know that he tempteth not him above their
strength, but always sweeteneth their afflictions in such
sort, that they shall not be as it were ever oppressed and
quite overthrown: and let us hope, that altogether like as
Isaack was upholden, and that God after he had afflicted
him, looked also again unto him to give him somewhat
wherewith to comfort him, so likewise must we wait, and
then we shall not be deceived, if we rest there. For God
knoweth our frailty, and there is no doubt but he will
always give us such taste of his mercy and favor, that we
shall have good cause to bless his name, and have no
occasion to grieve ourselves in such sort, that we know not
how to comfort ourselves anymore in him. But the
principal point is, that Esau took two wives from among the
Hethites. Here we begin to see already that Esau was not
only once profane, but that he went on in that course, and
gave himself wholly thereto, as we have showed heretofore,
that after he had well filled his belly with the pottage, that
Jacob his brother had prepared for him, and when he had
eaten and drunk, he went his way, and despised his

birthright. Moyses also rehearseth now that he took two wives from amongst the Hethites: for if he had had any remorse within him, and that he had esteemed the promise of the spiritual inheritance made unto his father, it is certain, that he would have holden himself as separate from all those people. For he knew full well, how his grandfather Abraham had behaved himself in that point, that he had made his servant to swear solemnly, that he should not take a wife for his son Isaack in the land of Canaan: he knew that his mother was sought after, in a far country, in Mesopotamia, because god would have this house as it were apart, and would not have it mingled and mashed with those of that country. What doth he therefore, when he taketh two wives of the inhabitants of Canaan, whom God had accursed? This was as much as if he had forsaken the promise of salvation, and as though he had renounced, to make anymore reckoning thereof than if it had not been worth a straw. Lo one testimony already how Esau made himself unworthy of his birthright: and this came to pass because he was not governed by the spirit of God, as also we have showed before, that God will so hold in and keep his elect, and in such sort ratify and seal in their hearts his goodness and fatherly adoption, that they shall soar up to him, and despise this world, to the end they may rejoice in those spiritual benefits he hath prepared for them: but contrariwise, he letteth loose the reigns to all those whom he hath rejected, in such sort, that they harden themselves: and although this be not done all at once at the first push, yet notwithstanding a man shall find in the end, that there is no seed of the fear of God, nor of godliness in them. This therefore is the thing we have to bear away upon this place.

And hereupon let us learn in suchwise to behave ourselves, that always we labor to sunder ourselves from them, that would draw us to destruction: For it is without all doubt, that if we live overfamiliarly with the contemners of god, they will soon defile us: their fellowship and conversation is a deadly pestilence. And so much the rather it behooveth us to walk with carefulness herein, taking good heed unto ourselves that we defile not ourselves with the filthiness of this world. And let us in the mean season acknowledge, that it is also a wonderful providence of God, that he would have Esau to take two wives in this country: For this was to this end, that he might be as it were cut off from the house of his father Isaack: he loved him dearly, and although his wives vexed him, yet for all that he could not withdraw his heart from Esau, knowing notwithstanding that God had rejected him. And herein he resisted God, without ever thinking upon the matter: but God wrought therein after another manner. When he saw such infirmity in his servant Isaack, he brought to pass in the end, that he must utterly forsake his son Esau. Mark then how god ruled all in such sort, that his church continued always in her smallness, as it were hidden under the earth, as though it had been nothing: there remained no more but Jacob, as we shall see oftentimes, and Isaack was half spent: he was three score years old, when his children were born, and now was Esau of the age of forty years when he took his wives: Isaack therefore was very old. And concerning Jacob, he was also forty years old, and yet was not married. And where then was this stock? It should seem that the Church must quite perish, and all the promises of God be utterly abolished: but although it were so small, that it was contemptible in men's judgments, yet we see that God so well governed his Church, that it remained pure and sound, and that which was profane was cut off from it: as if a house should be swept, and the sweepings be cast out of doors. So fell it out that Esau was rejected, and that Jacob remained alone, as also the heritage was appointed to him.

But now let us fall down before the high majesty of our good God, with acknowledging of our faults, and praying him, that he will make us to feel them in such sort, that it may serve to make us continually to mourn before him, and to ask pardon thereof in such sort, that we may labor to resist it, and more and more be withdrawn from it, until we shall be thoroughly clothed with his righteousness. And that he will support us in our weaknesses, so as we leave not off to call upon him as our father, although we fall many ways. So let us all say, O almighty God, heavenly father, etc.

❧The eleventh Sermon of

Jacob and Esau, Genesis 27.

3.   *Nowe it came to paſſe when Iſaack was very olde, and his eyes began to be darke that hee could not ſee, that calling Eſau his elder ſonne, he ſaid vnto him: My ſonne, who ſaid vnto him, Loe here I am.*

4.   *Then he ſaide, Behold nowe, I am waxed olde, & I know not the day of my death:*

5.   *Therfore take thy implements vnto thee, I pray thee, thy bowe and quiuer: and goe into the fields, and hunt ſome veniſone for me.*

6.   *And prouiding ſome delicate diſhes for me, euen as I loue, bring them vnto me, that I may eate, and my ſoule may bleſſe thee before I die.*

7.   *(Nowe Rebecca heard Iſaack when hee ſpake thus vnto Eſau) Eſau went therefore into the fielde to hunt veniſon which he would bring.*

8.   *But Rebecca ſpake vnto Iacob her ſonne, ſaying: Loe I heard thy father ſpeaking vnto Eſau thy brother, ſaying:*

9.   *Bring mee veniſon, and prouide mee ſome daintie diſhes which I may eate, afterwardes I will bleſſe thee before Iehoua, before I die.*

E SAW YESTERDAY, HOW ESAU by his marriage, showed sufficiently enough, that he had no great care concerning that blessing which had been promised to the house of Abraham his father: For this was the stock which must possess the land of Canaan. It must therefore needs be, that the people which dwelled there then, must be quite rooted out: and this land be wholly dedicated to the people of God. Likewise, it must be purged from all pollutions. Lo how Esau mingleth himself amongst them, whom God had already condemned: this therefore was a sign that he was fallen from God, for otherwise he could not have drawn near to that people. And if he would have been an heir of the promise, he should have always kept himself as one listed [*pleased*] and chained in, and not have mingled himself, which was no other thing but to stop the course of the grace that was promised. But as we have seen, he took wives from amongst the Hethites. Mark then how he renounced, as much as lay in him the grace of God, through which the whole stock of Abraham must possess the land of Canaan for an inheritance. But there was yet a second fault: For he took two wives, which was contrary to the law of marriage, as we have seen. For the sentence which God had pronounced to rest upon, was, that a man shall *have an help*, and not two nor three. And further, when Eva was created, and that she was given to Adam, it is said[†], *that they should be two in one flesh*. Mark then the rule which men

---

† *Genesis 2:24*

ought always to keep. So then we see that Esau even brake the bounds of all honesty, yea of nature itself, and that he was as a beastly man in this behalf. It is true that his grandfather Abraham had two wives: but herein he was to be condemned.

And besides it was not his desire that provoked him thereunto: but, his wife through overmuch haste, brought him to it. And when everything shall be well weighed, it was an inconsiderate zeal that he had to enjoy that which God had promised him: that is to say, that his seed should be blessed. Now he had no children. He took therefore a second wife: but this was (as I have said,) to pervert the order that God had established. He committed evil therein: but in Esau what can we allege, but that he was a dissolute man, and had nothing but vice and wickedness in him, so that he could not distinguish between marriage and whoredom? And this is the cause that he took two wives. Now it is very true that in this time, marriage was ill kept amongst the peoples of the East: For they were always much given to their fleshly lusts: in such sort, that beyond that which is called polygamy (that is to say, plurality of wives,) they committed incests also very commonly. And this was a nation very beastly in this point, that they made no accompt [*account*] to profane marriage: but this custom doth not therefore excuse Esau. And so, let us mark well, that this shall be no excuse before God, when we shall say that every man doeth so, and that we have a great sort of companions: let us not think to be free thereby before him. Notwithstanding when vices do reign in a country, and men make a law against them, if some neglect them, every man flattereth himself, and every man taketh for his warrant those which have led him to destruction. And (say they) such and such do it well, and after when men come unto them, and say to them: wherefore do you so? O see such a one did it well. But we shall all be put in a bundle together, and God knoweth very well how to writhe [*twist, intertwine*] us up altogether like thorns, when we shall make a cloak of their vices, who ought when they do evil to be an example unto us, to make us flee them. But notwithstanding all this, that Isaack is yet blinded with the love of his son Esau: he saw him now too degenerate out of kind, because that he wallowed (as it were) a Swine upon a dunghill, because he made a covenant with those people whom God had rejected: and farther perverted the order and institution of marriage: yet notwithstanding his father beareth all this. It is said, that the wives of Esau did as it were spur him, and that his heart was wounded therewith: but so it is, that the love of his son did always hold him back.

Now there might well be some virtue: but this meaneth not that everything was therefore praiseworthy in him: no he wanted [*lacked*] much in that behalf. For he should have had his son, how old soever he had been in detestation, forasmuch as he was so estranged from God, and because as much as lay in him, he had made the promise of salvation of no effect. For what might have become of the Church, if the stock of Abraham had been joined with those people? Isaack therefore ought to have been more touched, to see his son so profane. And seeing he saw this beastliness in him, that he made no matter of it, to have two wives: and he would have had them by dozens, if he had been able to have kept them. When therefore he beareth with these faults in his son, it is very certain that he

offended God.   For unless fathers use severity and
correction when need requireth, when they see their
children to be so wicked they are guilty, inasmuch as they
fail in doing their duty.   Our Lord hath given them
authority over their houses and offspring.   And wherefore,
unless it be to the end to keep them in awe and to restrain
them, that they may render an account, when any evil shall
be committed in their family?   Lo then a fault shameful
enough in Isaack: but yet he exceedeth farther in doting so
upon his son Esau.   It is said, that his eyes began to fail
him, forasmuch as his sight was dim: but it is certain that
this foolish love which he bare to his eldest son blinded
him, much more than his age, or the lack of his bodily
senses: For he ought to have marked (as the truth was) that
God had preferred Jacob before Esau, and yet nevertheless
he resisteth it, as we have seen before, when it was said that
he loved Esau, and that Rebecca loved Jacob: and this love
of hers was an obedience that she yielded unto that
heavenly revelation.   For GOD had pronounced this
sentence before, *That the elder should serve the younger.*
Rebecca was a great deal better advised than her husband.
But he continueth still as we may see in this place, and it
seemeth that he would have resisted God.   It is very certain
that his purpose was not such: But he is in suchwise
ravished by his affection, that he forgot himself, and had no
discretion and judgment.

   And hereby we may see, how we ought always to
suspect our affectionate passions.   For they rush upon us
always to butt against God.   As a Bull chased pusheth with
his horns, so our appetites and desires drive us, and ravish
us, in suchwise, that we make war most notoriously against

god, yea without ever thinking upon it: it never cometh into our memory, This is forbidden me, God hath condemned and rejected it. We have therefore many times our senses so incumbered, that we keep not either the way or the path. And hereof we see an example in Isaack. For all the time of his life, he was as a looking glass of holiness, and led as it were an Angel's life, keeping himself in the fear of god: but herein so faulteth, that god is nothing with him. He treadeth under his foot that which he had understood by his wife: that is, that now the right of the firstborn was given unto Jacob. Nevertheless he passeth beyond that. Now this is a wonderful strange thing for he was notwithstanding the minister of god, and a prophet: and as soon as he had charge to give the blessing to him to whom God had ordained it, yet he dealeth as if he had been the keeper and appointer thereof. God had done him this honor, as if he should have said, I will bless him whom I shall think good: but the testimony shall come out of thy mouth. Thou shalt be a messenger: especially that which thou pronounceth, shall have authority of justice: it shall be authentic, which I will ratify in heaven. God had done him this honor: and yet he leaveth himself to be so snared in ignorance, that he goeth quite contrary, specially from his duty, and from that which his office required. This at the first show should seem a thing intolerable: but God, who by his wonderful counsel directed him in such sort in this matter, that he turned darkness into light, and showed that this was not a thing according to man's fantasy, that the inheritance of salvation should come unto this man or to that man: but that in despite of all men, he must have it to whom it was ordained and established to hold it, and that it must have his effect. But because all things cannot be understood at once, let us follow that order in rehearsing of it, which Moyses useth, and afterwards we will gather in the end, the profit that this History bringeth unto us. It is said that Isaack seeing himself now to draw towards his end, forasmuch as he was transitory. He saith unto his son Esau:

> *I know not the day of my death: and therefore go*
> *and hunt Venison that thou mayest provide me*
> *meat according to my appetite, and which I love,*
> *and my soul shall bless thee,*

Isaack in saying that he knew not the day of his death, signifieth, that he saw himself to draw near to the grave already: For there is none that knoweth the day of his death. God would always hold us in suspense and doubt concerning this, to the end we might always be ready. Death (as it is said in the common proverb) is sure to all, but the hour of death is unknown unto us: and this is very profitable for us: for we see how men are given to their pleasures and are merry whiles that they think to have some truces or some release. And what should this be, if we knew certainly of the end of our life? Everyone would bend himself to all kind of evil, and God should be despited even to the end. But when our Lord holdeth us short in such sort, that from the womb of our mother we are still besieged with death: as we see of young infants, who die before they come into the world: so far is it off, that we cannot live even the minute of an hour, but that as soon as we are born we are subject to death, as our frailty declareth. For with what a number of diseases are we compassed? And to how many dangers and hazards is our life subject? So then, there is neither young nor old that should not say by good right, that he knoweth not when he shall die but the meaning of these words is as I have said: to wit, that Isaack knew well that he could not continue in the world. And indeed, although young people and they which are strong and in the flower of their age, ought to prepare themselves to forsake the world, and every hour to die, while they live: yet do we most fail herein, albeit our nature warneth us to give ourselves no more to the world. So that we have to gather of this drift of Isaack, that as every man seeth himself weak and transitory, so that he draw his legs after him, where he hath lived long, that this (I say) should stir us up so much the more to prepare ourselves to die. Now it is very true that he spake here to no other end, but to bless Esau: but so much this admonition importeth, that when we see death to approach, that we learn freely to yield up ourselves into the hands of God, and to glorify his name in such obedience, that we live no longer to ourselves: and after we shall have disposed of everything in such sort, that there be nothing that hold us or let us, from going cheerfully forwards when we shall be called. But when he speaketh of the blessing, this is not to be understood of common prayer. For there is no doubt, but that Isaack prayed everyday for his children: and it is said here: *That I may bless thee before my death.* We may then gather that this blessing whereof Isaack speaketh, was had in special regard: and indeed (as I have said) Isaack was as it were the warden and keeper of God's promise: and this treasure was committed into his charge and credit, to bless. And mark why the Apostle saith[†], *The lesser was blessed of the greater*, because it must needs be, that in this case he must have his authority from God. This was declared more plainly in the time of the law: For the priests were ordained, not only to teach the people, and to offer up sacrifices: but also to bless, and the very form thereof was set down unto them. And oftentimes when Moyses speaketh of this office, he setteth the Priests whom God had chosen to bless. But they do this, in respect of their own persons, no otherwise than as figures: but this was to show that it belonged to our Lord Jesus Christ, to be a witness unto us of the blessing of God, and to ratify it towards us: as also he showed when he ascended into Heaven, and that his hands were lifted up, he blessed his disciples. He showeth therefore that the truth and substance of these figures of the law, was fulfilled in him. Now he was so, before the law was written: for God would that Abraham should be the father of the church: and for this cause he blessed Isaack, as if the heritage had been resigned to him, which had been promised to him. Isaack now must do the like: for he received not the blessing for himself, but to the end it should always remain in his house. He must therefore be the minister of the grace of God: as we yet see at this day, that he communicateth his benefits and spiritual gifts amongst us, by the hand of those whom he hath ordained to this purpose. Men therefore cannot forgive us our sins, and yet nevertheless our Lord Jesus Christ useth this figure of speaking: *To whomsoever you shall forgive their*

---

† *Hebrews 11:20*

sins, they shall be forgiven. Now yet for all that he hath reserved this to himself as he protesteth in Esay: *O Jacob it is I and none others that take away thine iniquities.* Now albeit God alone hath this power to forgive sins, and to purge us from our spots: yet nevertheless, he doth this by the hand of men. We have in Baptism an infallible token that GOD will not lay our offences to our charge: but that we are as righteous and clean before him: and farther we have an earnest, that he will renew us by his holy spirit, to the end we should walk in all purity. Now this cannot be given us of men: but yet GOD maketh them herein as instruments, and all through his favor. Again, Is it in the power of any mortal creature, to make us partakers of the body and blood of our Lord Jesus Christ? And yet nevertheless in the supper when the bread and the wine are distributed, it is certain that this is not a vain and empty figure, but that all is accomplished, and that our Lord Jesus Christ showeth himself faithful in this: For it is he which giveth it: and it were too much to attribute it to those who are and can do nothing, to say, that they have our Lord Jesus Christ to communicate to them which come unto them to receive a morsel of bread, and a drop or two of wine. And indeed this is well showed unto us, when he saith[†]: *My flesh is bread from heaven.* And he giveth it after two sorts: one is, that which he gave, when he offered up himself to his father for the cleansing of sins. *The bread which I will give unto you* (saith he) *is my flesh which I will give for the life of the world.*

Lo then two kinds of giving: for he gave his flesh,

---

† *John 6:51*

when he offered it up for the satisfaction of all our faults, to the end that God might be appeased towards us, and that we might be released to become righteous. Now the second giving is that which he maketh daily. Now if it belong to Jesus Christ to give himself unto the faithful, who receive him by faith, it followeth then that this ought not to be attributed to men, not as though they had this power: but only that Jesus Christ surceaseth [*ceases, desists*] not to apply this thereto. And thus it hath been in all times: For God hath evermore reserved to himself the praise of men's salvation: but this letteth [*hindereth*] not, but that these may be instruments by whom he worketh. Lo then how this maketh for Isaack, to show that he must pronounce the sentence of the blessing whereunto he was ordained. And indeed we see this in the doctrine of the Gospel: for what is the preaching of the Gospel? *It is the power of God to salvation to all believers* (saith Saint Paul[†]:) and there he speaketh of that word which proceedeth from our mouth. What, the power of God? Why, it is nothing in itself. It is true: but it pleaseth God to display his power by the means of men, and would that his word should have such effect and power in the working, that it be as it were a key to open unto us the kingdom of heaven: as also he hath compared it to the keys of the kingdom of Heaven.

So then, let us mark well that Isaack speaketh not here of any common blessing: that is to say of prayer, as when we bless one another and when we pray that God will show mercy to our neighbors, and that he will give them

---

† *Romans 1:16*

that which he knoweth to be fit for them. And thus much concerning blessings. But Isaack knew that he was ordained the minister of God to dispense that treasure that was committed to his charge. And this is worthy to be noted, to the end that we have not the doctrine that is preached unto us, knowing what it importeth. For there are many fantastical men[†] that refuse all inferior means, and would without wings mount up above the clouds. And is not God, say they, sufficient to teach us? Is it not he that giveth faith? And is the holy Ghost in the hands of men? what need have we to be preached unto? And to what end is it to read so much? All this is superfluous: For God can sufficiently inspire us, without having our ears so battered with the tongue. For he hath all that is needful for our benefit and salvation: and he will bring it to pass. And must men then hold him as it were bound to them? And must the power of his spirit be mashed and mingled with those inferior means as though he were not at liberty? Lo what these fantastical spirits say. Now they consider not that God is not tied and bound to men, when he useth their service: for he doth it as it seemeth good unto him. It is true that faith ordinarily cometh by hearing, as Saint Paul saith: so that we cannot have faith unless it be by men. And cannot God as well do it otherwise? The question here is not of the power of God but of his will, and of that which he hath ordained. And therefore when we shall say, And cannot God do this and that? he can do it: but seeing he will that it be otherwise, we ought to rest there. So then, let

---

† *These be the Anabaptists that refuse the ministry of the word, and will be taught immediately from God.*

us learn to receive this doctrine which is daily taught us, with all reverence, knowing that when we shall have this testimony, that our sins are forgiven us, all is ratified in heaven: as if God himself should speak: For he will not have us to esteem his truth according to men, who are brickle and liars and amongst whom there is nothing but vanity: but he will have his truth esteemed for itself sake, and for its own nature. And in the meantime, let us have this sobriety and modesty therein, to submit ourselves to the order which he hath established. And thus much concerning this word of blessing.

Now here Moyses beginneth to rehearse how Rebecca found out a subtlety and craft to rob Esau of his blessing, and to translate it to Jacob: and after that we have spoken of the vices of Isaack, we see the like in his wife Rebecca: and yet nevertheless they both believed in God: notwithstanding that it was so darkened and bewrapped [*wrapped up*], that it could hardly be discerned. That Isaack had a true faith: and that this proceeded from a true zeal, it appeareth plainly: For if he had not been thoroughly persuaded hereof in himself, that the heritage should be given him which was promised to him, and to his seed concerning this blessing: What had this been? Surely but a crafty part and a thing of nought. Isaack therefore must needs be resolved, howsoever he saw himself as it were already in the grave, his life to be spent, and to have but a day to live: howsoever this were, yet nevertheless he always held this sure which was said unto him: to wit, that his family should be blessed, and that GOD had chosen him, and that this was not in vain, and that albeit he saw not the fulfilling of these promises in this world, yet

notwithstanding that god was in heaven, and that neither
he nor his should be deceived: but yet they must wait for
this. Wherefore Isaack having sought all the time of his life
against all the temptations which might have overthrown
him, doeth yet in death persevere in faith and patience, and
doth this honor unto God that he doth boldly trust in him.
For whosoever trusteth in God shall never be confounded.
Isaack had this, and this was a very excellent faith. For see
a poor wayfaring man: it is said unto him, *thou shalt be the
heir of this country*, and yet notwithstanding he had no water
to drink as we have seen. Now notwithstanding death doth
threaten him: yet knoweth he not when it shall be, saving
that he is altogether ready for it. And yet for all that he
despiseth both Satan and the world, and remaineth
steadfast in this, that God will not deceive him: and that it
is all one to him whether he die, or whether he molder in
the ground: so that the truth of God may yet continue, and
have his full virtue and power. Lo Isaack then who seeketh
not for the world, but forsaketh all his senses and remaineth
steadfast: and doubteth not but that god had mercy on him
and on his stock. Herein as I have said we have good cause
to praise him: and yet in the meantime he was so blinded
with the love of his son, that he fought against God, though
he never once thought thereof. This was not a manifest
rebellion nor of willful malice: but it was because he was
sluggish and knew not his office but in part. He knoweth
very well that God would advance him to such a dignity,
that he might be the messenger and witness of this blessing:
He knoweth this, and notwithstanding on the contrary part
he is deceived. He had therefore in this case a particular
Faith: he had a good zeal mingled with the affections of the

flesh.

But let us come to Rebecca. Rebecca behaved herself here with with foolish rashness: for what an attempt was it, for the blessing of God, to be profaned through craft and lying? yea, (I say) lying so foul as nothing could be more. The matter was here of the salvation of the world, the question was of having Jesus Christ whom GOD should send for a Redeemer. But how proceedeth Rebecca therein? It is certain that a thing of such importance ought to be handled with all fear and lowliness: what a thing is it then that she cometh so foolishly to attempt that which seemeth good unto her, in so excellent a work of GOD and which surmounteth all others? For Rebecca knowing well that the blessing which she sought for he son Jacob imported that he should be head of the Church during his life, and that of him should come our Lord Jesus Christ: doth notwithstanding overthrow it, that she careth not to lie, to falsify, to pervert all: and also it seemeth, that she setteth out the grace of God but in a mockery and contempt: For this was to make it to be basely esteemed, to say, that it should come bewrapped [*wrapped up*] about the neck of her son, and in the hands of skins, coloring that he is hairy, and seeming to rob Esau of all his ornaments: and again that she maketh her son to lie: and farther Jacob, who went to seek a Kid which she causeth to be fod [*fed*], and maketh him believe that it is Venison: And after that he had the smell of the garments of Esau: to be short it might be said that she would have overthrown the election of God.

Lo therefore very foul faults, and yet all this proceedeth from an excellent faith, if ever there were any. This is very strange: But we may easily judge it. Whereto then had Rebecca regard? She loved her Son Jacob, and what should it avail him to have been blessed through deceit? For this was neither to get him riches nor profit in respect of the world: yea which is more she layeth him open to the wrath and curse of his Father: Again she knew Esau who was full of venom, full of fierceness, spite and wrath: and indeed we shall see afterwards, that Jacob was in danger of his life: Rebecca knew all these things, notwithstanding she setteth fire on her house, where she might have kept her darling with her, to have been always with him, to have administered that unto him which he might have needed in the world, without putting him in any such danger. But what did she? she had printed this in her heart that the birthright belonged unto Jacob, as GOD had promised her, and so she would obey God, and esteem this birthright, although it was nothing accounted of amongst men: as we shall afterwards find, that Jacob called Esau his Lord, that he humbled himself before him, yea, even to the bowing of the knee.

Now although that this same birthright were worth nothing in respect of the world, yet doth Rebecca greatly esteem it. See then undoubted and sure testimonies of a great and exquisite faith which was in her, that she would obey God in despite both of her husband and all that he had: so that she might execute that which God had pronounced, she passed not: And that she esteemed these spiritual blessings more than anything which was in the world. Lo then the undoubted marks of her faith, she had so great zeal that she forgot herself and regarded not any whit whatsoever mischief might come upon it. And why so? forasmuch as she conformed herself to the will of God: and forsook her eldest son, and cast off all motherly affection: and knowing that he must be cut off: very well saith she, let him go as a rotten member forasmuch as God hath so ordained. We see here in Rebecca notable virtues mingled with vices.

And hereby we are admonished to walk in fear, albeit that God give us a singular affection to meditate upon him, notwithstanding we shall always be in such sort bewrapped [*wrapped up*] in darkness, that when we imagine to do the best we can in the world, yet there shall be cause for us to amend when GOD shall call us to a reckoning. And in good sooth [*in truth*], there is not anyone which doth not prove this to be true: for although that this be our mark, to strive thither whether God hath called us, yet do we make so many false steps that it is great pity to see: and they which run more swiftly to bring themselves in order to God, yet for all that, they go out of the way and have may outlopes and crosspaths, and God suffereth them to the end that we should not have whereof to be proud. For if virtues themselves be faulty before God, alas what shall those vices be which are altogether condemned? Do we labor to do well, do we enforce ourselves thereunto: yet notwithstanding we shall offend GOD. And why so? It is because there is such infirmity in us, and we are wrapped in ignorance: Although that GOD enlighten us, and that we see the way well, notwithstanding, yet such clouds do oftentimes come before our eyes, that instead of keeping of our way, we stray either on the one side or on the other.

Mark how faulty the virtues of the faithful are, to the end that we may learn, only to rest ourselves in the mere goodness of God, and to the end it would please him to pardon our offences, and also to accept that for righteousness which he might justly condemn. How then is it that our works are acceptable unto God? how is it that he calleth sacrifices of a sweet smelling savor, and that they are so acceptable before him, that they shall have a reward? Alas, it is not any merit as the Papists imagine: but it is because that God hath justified that, which he might rightly reject, and accompt [*account*] as it were abominable. So let us mark that in the faith of Isaack, we may behold the imperfections which are in us, whiles that we live in this world, albeit that God have renewed us in part by his holy spirit, and again let us know that God worketh in such sort that the evil which is in us, hindreth not him to accomplish his work even by our mean. As for example, If we will search till we find an Angelical perfection in a mortal man, there shall never any be found that hath it, neither was ever any found who was not tainted with some kind of fault: and therefore the Priests which were figures and representations of our Lord Jesus Christ, first of all asked pardon for their offences, although that they made intercession for the people, and were as it were mediators, and that by their sacrifices they abolished sins: yet notwithstanding must they begin at themselves. But now by the way if we will seek ministers of the word, in whom there is no fault it is certain that we cannot find any: and it must needs be that the most excellent men be examples unto us, of the brickleness [*fragility, brittleness*] and weakness of men. But now if we will conclude: and how then shall I find my salvation by their means? For I see yet that they are full of imperfections. But let us learn (as I have said) in the person of Isaack that God leaveth not off to accomplish his work, although there be yet ignorance in them, who out to lead us, who when they distribute unto us spiritual gifts, which they have committed unto them, and whereof GOD hath made them keepers, although they be not altogether such as they ought to be: notwithstanding we leave not off to make our profit of them: for God useth and ordereth them in such sort in this work which he will do, that his grace is no whit hindered, because a man might find things to be bettered in them. This therefore is the thing that we have yet to mark upon this place. But to be short, we see that the faith of the children of God shall oftentimes be weak and entangled, not as the papist have imagined: for they call an entangled faith beastliness, when a man shall say, O, I believe in my mother's god: I know not what the whole Christianity meaneth: But lo it is enough for me to go simply to work: and I believe as our holy mother the Church believeth: and indeed the wiser sort of Priests will say, I believe in the god of my Chambermaid: because she believeth in god who maketh Cabbages to grow after that she hath planted them. See the implicity and folded faith of the Papists, which is a very sorcery of the Devil: but the entangled faith of the children of GOD, is because they be holden in ignorance. But yet notwithstanding there is some light: but what is that faith? It is an understanding which we have of the goodness and favor of GOD, after that he hath illuminated us by his holy spirit and by his word. For faith cannot be without these two things: that is to say, without the word of God: I say as God hath set in order in his church: and after it cannot be without he gift of the spirit: For the word of god should be preached unto us both morning and evening, and we can profit nothing therein, unless God do open our ears and enlighten us, forasmuch as we are miserable blind ones. The Sun shall always shine upon us: but they that are blind discern not between the day and the night, to them both are alike. And even so is it with us: that if GOD illuminate us not within, when he sendeth his holy word, to show us the way, we should always remain as poor strays, or lost sheep.

So then, it behooveth that our faith have light in itself: but yet I say, that this light is compassed and entangled with great darkness: For we behold not God face to face, and we are not capable to comprehend his secrets: and this is sufficient that we know them in part, and that we have some taste of that which shall be revealed unto us in perfection, than when we shall put off our flesh, and shall be translated into that heavenly glory, to be companions of Angels. Lo then briefly what we have to learn upon this place, to wit, that our faith, although it be great and exquisite, yet nevertheless it shall always have some weakness, and some imperfection and ignorance mingled with that, which God hath given us to know. Now hereof we may gather, that when the scripture pronounceth that we are justified and saved by faith, it meaneth not, that it is by the desert of faith: For if it were so that our salvation were founded upon the dignity of faith, then must our faith be perfect. For if our faith be weak (as I have already said) and that we have but only a part of it, then should we have but a part of salvation: and further it should be shaken, and we should always be wavering and in doubt. But when it is said that we are saved by faith, it is because we accept the mercy of god, which we ought to esteem fully sufficient for our salvation. Our faith is imperfect: yea but when there shall be never so little a spark, yet nevertheless shall the

goodness of God supply that which is wanting [*lacking*]:
even as we now bear this corrupt lump, not only in our
bodies, but in our whole nature. But we know that our
souls go unto death, and in the mean season where is our
life? It is in us. How? In that we have received the spirit of
God, saith Saint Paul in the eighth chapter to the Romans[†].
And have we the spirit of God in fullness? No not so: There
is as it were but one spark or drop of it: but this saith he is
life: and shall swallow up all whatsoever belongeth to death
in us, and shall make it of no effect. Let us mark then that
although our faith be very little, and that in respect of us we
conceive not the hundredth part of the benefits which God
offereth unto us, yea and that we do not so much as by a
lick, taste his grace, yet nevertheless we must not therefore
despair to be saved through faith. For the matter is not as
I have said, of our estimation, or of our paising and
weighing it in our balance, that is to say, if we have an
excellent faith to obtain the grace of God, and that which is
necessary for our salvation: but the question only is, that
when God hath declared that he will be our father, that we
embrace this promise, and stay ourselves thereupon. And
if there be any doubts or distrusts, that we resist them, and
that we hold this conclusion, O we are yet sure that God
will not disappoint us. Mark then what we have here to
hold, as well by the example of Rebecca, as by the example
of Isaack. But Moyses saith now expressly that Jacob
refused, saying:

---

† *Romans 8:1-27*

*And how shall this be? I am not hairy as my
brother is, and if my father shall find the deceit, he
will curse me.*

Here we see as it seemeth, two great vices in Jacob:
The one is, that he feared his father more than God. It is
true that it might so be judged thereof: but when all shall be
well marked, it is certain, that it was the fear of God that
moved him thereunto. For concerning the curse of his
father, he was no otherwise careful of it, than in this, that
it was imprinted in his heart, that his father was established
to be as it were a witness of the promise which God had
given unto him. Seeing therefore that Jacob had this, it is
a sign that he rested not upon anything from man: but that
in the person of his father he considered that which God
had decreed. The other evil was, that he doubted. Now we
know that in our life if we be not well certified, we shall not
remove so much as one finger, to the end we sin not, and
that God be not offended. And why so? Obedience is more
worth than sacrifice. When therefore we shall attempt to
do anything, not knowing whether it be lawful for us, and
whether God do allow it: this is as much as if we should
despise God: so that we should not know how to eat or to
drink, or to be short, to do anything: no not so much as to
remove a mote, but that all our actions should be
condemned, and that god should have them in utter
detestation: and Saint Paul also pronounceth it. For by this
word of faith he understandeth certainty in the fourteenth

to the Romans[†] that we be assured that that which we do is
permitted of God, and is agreeable to his word. But see
Jacob who saith, how shall this be? I am not hairy as my
brother is. He doubteth: that therefore is a sign that after
that he hath obeyed his mother, he should commit evil, and
that all that he should take in hand, should be nothing but
confusion, and that god would detest it. And surely so had
it been if he had always remained doubtful, that whatsoever
he should have done, being of sin, it should have been to
provoke the wrath of god: but we shall see by that which
followeth that he was confirmed. But the answer which his
mother giveth him, is:

The curse be upon me.

But she was not so lean and so dry as here she is set
forth unto us, but she showed him that he was chosen of
god, and that the birthright belonged unto him. And indeed
we shall see how he was confirmed, and that he feared no
more when he was before his father. Thus then it may
easily be gathered that Jacob was confirmed, to resolve
himself and to know that the blessing which he sought,
could not be disappointed: in the meantime
notwithstanding we cannot excuse him, but that he fell
foully, even in the very beginning. The matter was here of
the building of his house, but Jacob doubteth and sticketh
here, not knowing whether it were good or evil. We see
then that he had a very evil beginning: and consequently

---

† *Romans 14*

that he had nothing in that case but confusion, had not god holpen [*helped*] therein. To be short, we see as well in Jacob as in Isaack and in Rebecca, that the grace of God came not unto them, nor had any entry unto them by their own wisdom, nor by their good means which they invented. Lo therefore the defaults which are here: but god hath outgone all their faults and offences, and wrought in such sort through his infinite mercy, that we have good occasion to bow down our heads, and to confess that there is none but only he upon whom all our happiness dependeth, and from whom it proceedeth.

But now let us fall down before the Majesty of our good God, in acknowledging our faults, and beseeching him that he will open our eyes, that we may always more and more know them, to the end we flatter not ourselves in them: but that we may sigh and groan to obtain pardon of him: and in the meanwhile that we may in such sort fight against all our carnal desires, that in the end we may be full framed to his righteousness, from which we are yet so far off. And that he show not this grace only unto us, but also to all peoples and nations of the earth, etc.

❧The twelfth Sermon of

Jacob and Esau, Genesis 27.

13. *But Iacob ſayde vnto Rebecca his mother, Beholde my brother Eſau is a rough hairie man, but I am glib and of a ſmooth skinne.*

14. *Peraduenture my father will feele mee, and I ſhalbe vnto him, as a ſeducer: and ſo I ſhal bring vpon me a curſe and not a bleſſing.*

15. *Vnto whom his mother ſaide, Thy curſe be vpon me my ſonne: Only hearken vnto my voyce, and goe thy wayes and bring it vnto me.*

16. *Therefore departing hee tooke it and brought it vnto his mother: and his mother tooke it and made daintie diſhes, euen ſuch as his father loued.*

17. *Afterwardes Rebecca taking the moſt precious garments of Eſau her eldeſt ſonne, which were with her at home, ſhee put them vpon Iacob her yongeſt ſonne:*

18. *And putting vpon his handes the skinnes of kiddes from amongſt the Goates, and vpon the ſmooth of his necke:*

19. *Shee put the daintie diſhes which ſhee had made, with bread in the hande of her ſonne Iacob.*

20. *So hee comming vnto his father, ſaid, My father: who ſaide, Beholde me, who art thou my ſonne?*

21. *Iacob ſayde vnto his father, I am Eſau thine eldeſt*

*fonne, I haue done as thou haſt commaunded mee:
nowe riſing, ſit downe and eate of my veniſon, that thy
ſoule may bleſſe me, &c.*

E HAVE HERE TO CONTINUE the purpose
which was yesterday begone: that is, that
God directed Isaack, Rebecca, and Jacob, in
such sort, that notwithstanding the faults
that were in them, he leaveth not off to put that in
execution which he had determined, concerning the blessing
of Jacob and rejecting Esau. And yet this is not to clear
Isaack for his part, as though he had not foully faulted, and
that the like fault had not been found in Rebecca and in
Jacob: but God passed them over. And so, we see that
GOD waiteth not upon men, neither dependeth upon them,
when the matter standeth, for the performance of his
counsel. It is very true, that he will use them to serve his
turn: but he showeth notwithstanding that he worketh all
alone and of himself: and when his creatures serve him as
instruments, it is no farther than it pleaseth him, and not as
though he were bound by any necessity: yea and albeit that
things in respect of men go quite backward as it seemeth,
yet this showeth that his power is sufficient, so that it
needeth no help from others.

Now we have said, that in this matter of Jacob it
may be seen how he fell into doubt: and this was contrary
to faith. It behooveth therefore that GOD on the one side
supplied this want [*lack*]. Concerning that, that it is said
that he should bear the curse: it is for that he knew that his

father was ordained to this, that he must ordain an inheritor, not only for worldly and transitory benefits, but of the promise which belongeth to the spiritual life. He knew this: and therefore he respected not only a mortal man, but the living God. Now touching Rebecca, she saith, the Curse be upon her. We see how she was ravished (as was yesterday handled) in such sort, that she spake, as it were at random: but there is no doubt, that in the meanwhile she wist [*knew*] not, that this could do no hurt. It is true that she regarded not her fault. For although she had a good ground to obey GOD, and so to deal that his election might stand in full strength: yet notwithstanding she ought not in the mean season, to have made such a craft to bear sway, wherein there was nothing but deceits and lies. For GOD (as we have said already) is able enough to accomplish his own work, and to bring his own counsel to an end: he needeth not to borrow anything of us. It is not lawful therefore by a stronger reason, to go about to advance his truth by our lies. But Rebecca doth it: so that in this behalf she cannot be excused. But this example is not here set before our eyes, to the end that we also should imagine the like: For it will fall out, that at all assays we shall be ready to mingle our fantasies, that our matters may go well: and this is even as much as if we thought not God to be wise enough, or rather as if he were not strong enough, or had not the means in his own hand, to bring matters to a good end and issue. But in so doing, we do (as a man would say) control GOD: to say, very well, let him work, but after what manner? Not according to his counsel, and according to his power and infinite puissance: but according to some light thing, and we will first of all have that thing done, which we have imagined and forged in our own brain. For we will say, I find this to be good, this will be a very good and necessary means. But are we so overwise? that we must straightway enterprise this thing, and that we must put our hand to the pie in such sort. But mark, God hath not so ordained by his word. Lo then a rashness not to be born. And yet is this very common, and everyone shall find of this vice in his seed. But so much the rather ought we to learn to add nothing of our own, seeing we have always this corrupt medley which we must either this way or that way drive out of our heads. And when we shall so have wrought after our own guise and fashion, we shall do nothing else, but mat and overthrow all. But if GOD doth not lay such faults to our charge, and doth yet nevertheless accomplish his work: this is not to the end we should boast ourselves therein: as oftentimes they which have overreached themselves, can say, O, it is falne [*fallen*] out well: yea, but this is because GOD hath pardoned this folly, and that nevertheless he leaveth not to support us, albeit we were not worthy thereof. Let us learn therefore in no wise to excuse our presumptions, when God shall make that to prosper which we have naughtily and wickedly attempted: but so much the rather let us magnify his mercy, when we shall see that although we have fought against him, and have gone about as much as lay in us to forslow his work, that he yet hath not left off to give it his course. This is that briefly which we have to bear away concerning this place.

Now it followeth after, that Jacob went to seek two kids, which he brought unto his mother, that she might dress some dainty meat, such as she knew Isaack loved.

And after that she clothed Jacob with Esau's garments, and put the skins so upon him, that it seemed he was an hairy and rough man.

But here men might judge, that this was a very childish deed, and a very toy, forasmuch as it was a counterfeit meat, for she took of a kid, instead of some venison: and after that the father had eaten and was well filled, he blessed his son, and that this was as it were a reward for his dinner: and again that Jacob came in a disguised habit, as if he had been upon a stage counterfeiting his brother Esau, under color of his garments, and had his poll, his neck, and his hands: and in all this nothing was seen but matter of laughter. But to the end that we should be kept in reverence, and make our profit of this history, let us learn to look unto God's election whereof mention was made before: For if we have not this foundation, it is certain that in all that Moyses rehearseth, we shall not find anything that may move us, or give us any persuasion, that this was guided and governed form above. But when we shall be resolved, that GOD had given the birthright to Jacob before he was born: notwithstanding we have to note, in seeing these things so sottishly [*stupidly, foolishly*] ordered by men of an unadvised zeal, that therefore we cease not to say: Lo God who is always unchangeable, although men through their sturdy boldness, and foolish presumption trouble and turn all upside down, yet neverthless must his counsel remain entire and perfect. This therefore is that we have to note, to the end we may make our profit of this history. Moreover, when it is said: That Jacob came to his father, and said unto him: *I am thy son Esau, eat and drink.* Hereby we may see how men harden themselves, when they have once attempted to do anything of an unadvised zeal, how they wax bolder and bolder. At the first Jacob doubted: If I (saith he) be found as a mocker before my father, he will curse me, but by and by he careth for nothing, he speaketh as boldly and frankly, as if it should have been said, that he was sure to be in Esau's place. But hereby we have to note, before we begin anything, to think whether we have allowance from GOD, and whether he will guide us: and to see that in all our doing and enterprise, there be nothing but mere obedience. For if we begin once (as they say) to break our bounds, and that we imagine to do this and to do that, howsoever at the beginning we had some scruple and did make great difficulty thereof, in the end we shall shut our eyes and pass further: and when all the objections of the world shall come before our eyes, yet we shall become obstinate.

Forasmuch then as men are so hardened in their foolish and rash counsels, and that we see such a notable example thereof in our father Jacob, so much the rather (as I have said already) must we take heed that we move not a finger breadth, till we know whether GOD will allow that which we do, and that we have taken counsel of his word: For then we cannot be too bold, when we shall be subject unto him, and when there shall be no foolish overweening [*high opinion*] in us to follow our own fantasy. But we can do nothing of ourselves, how small soever it be, which is not too much. And therefore (as I have said,) let us learn to begin well, to the end, such an end may follow as we should desire. But in this which is here contained in Moyses, we may have a figure which shall not be unfit: and that is, that although Isaack was deceived, that Esau was not there, and that Jacob through his slights obtained his blessing, yet for all this, we have here an image of that blessing which is given unto us of GOD: For it is said in the first Chapter of the Ephesians[†], *That we are blessed with all heavenly graces and spiritual gifts.* And after what sort? Saint Paul addeth, *in Jesus Christ:* For if GOD should look upon our persons, we must be his enemies, and he must needs detest us by reason of sin. Seeing therefore it is so, it behooveth us to be blessed without ourselves: that is to say, in the person of our head.

And moreover, we must be clothed with the robe of our Lord Jesus Christ. For what can we bring, but altogether filthiness and pollution? We are wholly made in inquity: therefore we must be as stink before GOD: but when we are clad with the obedience of his only Son, O then, Lo a sweet savor, wherein we are acceptable unto him. So that although (as I have said already) in respect of men, there was nothing but confusion, (and as they say) all was jumbled together, yet nevertheless we may apply this to our profit. Jacob was a looking glass of the whole Church: and yet were we blessed in his person, as he was blessed in the person of his elder brother. For the question is not here, of finding it altogether like. If a man say that Esau resembled not Jesus Christ: it is very true: but yet in comparison, it needeth not that every part and parcel agree together: it is sufficient, that we see some agreement and likeness in part: as it is said, that the coming of our Lord Jesus Christ shall be as a thief in the night. And what? will he steal? It were

---

† *Ephesians 1:3*

a foolish thing to think thus: but it is enough that we see, that they which are asleep in the world shall be taken upon the sudden. So now when he speaketh of the birthright of Esau, and that Isaack represented the person of God, and that Jacob was blessed under the robe and countenance of his brother: herein we see, that that was accomplished which we alleged even now: to wit, that we shall be put back if we come in our own name, and in our own person, to get favor before God: but when we shall come there under the shadow of our Lord Jesus Christ, who is the firstborn amongst all the Children of God. See how we are received. But notwithstanding it is said:

> *That Isaack demanded, who art thou my son? I*
> *am thy son Esau?*

But herein he trusteth not himself, and though it may appear, that there was some fraud: For he saith unto him:

> *Come near unto me, that I may feel, whether thou*
> *be my son Esau or no.*

We see here that Isaack doubted, and yet nevertheless, the blessing ceased not in respect of god, to have his virtue and effect: as also it is said that he blessed him in the presence of God. But it is very true that if we have our eyes fastened upon Isaack, we shall say that this act was ill guided, and that he deserved not to be accounted in any degree of perfection: but that God wrought it, (as I have said) and not only when the inferior means failed, but when they were contrary, and that it seemed, that this had been utterly to abolish that, which was determined. But so much the rather it behooveth us well to note, that howsoever God use men in his work, and doth them this honor to serve therein as instruments, yet is there nothing on their part: and we may say: *He that planteth, and he that watereth is nothing*[†]. But here Isaack instead of planting and watering, did rather pluck up, and cut off the blessing of God to make it barren and without fruit. But howsoever it was, yet was God therein served. For whether he had planted or watered, he had done it but in part: but he did it not wholly and as he ought: and yet in the mean season (as I have said) the goodness of God surmounted, whatsoever was faulty and vicious in his creatures. Howsoever it were, we may well say that Isaack in doubting deserved to be deprived from that state and office which was given him, that is to say, that he had lost the grace of God, wherein the salvation of the whole world was included. Lo the treasure which was committed unto him: but he by his unbelief deserved to be stripped of it. But God would not so have it. And to whom shall we attribute this? It must needs be that his mercy be here magnified, seeing that in man there is not only not any help thereto, nor anything that answereth unto it, but quite against it. And yet let us note, that none was more dulled of God than he was. It is true that we saw before, that he had dim eyes, and that he was so weak with age, that he was as a man half dead: but yet this came not to pass naturally, that hearing the voice of Jacob, he was so

---

† *1 Corinthians 3:7*

foully deceived that he once thought not, There is some fraud in the matter. He doubteth thereof, and yet nevertheless goeth on, and albeit it were against his will, yet he blessed Jacob instead of Esau. It must needs be therefore that God dulled him, so that it was not of age only. And this is that which I have said, that God guided his work so, that although men hinder and let it and it seemeth to have been, as if they should draw quite contrary, nevertheless the end and issue was such, that it appeareth that God executed that which he had pronounced, following his secret election, which was made before the creation of the world. And so we know in all that Isaack did, there was nothing but a kind of sottishness [*stupidity, foolishness*], that he was so dull: he had no understanding, he discerned nothing, nor had any judgment, and yet notwithstanding God maketh this to prevail. After what manner? How is it that he maketh the bread which we eat to be of strength to nourish us? when we shall have well eaten and drunk and shall be refreshed and satisfied, so as he which neither can bow his arm nor his legs, shall have new strength to travel. Shall we say that this is because the bread hath any power, any life, or any moving? But when we see that the bread giveth us that which it hath not, and the corn and wine and other meats: this is to show us that God useth not his creatures in such sort, in any work that we should occupy ourselves in that which we see with our eye: but that we should always bend to this, that as he disposeth the order of nature, and likewise guideth and governeth us, yea and that against nature: that many times he will work quite contrary to that, that is accustomed unto us, in such sort that we shall be astonished thereat: and chiefly when the question is of our salvation. And yet must not we imagine that we bring anything thither for our part: but that it is God that must accomplish all, who began it and will perform it. And moreover if he work after a strange and unwonted manner, and that there be nothing but an outward show of folly: let us know (as Saint Paul saith†) that the *folly of God is greater wisdom, than all the wisdoms of the world.*

Now he calleth it the foolishness of God, after our opinion: because he worketh in a contemptible manner, that we might be ravished therein thinking, What is this that God will say? It seemeth that he jesteth and mocketh. We will conclude thereof even so. And this is the cause why Saint Paul saith, *that it is folly*, because men rest themselves upon their outward senses. But howsoever it be, this surpasseth all the wisdom of the world. Mark then what we have to bear away. And when we shall well remember this lesson here, we shall not be as a great sort of giddy heads, who take all these facts at adventure, and thereupon mock themselves, as though all that were here rehearsed by Moyses, were nothing else as a man would say, but foolish trifling.

But when we shall have learned this which is here showed us, by Saint Paul, it is certain that we shall have another manner of sobriety, and that we shall not give over to adore the secret of God, although at the first show he glorify not himself: but we shall always look to the beginning and to the end, and not to those means which may give us occasion, and engender [*beget*] in us some

---

† *1 Corinthians 1:25*

offence, or which may swallow us up. To be short, we see
that God directed Isaack in such sort that he was altogether
blind: we will not say therefore that god gave Isaack here
any fight to the end he might do that which appertained to
his office, knowing well the cause why, and knowing all the
proceeding of the matter: but he was blinded, and yet he
held him as it were by the hand, and led him as a blind man
which seeth nothing. And indeed we see in the Church,
something that answereth to this, or else comes very near it:
for (as it was said yesterday) *The preaching of the Gospel is the
power of God to salvation to all believers*[†]. When therefore we
preach the grace of God whereby we are reconciled,
inasmuch as our faults are pardoned us in our Lord Jesus
Christ, and that the blood which he shed for us, is the true
purgation thereof, to cleanse us: Lo then God who openeth
the Heavens, and calleth us unto himself, albeit the word
proceed from the mouth of a man. But in the mean season,
I know not to whom this shall be available: For everyone
shall be a witness of his own faith: and when I speak and
have not received my part therein, woe be upon me: and I
should be more than blind: as also they have been who shall
have preached the Gospel, and shall be witnesses of the
grace of God, and shall draw poor sinners to salvation,
notwithstanding there is nothing remaining for them but
condemnation. And why so? For they are as Players in
whom there is no affection nor zeal. So then, God will be
served oftentimes of a people who are worth nothing, who
are as dogs, and the very offscouring: and yet

---

† *Romans 1:16*

notwithstanding they are as the ministers of his power, to draw those to salvation, that are in the way of destruction. Moreover there are mercenaries that preach for their belly, and have no other regard but to themselves, or else would make themselves to be very well esteemed: and yet are these nevertheless the instruments of God for the salvation of all believers. And oftentimes the best, they I say, that acquit themselves most faithfully to do their duty, to call poor sinners to salvation, to be guides and examples to all others: these shall not yet find what God will do. And why so? They sow the Seed and know not how God will make it profit: and oftentimes they ween [*think*] to bless, and they curse. And wherefore? Because it must needs be that the vengeance of God be prepared for all contemners. The Gospel is preached, to the end we might find God merciful to us all: but there are many that through their contempt and ingratitude heap upon themselves their own damnation: For the gospel shall be unto them *a savor of death unto death*, as Saint Paul saith[†]: that is to say, a deadly savor, that only the breath shall be enough to swallow them up: as we see yet at this day: that God worketh by the ministers of his word, that some are altogether blind, other are blind in part: For the hirelings of whom we have spoken, they are altogether blockish and know nothing: But the good and faithful Ministers, although it so be that they know that they have their eyes dim, yet they are ignorant how God will make their labor to profit, or in what sort: and oftentimes their purpose is quite overthrown. This then is

---

† *2 Corinthians 2:16*

that we have to learn. And in the meantime, seeing god
hath declared unto us that his word is the open way to the
heavenly life, and that he will ratify all that which shall be
pronounced hereby men in his name: let us keep us to that
and not doubt (whatsoever want [*lack*] shall be in us, as well
concerning him that speaketh as him that heareth): that yet
nevertheless when we shall receive this word by faith, and
it shall be faithfully and in truth handled unto us, we shall
be partakers of this blessing. And herein we may see the
beastliness of all those false wretches of the papacy: for
mark whereupon they have founded that Idol which they
have, to make a god of a morsel of bread: they say if a Priest
have no intention to consecrate, it is nothing, and in that
the bread is turned into god, it is by the intention of him
which consecrateth: so as they must be Idolaters in all their
Masses (I speak of their own doctrine) if they make not this
condition. For what know we (say they) whether the Priest
which consecrateth, doth his business as he ought, and
whether his mind be upon his kitchen or chambermaid: for
in so doing the bread remaineth bread: there is no GOD:
and why so? For say they, if his intention be not there it is
nothing. But it is very true that they show very well how
one error draweth another: for because it seemeth to them
that there is a change made of the bread into the substance
of our Lord Jesus Christ, for which they have invented that
same charm: they add straightway the intention: but
notwithstanding we see that they know nothing of the
nature of the Sacraments. I leave now to speak of this
conversion which they imagine, and call transubstantiation:
but if he that ministereth the sacrament: and hath this
charge and calling, hold the people bound to his intention:

what shall this be? A wicked man that shall baptize, he
may mock God, and by this means quite make frustrate the
sacrament, and after when he shall minister the sacrament
of the Supper, the poor people shall therein be mocked, who
come thither to seek a pledge of their salvation: he therein
manifestly despiteth God. To be short, they must hold the
power of God, (which he most notably setteth forth in the
sacraments) shut up in their fist. And what a blasphemy is
this, and how detestable? But see how far they are come.
For it is certain that in the Mass, if they had an Angel there,
yet it should never cease to be a devilish thing: but
contrariwise if there were a devil in the supper which is
ministered, yet it could not let God from accomplishing his
work. We must not look to the worthiness of him which
giveth the bread or the wine in the supper: But God hath so
instructed us therein, that he hath given power to the visible
sign: It is he that worketh by his holy spirit, so as we be not
deceived when we come thither, but shall be truly united
and joined unto him. Lo then what we have to bear away
upon this place, to make our profit thereof. But now let us
come to the blessing which Isaack gave. After he had kissed
his son he saith:

> *Lo the savor of my son is as the savor of a field*
> *which God hath blessed.*

Albeit we see that he was deceived: yet under the
savor of this borrowed garment, he accepteth Jacob his son,
as if he had been his firstborn. Lo then how the savor
whereby we are accepted unto God, proceedeth from him
which is the firstborn in the house, to wit, from our Lord

Jesus Christ. Moreover he addeth:

The Lord give thee, the dew of Heaven, and the
fatness of the earth, abundance of wheat and wine.

Here at the first show a man would judge, that this
blessing imported nothing but that Jacob should be fat and
well nourished: For Isaack mentioneth not here any spiritual
gifts, as we have showed before, that it was not for any
earthly commodities, nor for riches, profit or pleasures that
Jacob must be blessed: How shall these things therefore be
reconciled? But we have to hold this rule that is given us in
the holy Scriptures: to wit, that the grace of God was always
clothed as it were with some figures, until that our Lord
Jesus Christ came. For when the fathers would obtain
pardon of their sins, they had some beast slain, and the
blood was shed: sometimes the fat was burned, and the
blood was sprinkled. And could a brute beast I beseech you
blot out our sins whereof we are guilty before God? How
could blood do it, that had nothing in it but corruption?
And again, when fat is burned it so stinketh, as it cannot be
abidden [*endured*], and what shall this make for the
pacifying of GOD towards men? What? but should a man
say in all these, that GOD would keep his people in earthly
things? but we must always come to that pattern which
Moyses saw in the mountain, according to which he hath
spoken, and mark also whither we are sent by Saint Paul
and by Saint Stephen. So then as the sacrifices imported
more, than they showed: so let us note, that in all the rest
God hath in such sort guided the people therein, that
always some obscurity was mingled among: For it must

needs be that this should be kept till the coming of our Lord
Jesus Christ, to the end that we should simply and clearly
see the grace of GOD and the spiritual life. It is said that
our Lord Jesus Christ is the first fruits of those that rise
again: And why so? we cannot attain unto that resurrection
which is promised unto us, and to that heavenly life, unless
we see him to march on before us. Our bodies returning
into dust, what can they promise us? The end of all men is
nothing but despair: it seemeth that all shall be abolished:
and (as Solomon saith) the death of a dog and of a man, as
touching the body shall be all one. So then if we look not
up to the kingdom of our Lord Jesus Christ, it is certain that
all here shall be as it were confused: but when we shall
know that he hath overcome death, and is ascended into
heaven, then we have an easy access. But it was not so
neither under nor before the law: for the fathers had not the
sight of our Lord Jesus Christ, but in a shadow. It is true
that they attained to that heavenly life as well as we: they
had one and the same spirit of adoption, they called upon
God for their father: but for all that this was afar off, and
these things were dark unto them. And thus, let us note for
this cause that they had no such revelation, as we have in
the gospel: For it behooved God to draw them by such
means as were fit for them. And this is that which Saint
Paul saith in Galatians four† that they were governed as
young infants, and that the law was like unto a tutor. For
although an infant be already the heir of his father, yet he
hath not the occupying of the substance, forasmuch as he is

---

† *Galatians 4:1, 2*

not able to take it in hand: but he is under the direction of his tutor: and though he do it, yet hath he no liberty to do it. Thus then although the fathers under the law were heirs of the kingdom of heaven as we are, yet so it is that they had this servile subjection unto it, under which they were kept as under a tutor. And wherefore? Because this honor as I have said must rather be kept until the coming of our lord Jesus Christ. If the ancient fathers had not been advanced by little and little, and as it were by degrees, to come to everlasting life, seeing these things were yet so dark unto them, and our lord Jesus Christ was so far off: what had this been? had they attained their purpose? Thus it behooved god to help them, and to reach out his hand unto them.

And in this respect was the land of Canaan as a pledge and gage unto them, that God had appointed a better inheritance for them, than in this world. For they might have returned to the country where they were born, which was more fertile than this of Judea, as may appear. Mark Abraham and Isaack pinched with famine and if they had looked to nothing but to have been nourished here upon earth, they would have forsaken that land of promise. But they rested there. And wherefore? to enjoy it after their death? Of necessity therefore, must they think of a more high thing than this visible earth, and they must take it in another respect, than to say, we have here all that we can desire. But they took the land of Canaan as a pledge that God gave them, until they should come into the possession of that heavenly life.

So then, when we see in this blessing of Jacob, that he speaketh of the dew of heaven, and of the fat of the earth, of abundance of corn and wine, it meaneth not that Isaack would only pray for this, that his son might be fed as an Hog in a sty, and that he should be fat and full here beneath: but he followed the order that God had appointed at that time: to wit, that he did give unto them pledges of a thing that was much more excellent. And that so it is, Isaack addeth a little after:

> *That his son should rule over his enemies, and that*
> *all nations should bow their knees before him.*

And by what right giveth he him this? Lo Isaack a poor stranger that must hire the land where he setteth up his pavilion, and must live as it were by the favor of another: and yet nevertheless he maketh his son here a King of kings, and all the world to come and do him homage, and that he shall bring the whole earth into subjection. We see then very well that he troubleth not himself with earthly things: but he joineth both together, to wit, he taketh earthly blessings as pledges, to the end to bring his son further off: and in the meanwhile he hath his path right that might lead him to the kingdom of heaven, as was promised him. Now we know that things are offered to us in our Lord Jesus Christ, that may make us forget both honors, and all highnesses, dignities, and nobilities of the world. This therefore is the thing we have to mark upon this place. It is true that even at this day it must needs be that those temporal blessings which we receive from the hand of God, should be unto us as it were pledges of his goodness: but they are sometimes more, sometimes less. For in respect that the ancient fathers had not the like light as we have, and were in shadows and figures: this is the cause why God would not so well testify his favor unto them, as he hath done unto us at this day. For in the gospel we have our Lord Jesus Christ: and it is said that we must be fashioned after his image. Now we know that he had nothing in this world, but all kind of miseries and confusions: for we see how he was crucified, so as it seemed that he had been utterly forsaken of god his father: he was in extreme distresses and anguishes. Thus then we must be fashioned to him after another fashion than they were, who were so led by figures. Furthermore, when we shall compare Jacob with Esau, we shall yet better know (as we shall find afterward) that when Isaack blessed Esau, that the blessing which he will use, will be a great deal more large and rich, than that which he useth here towards Jacob his son: and yet nevertheless, this was not to bless him to that heavenly life: but he saith unto him: My friend there be not two blessings, seeing that is taken from me, it must stand, and God hath blessed him whom I have blessed, forasmuch as he hath appointed me the minister thereof, it must needs be that it even so stand, as it hath been done, I have no more right in it: I must hold myself contented to have blessed once: and yet afterwards he blesseth Esau notwithstanding. And how? What, is there any contradiction? no not so: but this is to show us, that there was not any other heavenly blessing, to say, that he whom he blessed should be the head of the church, and that Jesus Christ should come of his race: this was no longer in the hand of Isaack, as he confesseth. But concerning the benefits of this world, and that which might satisfy the creatures, he gave him more abundantly, than he did to Jacob. Now then we may easily see, that Isaack speaking here of the dew of Heaven, of the fat of the earth, and of great quantity of corn and wine, he meaneth not that his son should trouble himself therein: but he simply setteth these figures before him, which were pledges (as I have said) to draw him further of: This therefore is the thing that we have to mark. And withal let us note, that when it is said that Isaack had declared:

> *The voice is the voice of my son Jacob: but the hand is as the hand of Esau.*

That God had yet purchased this for him. It is true that all this was done through error: but yet besides this error he had some certain knowledge: and the Lord did in such sort advertise him of it, to the end to show that the blessing belonged to Jacob: as also in truth in must be reserved for him, although this had not come to pass: that is to say, albeit Rebecca had not used this ill deceit, yet God know full well how to hold Isaack's mouth, as also he held the mouth of Balaam. Behold Balaam who was a liar, who was hired, and came also the curse the people of God, if it had been possible for him, to the end to get gifts of Balak. But nevertheless God did so turn his tongue that when he thought to curse, (maugre his beard) he blessed them. But Isaack was not as Balaam: For his purpose was not to resist GOD, nor to abolish his election: but he was blinded with a foolish love which he bare unto his Son, (as we have said): and our Lord could well enough govern his tongue when he would, to cause him to bless Jacob: but now when he imagined to bless his son Esau, yet nevertheless doth GOD draw this from his mouth, *The voice is the voice of my son Jacob.*

Now this was the principal and chief of the blessing, even the voice: For Isaack gave nothing of his own: but he was a witness of the favor of God, and as it were an Harrault to publish it. So then, forasmuch as he found nothing of Esau but the apparel and the touching, he must not rest himself thereupon, forasmuch as he found the voice in Jacob. By this we may see that God would even now already allow it, although that Isaack knew not what he did, nevertheless the blessing must be turned to Jacob. Thus much concerning this word. Moreover for the conclusion let us mark well when it is said, that all people shall be subject to Jacob: that this is not to the end that he should have any earthly Empire or dominion in this world, either he or his. It is true, that they ruled in the land of Canaan: but howsoever it was, yet did not they bring into subjection all nations. In the time of Solomon, it is true that God exalted his people far and wide: but this was in a figure: for it must come unto our Lord Jesus Christ, who is the head both of men and angels. So then that which Moyses here rehearseth of the sovereign dominion, it is certain that it cannot agree, neither to Jacob nor to his Children, nor to all their posterity, until that we come to our Lord Jesus Christ. And this is the cause why it is expressly said, that he should be the head of his Brethren, and that his mother's sons should bow down before him. This was not in respect of Jacob's person: he had but one only brother, who bowed not himself before him: but rather made him afraid, as we shall see after: but we see the accomplishment of all in our Lord Jesus Christ: and this was not for himself, but it was for our good and for our salvation, that he received all power from God his father, to the end that every knee should bow down before him: In him also it is altogether that we are a priestly kingdom, so that we acknowledge him as our king and our head to worship him.

But now let us cast down ourselves before the majesty of our good God, in acknowledging of our faults, and praying him that he will make us in such sort to feel them, that it may be to humble us before him, and for to make us to ask pardon of him, and also for to hate ourselves, and to be displeased with ourselves in our own vices: and pray him that it would please him in such sort to reform us, that we may grow up more and more in all holiness and obedience of his righteousness. And that he would support us in our weaknesses, in such sort, that he leave not to accomplish the promises that he hath made unto us, although that on our part we do not only slack them, but seem also utterly to thrust them from us, that notwithstanding he will not leave, to stretch out unto us a strong hand, until that we be come unto the mark which he hath set before us: that is, till we be partakers of that glory which he hath purchased unto us through our Lord Jesus Christ. And that he will not only show this grace unto us, but unto all peoples and nations of the earth, etc.

&The thirteenth Sermon of

Jacob and Esau, Genesis 27.

31.   *Iſaack ſaide, accurſed be euery one that ſhall curſe thee, and bleſſed be he that ſhall bleſſe thee.*

32.   *Nowe as Iſaack had made an ende of bleſſing Iacob: it came to paſſe I ſay, that Iacob being ſcarce gone forth from the preſence of his father Iſaack that Eſau returned from his hunting.*

33.   *Therfore he alſo brought vnto his father delicates prepared: and he ſaid vnto his father, let my father ariſe and eate of the veniſon of his ſonne, that thy ſoule may bleſſe mee.*

34.   *Now Iſaack ſaith vnto him, who art thou? he ſayde, I am thy firſt begotten ſonne Eſau.*

35.   *Then Iſaack trembled with a wonderful feare and ſaide, who is that which brought vnto me veniſon euen nowe, and I haue eaten of all before thou cameſt, and whome haue I bleſſed? alſo he ſhalbe bleſſed.*

36.   *Now Eſau hearing the words of his father, cried out with a wonderful great and bitter crie: and he ſaid vnto his father, bleſſe me, my father bleſſe me alſo.*

37.   *Who ſaid, thy brother came through crafte, and hath taken away thy bleſſing.*

38.   *And he ſaide, howe rightly is his name called Iacob! for he hath ſupplanted me nowe the ſecond time, he had taken my birthright, and loe now he hath taken my blessing also, &c.*

ESTERDAY WE STAYED AT THIS WORD concerning the blessing which Isaack gave unto his son Jacob, to wit, that whosoever should bless him, should be blessed: and whosoever should curse him, should be accursed. But it is very certain that this was not in the hand of any mortal man: for it belongeth unto God to punish those which do any wrong to his children: and besides that, it is forbidden us to seek revenge, it is not in our power to bring to pass that our enemies have their reward. Now therefore it is very certain that Isaack pronounced here the sentence of god, and that he spake not in his own name: but was authorized as a prophet. And indeed we have seen that this was pronounced from the mouth of god to Abraham in the twelfth Chapter[†] *I will bless all those which shall bless thee, and I will curse all those which shall curse thee.* God reserved this unto himself. But now how is it that Isaack presumeth to speak after the manner of god, unless because he knew that this inheritance was left unto him, and so he resigneth it unto his son, to the end that after his departure he might be the possessor thereof? We see then briefly that Isaack speaketh not in this point rashly, although that he had many foul faults, yet notwithstanding he was grounded upon that which God had promised him, and he knew that

---

† *Genesis 12:2, 3*

this office was committed unto him. And thus he doubted not to curse all those which should curse his stock.

Now seeing it is so, this was not man's word, but a sentence given by the power of the holy ghost. We have then first of all to learn, that if we be knit together with Jacob by faith, that God taketh us into his custody, upon such condition, that all they which shall hurt us and shall do us any scathe [*harm*], they shall fight against him: for he defendeth us as the apple of his eye, as he hath also spoken thereof. And what a benefit is this, that God taketh all our quarrels, and becometh the enemy of our enemies, that none can lift up so much as a hand against us, to do us wrong or violence, but that he by and by setteth himself against him, as if that were to violate his own majesty? When therefore God cometh so low, that he declareth that we must address ourselves to him and stay upon him, as oftentimes as any wrong is done unto us: what better thing can we desire? Thus therefore let us learn to be patient in all our afflictions: and if we be unjustly persecuted in this world, let us know that nothing shall escape unpunished, but that all our adversaries must come to an account. They may imagine for a time that they have gotten all: but as sure as God dwelleth in heaven, their reward shall light upon their own heads, and they shall know that in imagining to trouble and torment us, they have violated the protection of God, and his safeguard. Thus much then for one point. And further, let us learn also by this place, to do good to all the children of God. It is true, that it is not lawful (specially for us) to do any wrong to our enemies, although they were the most wickedest men in the world: but yet we do see that God hath his faithful ones in his tuition, and they cannot be touched the breadth of a finger, but God setteth himself before us to be our buckler: and declareth that he will curse all those that shall curse us. We have therefore the more occasion to abstain from doing all injury, and to take good heed, that they whom he hath so received to himself, be not violated nor offended by us. And contrariwise, when we see the children of God to have need of our aid and help, although we look for no recompense of them, after the manner of the world, and that they have no means to show any, or be unknown unto us: when it is said that God will bless us, let us learn to employ ourselves therein, seeing that our reward is prepared for us in heaven, and that we cannot be made frustrate thereof. This therefore is the sum of that we have to learn out of this place: to wit, that we take good heed, that we do no wrong to those whom god will maintain: for seeing that they are in his keeping, it is certain that we must come to a reckoning, when we shall do them any wrong. And withal let us endeavor always to do good unto those, whom God offereth unto us: and seeing he declareth unto us that he will accept all, as if it were done to his own person, let us not think that we have lost anything, although the men to whom we do good, be not able to requite it: for if they be poor and destitute of all ability, or rather have no occasion to show that they are not unthankful: nevertheless let us know that God doth receive with his own hand, all that which we have done, in supporting those which were destitute and had need. When we have this I say, we shall have enough to content us. But if we desire that god bless us in such sort, let us first take heed, as I have already touched, that we be the true children of Jacob, not of the carnal race but by faith, and that we be regenerate by the same spirit, that we may have the testimony of our adoption imprinted in our hearts, and as it were sealed, to the end we may have full assurance thereof: and that in this trust we may cry out unto God. Now to the end we may do this, we have to praise the head of all, that is to say, our Lord Jesus Christ: who as Saint Paul saith[†], *is God blessed forever*, when he spake of his human nature, and that he was descended of the stock of Abraham, and yet he saith nevertheless that he *is God blessed forever*. Now we have to bless or praise him, not after the manner of men, but to glorify him as he deserveth. And moreover when we pray unto God for the advancement of his kingdom, we say as that prayer is suggested unto us by the holy ghost[††]: *blessed is he that cometh in the name of God: O Lord make thy kingdom to prosper, O Lord increase the kingdom of David*. So then this is the way to make us partakers of that which is here recited by Moyses: to wit, that God beareth such special favor and singular love towards us, that not only he blesseth us: but if any do us good or evil, he accepteth this as done to his own person, and will recompense them that have pity upon us, and shall help us in our necessity: and again he will revenge our cause: and although we be patient in all the wrongs and outrages that men do against us, yet nevertheless he will keep us and stretch out his arm to chastise all those who shall unjustly oppress us. Lo then the sum of the matter, concerning that word that was left for us. Now it is said:

---

† *Romans 9:5*

†† *Mark 11:9, 10*

That Jacob was even hardly gone forth from his father, and that scarcely he had obtained that he went about, but lo Esau returned from hunting, and brought meat to his father, he brought it unto him being upon his bed.

If we shall consider that which is here rehearsed by Moyses, according to the outward show, it is certain that Esau was worthy to have been blessed. For he diligently performed that which was enjoined him by his father: and discharged himself of his duty. And wherefore then was he bereft of his birthright? But see wherein we are oftentime deceived: that is, because we regard that which we see with the eye. But God regardeth the right and truth, as Jeremy saith. So then, let us not think that GOD embusieth himself in the outward show, which indeed is nothing: and yet notwithstanding we are wont to be ravished therewith, in that we are sensual men. To be short, that which hath the goodliest glister and show before men, shall oftentimes be rejected before God, as the Painims [*pagans, heathen*], they set great price upon their virtues in the outward show which they had: but we must come further: that is to say, we must know that God soundeth the hearts and secret thoughts. So an act may be highly and greatly praised and esteemed, and yet nevertheless shall displease God: For if the affection shall not be right, there is nothing but hypocrisy and a double courage in it, or else the end shall not be well ordered. For let us put the case that a man giveth himself to virtue, and yet hath this foolish arrogance in himself, to get reputation, and that men should clap their hands at him in the judgment of the world: he hath now already received his reward, and because he is led with ambition, it must needs be that all that he doth and taketh in hand, must be rejected of God. And why so? Humility is the foundation and root of all virtues. As long therefore as men do seek to merit by their own virtue, it is certain, that if they were Angels in outward appearance, yet all that proceedeth from them, is nothing else but baggage and very filth. So let us learn, that when we see how Esau behaved himself so to the eye, and that he failed in nothing, and yet notwithstanding that he was cast underfoot, and that God made no reckoning of him, let us learn (I say) not to give ourselves to foolish ambition to be seen of men, and to be well thought of: but let us walk in simplicity and uprightness before God, let us know that if the heart go not before, that all the service that we can do unto him, shall be justly rejected. Mark shortly that which we have to hold, concerning that which Moyses hath rehearsed here, touching the obedience which Esau rendered unto his father. Now there is also to be noted further, when we shall make comparison of him with Jacob, we shall find that which was showed before, to wit, that Jacob was not preferred, but by the free goodness of god of which thing there appeareth no reason unto us, for lo Esau which went to hunt, who lied not, who deceived not his father, and did not thrust in himself craftily, neither by any deceit or indirectly: he had none of all this. But what doth Jacob? he deceiveth, he lieth, and dealeth dissemblingly, and presenteth himself as it were his brother Esau: there was nothing in him but craft and theft concerning this matter, and further, he doth greatly dishonor his father, to make him believe one thing for another. We might well say then, that Jacob deserved to be rejected and cut off: but nevertheless GOD would that he should have the birthright. And whereupon is this founded unless it be upon his everlasting counsel which we cannot comprehend? And so let us learn to humble ourselves: notwithstanding that the reason be not declared unto us why god should rather accept Jacob than Esau, and take the birthright from the greater to give it to the lesser. Albeit then that we know not what moved and induced God to this, yet notwithstanding let us hold for most certain, that he doth nothing but most justly, because his will is the rule of all righteousness: he is subject to no law, and much less to our fantasy, to do those things that seem good unto us: but so far off is it, that though we were able to dispute and to allege all the reasons that possibly we could conceive, yet the only will of GOD, shall overcome all the reasons in the world: and all that which shall enter into our brain, must of necessity be overthrown: as it is said, that he shall always be justified, yea albeit men condemn him. For they rather have this devilish pride to murmur against that which he doth, and to find somewhat to say against it, and to bring forth their reasons: but when they shall have prattled peddlers french as long as they can, yet shall the justice of God remain untouched, and they which have durst rather to slander it and bark against it, they shall remain ashamed and confounded. Lo therefore yet another principal point that we have to hold in this place.

Now it is said, that Isaack asked first, *Who art thou?* And hearing that it is Esau, he was astonished, yea Moyses further addeth more, with a wonderful fear. If Isaack had not known how much worth that blessing had been, and that it should be confirmed by God, if he had not known, that he being called to the dignity and office of a Patriarch, must be a witness of the inheritance of salvation, he had not been so astonished: For he had done as other men used to do. I have been deceived by my son. He had stormed and chaffed against Jacob, yea and he would have cursed him: and he would nevertheless have concluded, O, I will keep my right, howsoever it be, this shall no whit prejudice me therein, and I have my authority frank and free. Lo then how Isaack might have used himself therein, after the common manner. But he knew that God had ordained him the minister, to cause that the inheritance of salvation should rest in his house: and he knew that he was but an instrument therein, and that this was not because God had resigned his office to him, albeit he had communicated it unto him. For if God communicate his authority to those, whom he hath established in the ministry of his word, this is not meant that he depriveth himself of it therefore, neither that he giveth over his right therein, in any sort whatsoever. Isaack knew then, that forasmuch as he was but an instrument of the holy ghost, that that which he had pronounced must stand: and there is no doubt also but that it was revealed unto him. For before he was as it were, restrained: the love which he bare to his eldest son had so besotted him, that he had quite lost the remembrance of that which we have seen before: For he was not ignorant of that which God had determined, *That the greater should serve the lesser.* And yet nevertheless, he is a man as it were altogether senseless and devoid of reason, always addicted to his son Esau, and thought not to yield himself to be governed by God. Now this was not of any deliberate and

set rebellion, (as we have declared before:) but it was love
that blinded him, and for that he marked not that he should
simply have rested in the will of God.   Lo how he
overhastily forgot himself.   So then, let us note that this
great fear whereof Moyses speaketh, was as if a man should
suddenly come to awaken a man making some alarm about
him, and as if he had been seized with some astonishment,
and thought this had been some message of death, and that
his enemies had been even come to his bed.   Lo in what case
Isaack was.   But here we have to note in the first place that
it is good that God awaken us very roughly, when we shall
be so sluggish, and that he come unto us everyday.   It is
true that we will think ourselves watchful enough, when we
shall hear the word of God, and will be zealous, and it will
seem that we are very wary therein: but all that we have
heard is quickly fled from us, and specially when we have
contrary things before us.   If we have been exhorted to
patience, and it seem that we have been therein so well
appointed, that there wanted [*lacked*] nothing: let one come
to trouble us, let us receive but some little blow, incontinent
we will be so enflamed with wrath and displeasure, that we
forget that which was spoken unto us.

Again, when we are exhorted to despise the riches
and honors of this world, if we be allured thereunto by our
adversary the Devil, we will be (as it were) asleep in them,
and all our senses will be wholly occupied therewith.   Now
if our Lord used any simple admonition, it is certain that it
is as if it were spoken to a man that were asleep.   And what
shall men profit thereby?   It behooveth therefore that God
awaken us oftentimes by force.   And so as often as God
shall scourge us, and that some shall be chastised after one

sort, some after another: Let us examine that which was in
us, and so we shall know that we were for a time blockish
and senseless, that we have known nothing of that which we
ought, or else that we were not so attentive therein, and let
us learn by the example of our father Isaack, that seeing our
Lord doth stir us up and would that we should deeply and
in good earnest think upon him, and that we should gather
up all our senses, which before were wandering: let us learn
I say to make our profit thereof: Lo this for one lesson. But
let us mark how Isaack willingly submitteth himself to the
will of God. I have already said, that they that will
maintain their reputation, will be willful: although they had
done the greatest evil in the world, yet they will always
maintain it. And lo this is the cause that so many people
plunge themselves so deeply, even unto the depth of the
bottomless pits: that is, they are ashamed to be reclaimed:
they would have the renown of constancy, and they think
that if they should change, that it should be cast in their
teeth, as a great lightness and inconstancy. Lo the cause
why men harden themselves in obstinancy with boldness
and presumption, to follow a thing, howsoever it be, and
take the bit in their teeth and will in no case bow, neither
to the one side, nor to the other. Now this is a vice very
common, and so much the rather we shall be subject unto
it, unless we come to that which is rehearsed here. Lo
Isaack who might have been greatly ashamed, for that he
was so deceived and abused: a man might say, look upon
this drunkard, when he is well whittled [*worn out with
fretting*], and that he hath eaten and drunk, he taketh one
for another: and farther, a man might have said, this was a
glutton, when he could not discern between kid and

venison: and again, it might have been said: What? when he blessed his youngest son instead of his eldest: being so deceived, and because he did this through error and theft: weeneth [*thinketh*] he that this shall be available before God? Isaack therefore might have had many respects to have been obstinate in his fact. But he forgetteth all, and knoweth that forasmuch as it was so ordained of God, that Jacob should be blessed, that it must remain, and no change must be made therein. We are then briefly taught that as often as we shall do any act unadvisedly, which pleaseth not God, or else if we shall exceed our bounds, and go beyond our calling, howsoever it be, that we always turn the bridle, as soon as we shall be warned, and that we follow not the matter, because this is manifestly to despite GOD. But especially we have to consider, although Isaack were carried with an evil affection, and although he forgat that which had been pronounced by GOD, that faith was not utterly quenched in him, albeit it was choked. This argument was handled yesterday more at large: yet ought it by the way to be further thought upon. For what moved Isaack to say, I have blessed thy brother, albeit he obtained it by deceit, shall he remain blessed yet? What lesson learneth he? It must needs be that he knew this before. Now he knew it: but as I have said already, the light of his faith was as a coal of fire that had been raked under the ashes: one should have seen nothing thereof, but let them remove a few of the ashes, and then lo the sparks appear by and by, and afterwards the fire showeth itself. Even so was it in Isaack: and this is not written only for his person, but to the end we should gather a general doctrine thereof: For oftentimes the like shall fall out and come to pass with us, to wit, that when we shall much loose the bridle to our vanities, that one shall be ravished with ambition, another shall be kindled to covetousness, to heap up goods, another shall have some foolish appetite: to be short, another shall be drawn away and estranged from GOD, by some manner of means: then lo our faith which is (as it were) dead. Now God suffereth it not to be altogether abolished: For when the word taketh lively root in us, it is an incorruptible seed. It cannot then be quite rooted out: but howsoever it be, it cannot be said that there was not one spark or drop of faith, in such sort that we be so cold, that we think no more of GOD, that the world hath quite overcome us. When therefore any do so wander, that they think only but on their lusts, a man would say that faith were quite dead. Now this may well be in appearance: but notwithstanding God yet reserveth some hidden seed: as we have said, that the fire may well be choked, and yet not altogether quenched, when it shall be raked up under the ashes. For all our affections, the riches, honors and pleasures of the world, are as ashes to choke up this light of God, which ought to guide and lead us. But our Lord having pity upon us, bringeth to pass, that a little after we acknowledge our faults: and whereas we were so cold, yea as it were altogether frozen, we begin to wax warm, in a good zeal, and to return unto him.

Lo then, how GOD accomplisheth that in his faithful, which we read here of our father Isaack. But this is not spoken to the end we should therefore tempt God, as though it were permitted unto us to suffer ourselves in such sort to be carried astray by the Devil, that our faith might be (as it were) asleep in our hearts and souls: For it will not always fall out, that God will awake those which are asleep, and call them again which are estranged from him. Let us learn therefore to walk in fear and carefulness: and specially when we shall find men so dull, that they shall be as it were altogether blockish, and that their faith shall be as it were dead in them: let us learn to fear so much the more. What holiness was there in David? And yet nevertheless we see that he was for a time, as a man quite desperate. Afterwards, having committed such an abominable fault, to have ravished the wife of another, and to have caused her husband wickedly to be slain with such villainous treachery, that he deserved to be thrown out from amongst men: after all this, we may see, what manner of Prophet soever he had been, what fear of God soever he had in him before: to be short, albeit he were a mirror of Angelical perfection, we see that he was as an Ox or an Hog, he knew nothing, he had no remorse, it seemeth that God had given him up into a reprobate sense, and had stricken him with a spirit of blockishness: yea and when the Prophet cometh unto him alleging this comparison, and speaking unto him of a neighbor, that through violence had oppressed a poor man: O he knew well to condemn others, and in the meanwhile thought nothing of himself, till that the Prophet[†] said unto him: It is of thee, it is of thee that I do speak. Until that the Prophet Nathan said unto him. It is thou murderer that hast done such a deed: until that he came to give him a blow with a club, as it were a chafed Bull, he continueth blockish in it: and forasmuch as the Devil had won him so

---

† *2 Samuel 12:7*

far that he was as it were drunken yea altogether bewitched, it must needs be that God even thunder against him.

When therefore we see such like examples as this which is here rehearsed unto us by Moyses, that Isaack the chief of the Church, is as it were blind herein, until that God had revealed it by force: so much the more (as I have said) it behooveth us to take good heed to walk in fear and carefulness: and in the meanwhile let us learn when GOD giveth us such pushes and spurs, to make us return unto him, whereas we were before as it were insensible, and have gotten through long custom such a strong savor: When god giveth us the grace (I say) to call back ourselves unto him, that we be moved as becometh us, and that it be not to wipe our mouth after we have said in one word, that we have faulted, as there are many: but that we follow that which is here taught us by Moyses that Isaack was afraid. And how? very greatly, yea wonderfully. For it is impossible, that we should come to repentance, unless we have a heaviness that must torment us and we be as it were in hell, to feel our wretchedness, and be therein confounded. Until so much be wrought in us, that we be come thither, it is certain that there shall be no repentance in us. This teacheth how we must practice this doctrine: to wit, That when our Lord shall have touched us, that on our parts we be as it were wounded to the bottom of our heart, and that we be so astonished, that we return no more to our slothfulness and negligence, wherewith we were for a time overwhelmed.

Now Isaack yet showeth his faith better in saying, *He shall be blessed:* For he knew that God had ordained him to this office, and that he spake not in his own name: For

the sentence of God cannot be called back: it behooveth
therefore that he kept him there. So we have farther to
gather of this place that we have already touched: that
Isaack here passed not his bound, although he had failed
through ignorance, and been deceived in the person, yet he
always kept a good principle: to wit, that he had executed
that which GOD had committed to his charge: and that
therefore this must remain concluded, and have his effect.
Now this is said for our instruction: For we know that at
this day our Lord would have the remission of our sins to be
showed forth by the mouth of men, he would assure us of
the inheritance of everlasting salvation, and also would have
his adoption to be declared unto us. Now we must needs
have whereupon to resolve ourselves: For if we have not full
assurance of our salvation, and if we cannot call upon GOD,
it is as much as to shut the gate of Paradise against us. But
in the meanwhile, Lo a man which speaketh and saith, that
he will pardon our sins, and yet he is a sinner himself.
Again, he promiseth us the Heavenly Life: and this is so
poor a creature so brickle as nothing more, that is nothing
but smoke: and yet will he open Heaven unto us, and is not
worthy to dwell in the earth: for who is he amongst us that
is worthy to be nourished here below at God's charges? So
then, when we shall cast our eyes upon them, that preach
unto us the word of God, by which they protest unto us
that God holdeth and avoweth us for his Children, that he
forgiveth our sins, that he receiveth us in the name of our
Lord Jesus Christ as righteous and innocent, it behooveth us
indeed to look more high: For if we stay ourselves upon the
men, it is certain that we shall always go out too far: and
besides we see that there are faults mingled in them, and

this shall be to shake us, and to lessen the authority of God, and in the end quite to overthrow our faith. So much the more therefore must we take heed unto this place, the which is written for us: that is, that when we shall be blessed, it behooveth that this hold and be made assured, as we have before alleged the promise of our Lord Jesus Christ[†] *That which ye loose in earth shall be loosed in Heaven, and that which you bind in earth shall be bound in heaven.* The Pope to ratify his tyranny hath falsely corrupted this place. For he will have a man to be bound to him, and to all that he hath invented: and again, to believe that he can do all, although he quite overthrow the authority of God, he would be feared and obeyed, and no man must gainsay him in anything whatsoever it were. Now this is too too detestable a blasphemy. But we know that our Lord Jesus Christ would not advance men's persons, so far as to make Idols of them, what then? he would give that certainty unto his word which it deserveth: For without this, what were it? As I have said, we should always be in doubt thereof, and never in quiet: but when we know that by hearing the promises of the forgiveness of our sins and of the free adoption of God, we hear that he inviteth us to him, that he openeth the door unto us, to the end we might have familiar access to call upon him: although it be a mortal man that speaketh unto us, yet in that we doubt not, it is as much as if Angels came down from Heaven, yea and more too: For Saint Paul[††] durst well to say, that if an Angel came down from Heaven

---

† *Matthew 18:18*

†† *Galatians 1:8*

and preached any other doctrine than that he had preached, that they should hold him for a devil: For he knew of whom he held his doctrine, to wit, that it was of God. So then let us learn to magnify that reverence which we owe unto the word of God, when it is preached to us, and highly to esteem that inestimable treasure albeit it be in earthen vessels: For who are we that we should preach the word of God? If a man would regard what is our condition, it is certain that all that we shall preach, shall come to nothing: but the treasure (as I have already said) ought always to be esteemed according to the dignity thereof, although GOD have put it in us, and we be but as broken pots, that have nothing but brittleness. Lo then that which we have to learn upon these words, *He that hath been blessed shall be blessed.* And how so? Had Isaack that Privilege therein, to say that that which he had pronounced should stand? After he had eaten and drunk, and further being a poor blind man, being so blockish that he knew not what he did: being so dull that hearing the voice of his son Jacob, he suffereth himself to be led as a poor beast: and yet nevertheless saith, It shall stand? Yea but acknowledging his fault, he is confounded, and nevertheless he continueth: For he knew whereto God had established him, and thereupon he giveth glory to God, and quite casteth down himself from his own understanding, knowing well that he had nothing of his own. And so, let us learn that Isaack so ordered himself, and in such sort rested upon the word of God, that he altogether renounced his affections wherewith he was beforetime carried away. In the mean season we have here a good rule concerning ourselves, whereby we are warned that when we shall be taught, although this be done by the means of mortal men who are sent unto us, that God doth accept us and account us for his own, that this ought to suffice us, and that we may despise Satan and all temptations, and all things that may come in our brain to shake our faith. And thereupon it is said, *That Esau cried out, yea by yelling and roaring, and that he howled as it were a wild beast,* and that he desired notwithstanding to be blessed: and that his father said unto him: Lo it must needs be that the first blessing hold: and that then he despiteth his brother Jacob, and said: It was right that he was so named. For we have declared before that Jacob's name was drawn from a heel, as if a man should have called him *Heelholder*: and this was forasmuch as he held the heel of his brother, when he should come forth of the womb. Now saith he, he hath given me a blow with his heel. As if a man should say, when a beast rusheth upon him, that he hath stricken him with his heel. Now Esau applieth this to his brother: He hath supplanted me twice now (saith he). And this word also cometh of *Tripping,* when a man giveth one secretly a blow with his foot, and maketh one to fall. He saith then, that he hath already tripped him twice with his heel. The first time when he took away his birthright, and now when he took away his blessing. Now here we have to note in the first place, that which the Apostle showeth[†] us, to wit that albeit Esau wept and mourned, notwithstanding he obtained no place of repentance: for he came thereto overlate. And this is according to the exhortation which we have made heretofore. It is said that we must not be

---

† *Hebrews 12:17*

profane as Esau was, that we must not given to the earth, nor to all that which concerneth our bodies and this transitory life, in such sort that we should forget the heavenly life. And why so? for (saith he) they which profane themselves, and defile themselves in their filthy desires they may cry: but they shall find no place of repentance, forasmuch as the gate shall be shut against them. Now it is true that this at the first show might be thought strange: For it is said, As often, and at what time soever a sinner shall mourn and ask pardon, that GOD will be ready always to receive him to mercy, which return unto him. Lo the promise is general.

So then, how is it that the Apostle saith, that we shall not find place of repentance, if we come too late: For there needs nothing but to mourn? But this shall be easily to be understood, when we shall have distinguished between the cries of the faithful and of the unbelievers. Both the one and the other shall indeed cry unto God: but in diverse sorts, for the faithful shall be touched with true repentance, when they cry and when they mourn: It is said likewise that David roared, and that his throat was as it were hoarse. Lo then the cries which the children of God throw forth: as it is said that he himself brayed like a Lion. And a little after we hear what Ezechias saith, that his speech failed him, and that he groaned in himself as swallows, and that he could speak no more: that he was so hoarse, that he knew not how to speak one word, distinctly pronounced: that he was as it were altogether thrown down.

We see then that the faithful have had this affection: but in the meantime they had repentance, which touched them to the quick for their faults: as it must needs be that they displease themselves therein, and humble themselves before GOD: and after this they conceived some hope to obtain pardon. Now the unbelievers they will bray enough, but in the meanwhile they leave not off to have their hearts hardened: tears trickle down from their eyes, but in the meanwhile they leave not off to be proud and rebellious against God: they have indeed some horror of his judgments, but this is but to set themselves in despite against him: for they never go so far as to hate their offences, and to be displeased with them: Low how it was with Esau. And therefore we have to gather that without repentance, these cries shall be rejected of GOD, and shall never come unto him. And when the Apostle speaketh of repentance, it is not that he meaneth that Esau had repentance: but he meaneth, that he obtained not mercy, and that God was not merciful to him.

And so let us take good heed unto ourselves, and let us detest this blasphemy which the Devil soweth in the world, That there needs no more but one good sigh. For lo those merry Greeks, when they shall be exhorted to return from their wickednesses: O I must yet a good while use it: and God is a good fellow: Lo yet another blasphemy as detestable, whereat even the very stones should cleave. And further, God is merciful. It seemeth to them that under the name of mercy they should hold God bound unto them: but it shall be dearly sold them. Yea lo they come so far that they say, O there needs nothing in the end but one good bulk, and one good sigh. Yea but who is that which shall give it? have we it in our fist? must not God work therein? when a man shall fall, albeit he have hurt himself, he may well recover himself: but if he have broken his neck, can he recover himself afterward? Now before GOD all our faults are deadly: and which is more, it is to put us and deliver us into the hands of Satan. And can a man rise up, when his neck shall be broken? as I have already said.

Now it is certain, that as often as we offend GOD, it is as if we break our neck, as much as lieth in us. And so, can we restore life to ourselves after we have lost it? Lo then, what ought to stir us up to walk in carefulness, and not to tarry till the gate be shut against us: but let us hearken to all the warnings that have been given us: and when God shall knock, let us open unto him. And moreover we have to hold that which is spoken unto us by the Prophet Isaie[†]: *Seek the Lord whilst he may be found: Call upon him when he is ready to hear.* It is true that the time maketh no great matter, that we should take any great advantage of it: but yet we must understand for conclusion, that this place of Isaye was fulfilled when the Gospel was preached, as Saint Paul declareth in the second to the Corinthians[††], *Lo the acceptable days, lo the time of salvation.* And likewise we must well mark the similitude, which is alleged unto us by our Lord Jesus Christ that we let not the occasion slip: but when God biddeth us that we come unto him, let us come unto him, yea hasting ourselves, and let us not draw our legs to come slowly, lest our unthankfulness in the end seclude us, and that the gate be shut against us. Let us take good heed, I say to all these exhortations, and so let us make our profit of them, that having found place of

---

† *Isaiah 55:6*

†† *2 Corinthians 6:2*

repentance before God, we may, after we have bewailed our faults, have our mouth open to rejoice in him, and to praise his holy name, for that he shall have been merciful unto us.

But now let us throw down ourselves before the majesty of our good GOD, in acknowledging our faults, praying him that he will in such sort make us to feel them, that it be not to keep us long in them, nor to slug or flatter ourselves in them: but in such sort to return unto our judge, that asking mercy in him we may there find it in him and that it be not only to the end that he enter not into accompt [*account*] with us, to impute unto us our iniquities and offences: but that by his holy spirit he will purge us and that we may be more and more reformed: and that he awaken us, that we be not obstinate in our faults: but that we think upon all the corrections whereby he would draw us from the evil way, wherein we have strayed, and that we make such profit of all the advertisements which he giveth us, that we be not ashamed to be condemned of him, to the end to obtain mercy. That not only he will show this favor unto us, but to all peoples and nations of the earth, etc.

The ende of these xiii. Sermons
concerning Iacob and Esau.

¶An Answer to certain slanders

and blasphemies, wherewith certain evil
disposed persons have gone about to bring the
doctrine of God's everlasting Predestination into hatred.

ROMANS 9.20

O man who art thou that pleadeſt againſt God?
ſhall the thinge formed ſay to him that formed it,
why haſte thou made me thus?

DEARLY BELOVED BRETHREN we must not
be amazed if the article of the everlasting
predestination to God, be so assaulted and
fought against by Satan's maintainers, seeing
it is the foundation of our salvation, and also serveth for the
better magnifying of the free goodness of God towards us.
On the other side those Dogs which bark against it thinking
to have a good and favorable cause are therein more hardy:
as in very truth there is nothing more contrary to man's
understanding, than to place the cause of our salvation in
the good will of God, in saying, that it belongeth to him
alone to choose us: without finding of anything in us
wherefore he should choose us: and after he hath chosen us,
to give us faith through which we should be justified. But
what? Inasmuch as he is not bound to the person, it is good
reason that he be left in his mere liberty to give grace unto

whom he will, and to leave the rest in his perdition. But I defer myself to entreat more largely of this matter, because you may have large discourse thereof in those Books which are imprinted: which ought to content you. Concerning the writing which was scattered about, to abolish this article of our faith, in very truth it deserveth no answer: being on the one side so full of ignorance and beastliness, that everyone ought easily to judge thereof: and on the other side so full of impudence, that it is a wonder how these troublecoasts and shameless deceivers, abusing so villainously the holy Scriptures should be hearkened unto: notwithstanding because I have understood that there are yet some simple and weak ones that are troubled therewith, I therefore thought good to take the pain to show them that will show themselves teachable: how they ought to resolve themselves, to the end they might be no more deceived by these deceivers.

In the first place, he that hath made that writing, were it *Sebastian Chastalio* or some such like: to show that God hath created all the world to be saved, he allegeth that he laboreth to draw unto him all that went astray: the which I confess in respect of the doctrine of faith and repentance, the which he propoundeth to all in general: be it to draw his elect unto him, or to make other inexcusable. God then calleth everyone to repentance and promiseth all those that return unto him, to receive them to mercy. But this meaneth not that he toucheth to the quick by his holy spirit, all those to whom he speaketh: as it is said by Isay in the fifty-third chapter[†], *His arm is not revealed to all those that hear.* To which agreeth the sentence of our Lord Jesus Christ[††], *None can come unto me, except my father draw him.* And the holy scripture showeth throughout, that conversion is a special gift of God. And indeed the place of Ezechiel[†††], whereof this troublecoast maketh his buckler, very well confirmeth my saying. For the Prophet having said, *that God will not have pleasure in the death of a sinner,* addeth, *but rather will that he return and live.* Whereby he signifieth that God biddeth and exhorteth all which are gone astray to return to the right way. But not that indeed he leadeth them all to himself by the power of his spirit. The which he promiseth not, but to a certain number, which appeareth as well in the thirty-first chapter of Jeremy[††††], as in the thirty-seventh of Ezechiel and in the eleventh[†††††] and throughout the whole scripture.

The second reason of this writing is, that all men are created to the image of GOD, the which he saith not to have been abolished but only subjected to evil. As though it behooved man at adventure to believe his simple saying. But contrariwise the Scripture showeth, that albeit there remain yet some trace of the image of God in us, yet that

---

[†] *Isaiah 53:1*

[††] *John 6:44*

[†††] *Ezekiel 18:32 & 33:11*

[††††] *Jeremiah 31*

[†††††] *Ezekiel 11 & 37*

the whole is disfigured, so as reason is blind, and the heart perverse: wherefore by nature we are wholly accursed. We see therefore at the least, that by the will and decree of God, we have been all subject to everlasting damnation through the fall of one man. Concerning that which this troublecoast addeth, that if we believe, we are delivered through Christ by the power of the gospel, and of the holy ghost: that serves for nothing, but to confirm our doctrine. For it behooveth that we always come thither, that none believe, unless those which are ordained to salvation. Acts thirteen[†] and all the scripture is full thereof. Wherefore this is as much, as if he should say, that the elect of God are delivered from that common damnation through faith.

The third article containeth an horrible blasphemy that if God have created men to damn them, his will and the Devil's is all one. They that speak so, show plainly enough that they are altogether mockers of God, and despisers of all religion. It pleased God that Job should be robbed and spoiled: to be short, all that is there attributed to the Devil, and to those thieves and robbers, it is said plainly, that it came not to pass but by the good pleasure of GOD. Must we therefore conclude that God's will and the Devil's are all one? But they that know that the judgments of God are bottomless, and shall have once known their own weakness, will adore them with all reverence and humility and know well to put a difference, although that GOD willeth the same thing that the devil doth, yet that this is indeed in divers respects. And so, that he deserveth

---

† *Acts 13:48*

always to be acknowledged righteous, although that his counsel be incomprehensible unto us.

Afterwards to abolish the Election of GOD, seeming as though he would confess it, he answereth that God hath not created nor predestinated any man not to believe, seeing he calleth everyone. Wherein he showed that he never yet learned the ABC of Christians, seeing he knoweth not how to distinguish between the outward preaching, which is done by the mouth of men, and the secret calling of God whereby he toucheth the hearts within. Now when it is commanded in the last of Mark[†], to preach the Gospel to all, this importeth not that God therefore worketh in all by the power of his spirit: and when it is said in the second Chapter of the first to Timothy[††], *that God would all men to be saved*, the solution is added by and by, *that come to the knowledge of his truth*. Wherefore then is it, that he himself would not at that present time, that the gospel should be preached to all? so far of is it that he hath enlightened all the world in the faith. It is marvelous that this shameless forehead, is not ashamed to allege for himself the tenth to the Romans[†††], where the text expressly setteth forth that all believe not the Gospel, because that Isay saith, *that the arm of the Lord is not revealed to all*. Also the sixth chapter of

---

† *Mark 16:15*

†† *1 Timothy 2:4*

††† *Romans 10:16, 20*

Saint John[†] where Jesus Christ expressly pronounceth, *that all that are given him of his father come unto him.* And touching that, that he saith, *that all shall be taught of God:* it is a special promise made to the Church: as also the Lord Jesus Christ was a faithful expositor thereof, saying[††]: *He therefore that hath heard and learned of my father, shall come unto me.* Whereby he showeth, that all are not inwardly called. According as a little after[†††] also he confirmeth the same. *Therefore I have said unto you, that none can come unto me, unless it be given him from God my father.* Notwithstanding this Rustic imagineth he hath well escaped, having spoken a word of predestination, without making any semblance of the text[††††] so expressly set forth, where it is said, *that God will have mercy, upon him on whom he will have mercy, and that our salvation is of the same mercy: and not of the willer nor of the runner, and that before the two twins were born, when they had neither done good nor evil: to the end the purpose of his election might stand sure, he had chosen the one and rejected the other.* Also when we believe that this proceedeth of that, that God hath chosen us: Thereupon it followeth, that the rest of the world remaineth blind. But because it would be too long to allege all, consider those places which are gathered in a little book that our brother master Beza hath made thereof, and

---

† *John 6:37*

†† *John 6:45*

††† *John 6:65*

†††† *Romans 9:11-18*

you shall be fully satisfied therein.

To show that the hardening of Pharaoh, proceeded not of God, he allegeth that which is said in the third and fourth of Exodus[†]. I have commanded thee, to let my people depart and thou wouldest not. But it followeth not thereupon, that God had not ordained Pharaoh to be glorified in his obstinacy and hardness, as he protesteth, Exodus ninth chapter. And Saint Paul allegeth it in this sense in the ninth chapter to the Romans[††]. This therefore is sottishly [*stupidly, foolishly*] concluded of this impudent fellow, that our will is the first and chief cause of evil. I confess indeed, that it is the near cause, and the true root of our condemnation. But to the end a man may grant him, he allegeth the authority of Amerbachius, who is a lawyer, and as skillful a Divine, as a Poticarie [*Apothecary*] is a good butcher.

Concerning Melancthon, if this Rustic rested not himself upon him, as he protesteth, but upon the Gospel, how proveth he by the Gospel, that God hath not ordained of his creatures? Touching that he imputeth unto us, that we put a fatal necessity as the Stoics do, it is a very villainous slander: For the Stoics, they made god himself subject to such necessities, making a net of obscure causes, wherein God was entangled. But we set the Lord and master in full liberty, attributing the sovereign Empire to his providence, to dispose of all things. Concerning that this Clown babbleth of Free will, it is sufficiently rejected

---

[†] *Exodus 3 & 4*

[††] *Romans 9:17*

throughout the whole Scripture. For Freedom and bondage are contraries. Now, that we are the servants, yea the slaves of sin, there needeth not that we allege one place alone, seeing the whole scripture are full thereof.

Notwithstanding, to give some color to his error, he allegeth that Jerusalem would not receive the grace of God, yea as though this proved Free will, to choose good or evil. You shall find throughout all my books, how I have taught, that we must not seek the cause of our perdition anywhere else but in ourselves, and in our perverse will. But it followeth not, that it is in us to change our will, which is altogether given to evil.

You shall also find that I have taught that which this troublecoast setteth down here to put out the whole light: to wit, that our will is the cause or means to come to salvation. Wherefore it needeth not to allege that Abraham believed God, and that it was imputed unto him for righteousness. For in very truth it must needs be that a man must accept the grace of God. But the question is of knowing what is the first cause. And this is the power of the holy ghost, through which we are drawn to the obedience of God, according as he hath chosen and adopted us for his children before the foundation of the world. Now in this behalf this vile dog showeth sufficiently enough, that he makes no accompt [*account*] of the holy scripture, the which as much as lies in him, he would abolish or tread under his feet. For in going about to declare how Abraham was saved by his will, he saith that this was of that will which God had put in man creating him after his own image. Whereby he utterly abolisheth the whole grace of the holy ghost: and goeth beyond not only the Papists, but also some of the Painims [*pagan, heathen*], in the impiety. For the Papists keep such a measure in magnifying their Free will, that they confess, being corrupted and depraved, we can do nothing, if God through his spirit and supernatural grace, do not help, drive and direct us. But concerning the holy scripture, it showeth us, that we shall always be rebels against God, until that he shall have changed and renewed us. And lo why Moyses said to the people Deuteronomy twenty-nine[†], that God had not yet given them an understanding heart, and seeing eyes. And therefore to the end he might be obeyed, he saith, that he would give them a new heart, taking away that stony heart, Jeremy in the thirty-first: Ezechiel in the eleventh and thirty-seventh[††]: and Saint Paul in the second to the Philippians[†††] say that God giveth both to will and to perform. And in the first of Saint John[††††] it is said, that they which believe, are not of the will of flesh nor blood: but renewed of god. And Saint Luke speaking of the woman, showeth well, how all are drawn unto faith: to wit, that God openeth the heart, to the end his word may be understood. Now it is certain that these things are not spoken of the common order of nature. And yet this villain dareth allege that which Saint Paul saith in the third

---

† *Deuteronomy 29:4*

†† *Jeremiah 31 & Ezekiel 11 & 37*

††† *Philippians 2:13*

†††† *John 1:13*

Chapter to Titus, that God hath saved us not according to our works, but according to his mercy: to infer upon that, that we have Free will, but not so constant. Now when Saint Paul speaketh in the third to the Romans[†] of the will of man, such as it is by nature, he deciphereth plainly enough, that there is nothing but perversity and malice: as also in the eighth chapter[††] he saith, that all our thoughts are enmities to God. Mark then how this agreeth with that which this troublecoast chatteth, saying that God renewed us, after that we have consented to his calling. And he is not ashamed to allege to the same purpose the fifth to the Ephesians, where he speaketh thereof as of the fables of Marlin: but contrariwise he saith in the same epistle[†††]: When you were dead in your sins, and the captives of Satan, and that ye were the children of wrath as others, God hath quickened you, etc. And in the first chapter[††††] he showeth well, that faith and regeneration proceeded from no other thing, than Free election. And indeed, it must needs be that God accomplish in us that which he hath spoken by his prophet Esaie, in the sixty-fifth chapter[†††††], I appeared unto them, which sought me not. And lo why John Baptist, reproving the rudeness and hardness of his

---

† *Romans 3:10-18*

†† *Romans 8:7*

††† *Ephesians 2:1, 2*

†††† *Ephesians 1*

††††† *Isaiah 65:1*

disciples, saith in the third chapter of Saint John[†], No man can receive anything, unless it be given him from heaven. And which is worst, this troubler is not ashamed also to bring this place, that God giveth both to will and to perform, to make us believe, that the grace of God followeth our good will: howsoever it be that Saint Paul in that place without leaving anything to men, would attribute the whole praise of our salvation to God: as he saith in the first chapter[††] that he which hath begun the good work of salvation, will finish it. Wherein it must be, that he make the grace of god to come after the tail of Free will.

     Now afterwards this troublecoast taketh great pain to prove, that there is a will in man, as though any man had ever denied it. But he should show, that that will is Free to choose good and evil. Now how proveth he it? By the seventh chapter to the Romans, saying that this place cannot be wrested. But herein men may easily judge, how his mind is froward and perverse, seeing that Saint Paul[†††] declareth there, although his will labored and strived to good, inasmuch as it was regenerated by the spirit of God, yet oftentimes he went but hopping upon one foot. He allegeth a little after the seventh of the first Epistle to the Corinthians, where he speaketh of a man's will, that hath a daughter to marry. Here is good stuff to found Free will. Concerning the thirtieth of Deuteronomy, where it is said:

---

† *John 3:27*

†† *Philippians 1:6*

††† *Romans 7*

I set before you this day life and death, choose you: Saint Paul in the tenth to the Romans[†] giveth a sufficient solution: that is, that Moyses presupposeth that God putteth his word in the heart. And lo why it is said, that this ought to be laid to the gospel. Concerning that of Ecclesiasticus which notwithstanding is Apocrypha, there he speaketh but of the outward doctrine, but the inward grace is a thing apart and by itself, That which is so ill favoredly jumbled together by this troublecoast, that under the shadow that Jesus Christ calleth all those that are heavy laden, he concludeth that grace is given equally to all. But he maketh no reckoning that Jesus Christ after he had preached more excellently than all creatures, saith by and by, that his father must draw them to believe in him.

In the end going about to salve that place of Saint Paul where it is said, that if a potter make vessels of earth as he seeth good, this showeth that God disposeth of his creatures: I pray you mark well, the goodly solutions that he giveth: that God ravisheth by miracles, or diseases both one and other as seemeth good unto him. As if Saint Paul spake not expressly there, that God according to his unchangeable purpose, either chose or rejected men, before they were born, or before they had done either good or evil: to show that it is neither of the willer nor of the runner, but of his mercy, that his elect are saved. Such premises are worthy such conclusion as he maketh, let us draw near unto God, and consent unto him, and he will draw near unto us. As though the first approaching were not, that he should seek

---

† *Romans 10:19*

us out, whilst that we are far from him. It is true that God
oftentimes useth this speech, Return unto me, and
I will come unto you: but this is to show
what is our duty and not what
our power is.

Praiſe be vnto God

FINIS.

General Index
(THE TABLE)

A

THE TABLE

B

THE TABLE

C

THE TABLE

𝓓

THE TABLE

THE TABLE

G

THE TABLE

THE TABLE

THE TABLE

I

##

THE TABLE

L

M

THE TABLE

THE TABLE

ℛ

THE TABLE

THE TABLE

T

THE TABLE

THE TABLE

Z

SCRIPTURE INDEX

Old Paths Publications, Inc.

A NEW JERSEY NON-PROFIT CORPORATION

...ask for the old paths... Jer. 6:16

ANNOUNCEMENT !!!

TO ALL OUR SUPPORTERS:

We are pleased to announce that *Old Paths Publications* has been approved by the Internal Revenue Service (IRS) as a 501 (c) (3) Non-profit Corp. Donations to *Old Paths* are tax deductible for federal income tax purposes. Gift receipts will be provided. There are numerous ways that individuals or groups can provide effective financial assistance. Information is available and will be sent to any and all parties requesting it. We encourage you to become a part of our on-going work and ministry with your prayers and support. Please write to us or give us a call and let us know of your willingness to help. Our stated purpose has always been as follows:

> *Old Paths Publications* was established as a ministry for the cause of Christ and His Church. We seek to offer timely titles for the purpose of edification and instruction.

In our day, where true Christianity is increasingly under attack, *Old Paths Publications* endeavors to bring together a united and confessional Reformed and Presbyterian thought, through the publishing of gospel truths given to us by the Spirit of God through His faithful elect, as they saw the fast approaching storm of Apostasy.

It is our hope and prayer that we may be of service to you, that our books might ring true to the Word of God, and that the Lord Jesus Christ might be exalted by all for His own glory.

Our specific activity as provided to the IRS will consist of the following:

To state, defend and disseminate (through every proper means connected with or incidental to the printing and publishing business) the system of belief and practice taught in the Bible, as that system is now set forth in the Westminster Confession of Faith and Larger and Shorter Catechisms.

To provide as education, the history and development of christian religious thought throughout the world, for study and as an aid for teaching in places of learning such as universities, seminaries and churches.

To promote the Christian Gospel as a means to orderly, charitable and productive living and for the general benefit of the family as an historic institution in itself.

THE FOLLOWING CLASSIC WORKS ARE ALSO AVAILABLE FROM OLD PATHS PUBLICATIONS

PASTORAL THEOLOGY
by Patrick Fairbairn

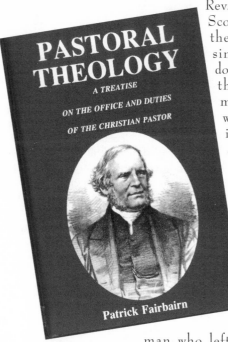

Rev. Fairbairn, a popular Scottish Presbyterian from the 19th century, had a sincere concern for the doctrine of the church and the relationship of its members. This classic work begins with his introductory remarks, a mere 38 pages, explaining *The Relation of the Pastoral Office to the Church, and the Connection Between Right Views of the One and a Proper Estimate of the Other*. Rev. Fairbairn, author also of the popular book Typology, was a humble man who left instructions that no extended memoir of him should be published by any of his friends. A brief and succinct Biographical Sketch was, however, produced and is found at the beginning of **PASTORAL THEOLOGY**. This brief record of the life of one with high merits as an author, and noble Christian character, is well worth the reading. **380 PAGES AND HARDBOUND WITH A DUSTJACKET WITH RARE PICTURE OF AUTHOR, AND SHRINKWRAPPED.**

Retail Price: $ 19.95 (Postpaid)

SERMONS ON GALATIANS
by John Calvin

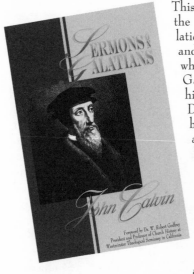

This work is a newly typeset edition from the 1574 printing of the English translation by Arthur Golding in its entirety and consists of two parts: the text of the whole of Saint Paul's Epistle to the Galatians as translated by Calvin himself, and the exposition of the text. Dr. J.R. Beeke says in his review of the book, "This is a landmark reprint...If a copy could be located on the used book market, it would sell for over a thousand dollars." The substance of the Epistle to the Galatians is this: because God had once condescended to enlighten men with the true knowledge of His Gospel, they are required to stand steadfast in the truth which they have embraced, and to show by their godly behavior that they be the children of light, so as they neither turn back again as renegades or as swine to the mire, nor be carried to and fro with every blast of doctrine like wavering reeds, or like little children that are soon weary of the things that they have, and fond of every new thing that they see. Calvin particularly addresses: free justification by faith, Christian liberty, the abolishing of Ceremonies, the force and effect of the law, and the pure walk of the Christian life. Emphasized throughout these Sermons is the historic and continuing reality of the troubling of the Church by the great deceiver Satan, who uses God's name against God, Christ's name against Christ, the show of the Gospel against the Gospel, and the countenance of Apostles and godly Ministers to overthrow the truth. This exposition is given that the wavering sort may in all goodness be confirmed, the weaklings strengthened, the ignorant instructed, the negligent warned, the forward encouraged, the slothful pricked forth, the corrigible amended, and the wilful and stubborn sort left utterly without excuse. This book contains a Foreword by Dr. W. Robert Godfrey, President and Professor of Church History at Westminster Theological Seminary in California. There is also an Index of Scriptures referred to by Calvin, and a Subject Index. This classic work presents Calvin not simply as a theologian but as a pastor as well. **990 PAGES AND HARDBOUND WITH COLOR DUSTJACKET INCLUDING PICTURE OF CALVIN, TOP STAINING, BLIND STAMPING, AND SHRINKWRAPPED.**

Retail Price: $ 49.95 (Postpaid)

SERMONS ON PSALM 119
by John Calvin

It has been over 400 years since John Calvin's 22 *Sermons Upon the Hundredth and Nineteenth Psalm of David* were published in a collected edition. Old Paths Publications has prepared a newly typeset edition from the 1580 printing of the English translation by Thomas Stocker in its entirety. The argument of this Psalm, the use thereof, and the instruction that we may gather by it is, to wit, that a faithful man is here taught to stir up himself to the reading of God's Word, and thereby to confirm himself accordingly. If David himself had done this, who of all others was the most excellent, how much more then ought we to do the like? Even we, which are so rude and ignorant, and far from so much profiting in the school of God as he? But because we are so cold, and have need to be spurred forward like Asses, David here shows us, what profit and commodity we may receive by this continual study, if everyone of us will apply ourselves to see and hear that which God has manifested unto us in his law, and in the Holy Scriptures. As he says in the Psalm, *Wherewithal shall a young man cleanse his way? by taking heed thereto according to thy word.* This book contains a **Foreword by Dr. James M. Boice, Senior Pastor of Tenth Presbyterian Church in Philadelphia, PA.** There is also an Index of Scriptures referred to by Calvin, and an extensive Subject Index. Through this classic work Calvin brings the reader to a clear and striking awareness: of his sinful and needy condition; of who God is; of the magnificence of the Word of God; and hence why we need to seek him and the mind of Christ through His Word with our whole heart! These sermons reveal not simply Calvin the theologian and expositor, but Calvin the preacher and pastor to those placed under his care. **600 PAGES AND HARDBOUND WITH COLOR DUSTJACKET, SEWN BINDING, TOP STAINED, BLIND STAMPED AND SHRINKWRAPPED.**

Retail Price: $ 41.95 (Postpaid)

PASTORAL THEOLOGY
The Pastor in the Various Duties of His Office
by Thomas Murphy

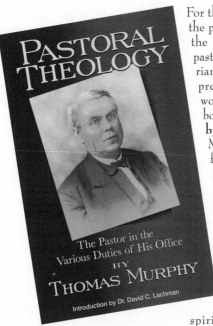

For those who have serious care for the pastoral duties of the minister, the Rev. Thomas Murphy, D.D, pastor of the Frankford Presbyterian Church, Philadelphia, PA, presented this comprehensive work in the year 1877. This book contains an **Introduction by Dr. David C. Lachman.** Murphy's fervent zeal for faithfulness, diligence and integrity in the work of the ministry can be seen when he says, *"There are special temptations to which, from its peculiar nature, the ministerial office is exposed...* Some are liable to be led away by spiritual pride, and then to become impatient of opposition, and to show a domineering spirit that is most offensive... Slothfulness is one of the besetting sins of this office, and that because of the habits of seclusion and the possibility of postponing duties, and because there is very often no other pressing impulse than the voice of conscience." "There was a great principle, a heaven-revealed principle, in the resolution of King David: *'Neither will I offer burnt-offerings unto the Lord my God of that which cost me nothing.'* To offer that to Jehovah which cost no sacrifice or effort, or is of no value, is unworthy his glorious majesty and the benefits we have received from him. And does not the clergyman violate that principle every time he goes into the pulpit and professes to serve God whilst preaching a sermon that has cost him no time or toil or thought? It is an affront to his congregation to preach such a sermon, but is it not a far greater affront to that glorious Being in whose name he speaks and who sees and knows all? For the preacher, who proclaims the words which God has given him, to slight his message is to slight the Author of that message...He thus shows the world what he thinks of the King who sent him, as well as of the message which he bears." **520 PAGES AND HARDBOUND WITH COLOR DUSTJACKET, SEWN BINDING AND SHRINKWRAPPED.**

Retail Price: $ 29.95 (Postpaid)

A TREATISE ON SANCTIFICATION
by James Fraser

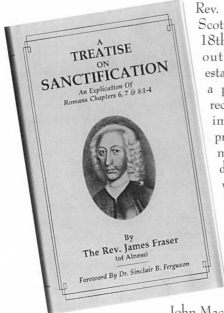

Rev. Fraser (of Alness) was a Scottish Presbyterian from the 18th century. From the very outset of his ministry he established a high reputation as a preacher, and was soon recognized as one of the most impressive and instructive preachers in a district where men of great and distinguished pulpit gifts were remarkably numerous. This 1897 edition of **A TREATISE ON SANCTIFICATION** (originally The Scripture Doctrine of Sanctification) was the result of the careful collation by Rev. John Macpherson of previous printed editions with the original manuscript. A foreword by Dr. Sinclair B. Ferguson of Westminster Theological Seminary and an interesting 20 page Biographical Sketch precedes what is avowedly a doctrinal commentary on Romans 6, 7 and 8:1-4. These chapters are themselves doctrinal, expressly devoted to the exposition of the Scripture Doctrine of Sanctification. The commentary deals with each chapter giving a careful introduction to each, treating of the general scope and contents of the chapter, and especially combating defective or erroneous views of the standpoint and intention of the apostle. Each verse is commented on separately, and the results of this exegetical study are then given in a paraphrase. This doctrine of sanctification is a subject critical to the Christian's understanding in every age, especially in our twentieth century where carnality has run rampant. A must purchase for those striving for sanctified living. **525 PAGES AND HARDBOUND WITH A DUSTJACKET WITH RARE PICTURE OF AUTHOR.**

Retail Price: $ 29.95 (Postpaid)

REVEALED TO BABES:
CHILDREN IN THE WORSHIP OF GOD
by Richard Bacon

Christians must follow the teachings of Christ and the Scriptures. This seems plain in and of itself. But do we truly apply this principle of the Christian life to our worship when it concerns the place of our covenant children? Does the Bible tell us who our covenant children are and does it give us commands as to their need for worship? What did Jesus have to say about the presence of covenant children in worship? Man's chief end is to glorify God and enjoy Him forever. We do this especially in the public worship where God's covenant people assemble to hear His Word. The children of the church are not excluded from that chief end. Richard Bacon deals with these questions and more. He is thorough, and conclusive in his approach to this subject, and clearly demonstrates from the Scriptures that children do belong in the public assembly of God, that they have certain rights as well as certain duties before the Lord that must be maintained. While the commands of Scripture require obedience from all who sincerely take the name of Jesus upon their lips, Presbyterian and Reformed Christians, by reason of their Confession, Church Order, and Reformation heritage, have an even greater responsibility to stand behind their profession. As Rev. Bacon states, "It is time for Presbyterians to become consistent with the theology of the Bible and to put into practice the theology that they claim to believe." **75 PAGES.**

Retail Price: $ 7.95 (Postpaid)

MANY VERSES!
THE IMPORTANCE OF READING THE SCRIPTURES IN REFORMED WORSHIP
by Ernest Springer

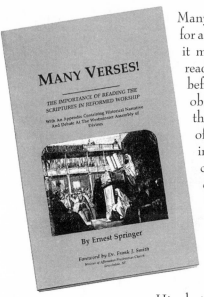

Many verses! What an odd topic for a book. Why in the world would it matter how much Scripture is read during public worship? But before this work is dismissed as obscurantist, consider the fact that the Bible is the very Word of God. It is hence inerrant, infallible, and inspired, and its character alone should command respect. But more than that, it is God's special revelation, particularly to His covenant people a love letter, as it were, conveying in a variety of ways the Lord's intense desire for union with His elect. In a direct manner, we who have been chosen from eternity have the opportunity to hear from our God's own lips all He wants us to know. This is not a privilege lightly foregone. Yet in a day when believers in formerly Communist countries are finally able to engage in public worship without fear of reprisal, we in North America are facing a time when the divine vision is indeed becoming rare even in churches that are professedly evangelical and/or Reformed. Perhaps it is because we don't believe the Bible anymore, or don't take God seriously. Whatever the cause, it is clear that we need an acknowledgement of the transcendent in our worship. One of the most crucial ways for that to occur is by an abundant reading of Heaven's communication to us. Ernest Springer makes a courageous, forthright polemic in favor of the historic practice of feeding the flock with "many verses."
75 PAGES.

IN THE SHADOW OF DEATH:
MEDITATIONS FOR THE
SICK-ROOM
AND AT THE DEATH-BED
by Abraham Kuyper

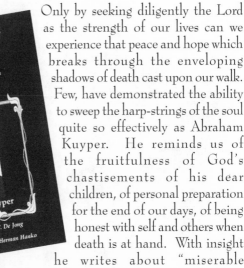

Only by seeking diligently the Lord as the strength of our lives can we experience that peace and hope which breaks through the enveloping shadows of death cast upon our walk. Few, have demonstrated the ability to sweep the harp-strings of the soul quite so effectively as Abraham Kuyper. He reminds us of the fruitfulness of God's chastisements of his dear children, of personal preparation for the end of our days, of being honest with self and others when death is at hand. With insight he writes about "miserable comforters," and "a last conscious moment." Even the more difficult topics are not avoided. That Satan plays a role in suffering, death is discussed as well as the "intermediate state" and the recognizing of loved ones in the state of glory. Each message is solidly grounded in Holy Scripture. In each there is instruction, consolation, at times much-needed warning lest sentimentality destroy a sense of sin's seriousness or the glory of our heavenly Father who works all things according to the counsel of his sovereign will. These meditations are intended to serve as a help in stimulating us to sit quietly in the presence of the living God who alone can heal the wounds which invariably disturb and distress the heart and so restore to us a peace which passes all understanding. A Foreword by Peter Y. De Jong and a Biographical Sketch by Herman Hanko. 375 PAGES AND HARDBOUND WITH A DUSTJACKET WITH STRIKING PICTURE OF AUTHOR, AND SHRINKWRAPPED.

Retail Price: $21.95 (Postpaid)

THE NECESSITY OF
REFORMING THE CHURCH
by John Calvin

According to **Dr. W. Robert Godfrey** (President & Professor of Church History-Westminster Seminary in CA), "**Martin Bucer**, the great reformer of Strassburg, appealed to Calvin to draft a statement of the doctrines of and necessity for the Reformation. The result was remarkable. **Theodore Beza**, Calvin's friend and successor in Geneva, called it the most powerful work of his time...Calvin organizes the work into three large sections. The first section is devoted to the evils in the church that required reformation. The second details the particular remedies to those evils adopted by the reformers. The third shows why reform could not be delayed, but rather how the situation demanded 'instant amendment' In each of these three sections Calvin focuses on four topics, which he calls the soul and body of the church. The soul of the church is worship and salvation. The body is sacraments and church government. The great cause of reform for Calvin centers in these topics." In an older edition of Calvin's writings, **Henry Beveridge** makes an observation worth noting, "The Treatise...embraces the great questions by which the Church is agitated at the present day. Indeed, in reading it, one is often led insensibly into the belief, that, instead of being the production of three centuries ago, it is a powerful protest written by some modern hand against the prevailing errors and threatened dangers of our own times." Whether Minister, Layman, Professor, Student, Elder, or Deacon, this Treatise is must reading for those who long for a return to the Old Paths of Truth from the Scriptures in their church. **130 PAGES.**

Retail Price: $12.95 (Postpaid)

EARNESTNESS IN PREACHING: ADMONITION FROM THE FATHERS
by Ernest Springer

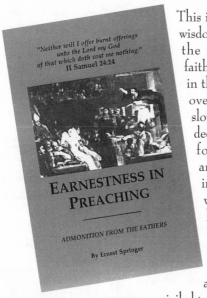

This is a short address flowing with wisdom from the past. It sets forth the requirement for sincerity, faithfulness, diligence and wisdom in the minister's use of the pulpit over against the "poverty" of slothfulness, laziness, craft and deceit. This is not simply a book for ministers, but it is an arsenal of suggestion for those in the pew who feel cheated by what pretends to be preaching by many who "hold the office". This collection of counsel from of old, speaks against, what the author maintains, is an illegitimate exercise of the awesome priviledge entrusted to the minister and is in reality a refusal of the direction of the Spirit of God by His Word. The Scriptures reveal a great principle in the resolution of King David, "Neither will I offer burnt-offerings unto the Lord my God with that which doth cost me nothing." This is not a study that seeks to prove the need for earnestness, rather as an assumed fact, it systematically presents commentator support in relation to the Scriptures, specifically the Fifth, Eighth, and Ninth Commandments, and certain Catechetical and Church Governmental Standards. You will find quotations from men such as John Flavel, Thomas Boston, Thomas Vincent, John Calvin, Zacharias Ursinus, Matthew Henry, Matthew Poole, Thomas Ridgeley, William Farel, Henry Ainsworth, John Owen, Charles Spurgeon, the Geneva Bible, Patrick Fairbairn, and Thomas Murphy. **48 PAGES.**

Retail Price: $5.95 (Postpaid)